Corporate Medievalism

Studies in Medievalism XXI

2012

Studies in Medievalism

Founded by Leslie J. Workman

Previously published volumes are listed at the back of this book

Corporate Medievalism

Edited by
Karl Fugelso

Studies in Medievalism XXI 2012

Cambridge
D. S. Brewer

© Studies in Medievalism 2012

First published 2012
D. S. Brewer, Cambridge

ISBN 978-1-84384-322-1

ISSN 0738-7164

D. S. Brewer is an imprint of Boydell & Brewer Ltd
PO Box 9, Woodbridge, Suffolk IP12 3DF, UK
and of Boydell & Brewer Inc,
668 Mt Hope Avenue, Rochester, NY 14620-2731, USA
website: www.boydellandbrewer.com

A CIP catalogue record for this book is available
from the British Library

The publisher has no responsibility for the continued existence or
accuracy of URLs for external or third-party internet websites referred to
in this book, and does not guarantee that any content on such websites is,
or will remain, accurate or appropriate

Papers used by Boydell & Brewer Ltd are natural, recyclable products
made from wood grown in sustainable forests

Printed in the United States of America

Studies in Medievalism

Studies in Medievalism provides an interdisciplinary medium of exchange for scholars in all fields, including the visual and other arts, concerned with any aspect of the post-medieval idea and study of the Middle Ages and the influence, both scholarly and popular, of this study on Western society after 1500.

Studies in Medievalism is published by Boydell & Brewer, Ltd., P.O. Box 9, Woodbridge, Suffolk IP12 3DF, UK; Boydell & Brewer, Inc., 668 Mt. Hope Avenue, Rochester, NY 14620, USA. Orders and inquiries about back issues should be addressed to Boydell & Brewer at the appropriate office.

For a copy of the style sheet and for inquiries about **Studies in Medievalism**, please contact the editor, Karl Fugelso, at the Dept. of Art+Design, Art History, and Art Education, Towson University, 3103 Center for the Arts, 8000 York Rd, Towson, MD 21252–0001, USA, tel. 410–704–2805, fax 410–704–2810 ATTN: Fugelso, e-mail <kfugelso@towson.edu>. All submissions should be sent to him as e-mail attachments in Word.

Acknowledgments

The device on the title page comes from the title page of *Des Knaben Wunderhorn: Alte deutsche Lieder*, edited by L. Achim von Arnim and Clemens Brentano (Heidelberg and Frankfurt, 1806).

The epigraph is from an unpublished paper by Lord Acton, written about 1859 and printed in Herbert Butterfield, *Man on His Past* (Cambridge: Cambridge University Press, 1955), 212.

Studies in Medievalism

III. Response

Volume XXI 2012

Two great principles divide the world, and contend for the master, antiquity and the middle ages. These are the two civilizations that have preceded us, the two elements of which ours is composed. All political as well as religious questions reduce themselves practically to this. This is the great dualism that runs through our society.

Lord Acton

Editorial Note

Although corporate culture has influenced virtually the whole of human history, perhaps never before have so many people been so attuned to that impact. Since the global financial crisis began in 2008, the business world has come under close scrutiny for its practices and values, especially its self-interest and self-promotion. Enormous disparities in wealth, growing unemployment, and feeble returns have led many critics to question the societal benefits of a strong business sector and to challenge community support for it.

Indeed, as academic salaries and retirement accounts are slashed, as colleges and universities eliminate tenured faculty members and sometimes entire departments, and as academic publishers collapse or are forced to reduce their offerings, even scholars outside of fields traditionally associated with business are concentrating on the influence of corporate culture. At the roundtable sponsored by the Medieval Electronic Multimedia Organization (MEMO) during the 2010 International Congress on Medieval Studies at Kalamazoo, Michigan, scholars of literature and the electronic arts found themselves discussing the many ways consumers have been manipulated by publishers, movie producers, and game designers. At the 2011 Congress MEMO was able to build entire sessions around that theme. And similar subjects have played a prominent part in many recent articles on (neo)medievalism, especially such *SiM* pieces as Veronica Ortenberg West-Harling's "Medievalism as Fun and Games" (2009), Brent and Kevin Moberly's "Neomedievalism, Hyperrealism, and Simulation" (2010), Harry Brown's "Baphomet Incorporated, A Case Study" (2011), KellyAnn Fitzpatrick's "Re(producing (Neo) medievalism" (2011), and Alexandra Sterling-Hellenbrand's "Performing Medieval Literature and/as History: The Museum of Wolframs-Eschenbach" (2011).

To my knowledge, however, (neo)medievalists have not yet addressed this important and timely topic in a direct and sustained fashion that seeks to reveal its range and common denominators. So I invited eight leading scholars in our field(s) to write about the influence of corporate entities on post-medieval interpretations of the Middle Ages. Though some of the authors asked for clarification of the terms and relationships in my call for papers, I refused because that was precisely what I wanted them to do. I wanted them to expose the many forms corporations may take and the many ways in which these entities may impact our subjects and us.

And I think they succeeded in at least indicating the range of such influences, not to mention the impact of the Middle Ages on contemporary corporate culture. M. J. Toswell notes striking and often disturbing parallels between modern businesses and medieval monasteries. Kevin and Brent Moberly discuss the resurgence of the medieval as a model for corporate ethics in the wake of 2008. KellyAnn Fitzpatrick and Jil Hanifan link guilds of players and a variety of other corporate experiences within medievalist video games to the companies that produce them. Harry Brown takes a similar tack with regard to cinema as he examines how medievalist films, and the corporations behind them, refract medieval economic and class structures through contemporary social and financial conditions. E. L. Risden explores a particular case of such reshaping in Hal Hartley's *No Such Thing* (2001), a *Beowulf* parallel in which the monster who probably devoured a reporter's boyfriend is overshadowed by the nefariousness of her boss and the media industry as they attempt to exploit the story. And Lauryn S. Mayer looks at George R. R. Martin's book series *A Song of Ice and Fire* as a medievalism that "paradoxically depends for its grip and impact on the recognition/denial dynamic governing corporate/community relationships."

At least some of these essays have direct relevance to one or more of the articles that follow them, and all of the essays invite us to search the articles for further variations on corporate influence. But, of course, each of the articles, as well as Clements and Robinson's response to earlier *SiM* essays on neomedievalism, has merits all its own and can benefit readers who have not seen the essays or are (otherwise) uninterested in the relationship between (neo)medievalism and corporations. Eduardo Henrik Aubert examines the first three centuries of post-medieval developments in the paleography of early medieval musical notation. Michael R. Kightley analyzes racial Anglo-Saxonism in Charles Kingsley's lecture series *The Roman and the Teuton* (1864) and novel *Hereward the Wake: "Last of the English"* (1866). Helen Brookman approaches Jessie L. Weston's medievalism through that author's late nineteenth- and early twentieth-century "fascination" with Sir Gawain. J. Rubén Valdés Miyares traces shifting roles in the cinematic sign of the grail. And Felice Lifshitz discusses the treatment of women in medievalist films, particularly in *Die Nibelungen* (1924) and *Excalibur* (1981) and particularly in relationship to vengeance.

As is true for Clements and Robinson, many of these authors are jumping into the middle of ongoing debates and overtly responding to earlier work in their areas of interest and in (neo)medievalism as a whole. But as with the essays, we hope these articles also initiate further discussion of their topics and open new subjects for investigation. All of our enterprises are to some degree corporate, and it is up to us to steer their drive for profit towards fruitful dialogue, including discussion of those motives.

Lives of Total Dedication? Medieval and Modern Corporate Identity

M. J. Toswell

In the Old English version of the *Monasteriales Indicia*, the sign for abbot is given as follows: *Ærest þæs abbudes tacen is þæt mon his twegen fingras to his heafde asette, and his feax mid genime* ("First, the sign for the abbot is that one puts one's two fingers to one's head, and takes hold of one's hair with them").[1] This might be more quickly explained as "lift two fingers to the head, and grip the hair." In a Continental version this sign is clarified, so that it suggests not the tugging of the forelock, but that the hair that is gripped to indicate the abbot should be above the ear.[2] The abbot was the head of the monastery, the leader of the corporate body of monks, and the spiritual and physical manager of the life of the monastery and its dependents. The dependents of a religious order could spread widely through a district, a country, and sometimes even beyond. Some abbots were powers indeed, and were among the significant figures in the land, traveling about with the king or high lord and witnessing charters as a matter of course. They had the kind of power over the monastics within their remit that a secular bishop could only hope for, though both fit elegantly into the pyramidal structure of the early Church. When Philip IV of France famously wiped out the Knights Templar (the Order of the Temple, admittedly not precisely a monastic foundation, but a spiritual order of the Catholic church organized very similarly, with the head or Grand Master serving as the spiritual leader of all his sworn knights and directing their every thought), he eliminated a church order that involved nearly every kingdom in Christendom at the time. The modern chief executive officer of a global corporation, in a surprisingly similar way, functions as the spiritual and physical leader of that corporation. If it is a small local business, then the CEO's role is not unlike that of an abbot, although nowadays signaling to indicate the CEO by lifting two fingers to the head and either tugging on one's hair (particularly on the forelock) or engaging in another finger movement is not often required. If the chief executive officer heads a large multinational corporation, then the similarities to the highly bureaucratic ecclesiastical structures propagated by the Roman church, and fully developed in all of Christendom by the eighth century, become quite striking. The *Rule of St Benedict*, with its emphases on obedience and blind faith and its precise calibration of rules and privileges, its careful analyses of human behavioral tendencies and development of formal structures to encompass them, is not so very far away from the management manuals that clutter the shelves of our bookstores, nor from the pyramidal organizational structure of a typical modern corporation (including a university). In a lighthearted way, without aiming to suggest some dark deep purpose to the parallels, this essay will consider how the organizational behavior of human beings in early medieval Europe bears comparison to that in the modern corporate and professional world.[3]

Although organizational structures were already developing in late antiquity and being laid out clearly by such early figures of the Christian church as Cassiodorus and Augustine, the first fully elaborated statement on the origins and structure of ecclesiastical offices is that of Isidore in the last years of the sixth century, the *De ecclesiasticis officiis*.[4] Isidore's concerns in the two books of this work were multiple: to establish a firm and clear system of clerical education, to ensure the moral virtue and discipline of those in the clerisy, to determine a structure for the liturgy and sacraments of the Church, and to organize and order the functions of those working and worshipping in the Christian church. Unsurprisingly, Isidore begins with the work of the Church and the instruments used in that work: the psalms, canticles, hymns, prayers, scriptures first, then the services and liturgical patterns. The rest of Book I works carefully through the feasts of the Church, the daily offices and services, and includes detailed analysis of the Eucharist in particular. In other words, Isidore begins with the study of what the work of the Church and its worshippers is. In Book II he turns to the behavior and workload of the members of the Church, beginning with the clerics, and working his way past bishops, presbyters, deacons, and other individuals working in the Church services to monks, and thence to devout individuals including penitents, virgins, widows, and married people. The last sections discuss the ways in which the members of the Church develop and manifest their Christianity, including baptism, chrism, confirmation, and the learning of Church doctrine including the Symbol or Creed. In other words, Isidore begins with a conspectus of the tasks involved in working for his corporation (the Christian church), moves on to a detailed consideration of the specific workload and tasks of each individual in the corporation, and concludes with a section on the training and education necessary for doing the work.

More particularly, Isidore discusses the role of the cleric, but in general terms, save for a detailed analysis of tonsure. His concern throughout the *De ecclesiasticis officiis* is with the moral rectitude and spiritual good behavior of his subjects, and details on duties and specific responsibilities can be thin. Each job description tends to begin with the biblical origin of the job, and then move to the spiritual purity of those doing it; "Guardians of sacred things," for example, in Book II chapter IX, are the Levites, those charged with guarding the tabernacle and vessels of the Temple, and Isidore continues with a description of their cleanness of mind and body, and their serious demeanor.[5] Some of his descriptions do suggest a concern with more mundane matters, however. The psalmists in Book II chapter XII are linked to their ancient predecessors, the cantors of the Old Testament including David and Asaph. Moreover, Isidore points out that the psalmists did not eat food the day before their chanting was scheduled, and that "[t]hey conscientiously used yellowish green vegetables for the sake of their voice." He notes that among the gentiles these cantors were called "beans."[6] Isidore's inclusion of this intriguing information suggests that, as modern corporations do, he cared for the physical as well as spiritual welfare of his charges. Incidentally, psalmists, by virtue of their being skilled in a particular art, are actually chosen by the presbyter without reference to the bishop. Then and now, musicians function as a breed apart – never quite part of the corporation but necessary to its smooth functioning. The other members of the monastic community, and in fact of the Christian community as a whole, receive relatively specific, biblically-based advice about their behavior patterns and their roles. Monks, for example, live a holy life in common, dressing, chanting, and fasting together as they form a sacred army.[7]

Slightly later than Isidore, and in the long run very much more influential, was the Rule of St. Benedict, the structure and organization of the cenobitic life that became the standard monastic system in the early medieval church. Benedict, like Isidore and the many other compilers of rules of Christian behavior, was concerned both to establish a good institutional organization and to foster spiritual discipline. In the Benedictine Rule, once again the spiritual work came first, with throughout an added and intriguingly acute psychological insight into how the individual would set him or herself to following the Rule; in other words, Benedict was well aware that the outer appearance of proper behavior might well hide an improper mind. Outer observance and inner belief had to be brought into a synchronized and spiritual whole. Having established this concern for the need to match heart and mind in true Christian devotion, and having worked through the spiritual workload of the monastic community, Benedict switches in the second part of the Rule – as did Isidore – to the more specific job descriptions. Benedict's job descriptions are, however, very much more specific than

those of Isidore, and reflect a very different sensibility. Benedict has a sense
of the monastic foundation as a functioning unit, and of the abbot in particular as the head of the unit. This becomes particularly clear in Benedict's
analysis of the role of the prior, someone who might be overtaken by pride
and a sense that he is exempt from the abbot's authority. Benedict therefore
states categorically that it is best: "for the abbot to make all decisions in the
conduct of his monastery. If possible, as we have already established, the
whole operation of the monastery should be managed through deans under
the abbot's direction."[8] The prior, then, is clearly an appointee of the abbot's
and even more clearly answers to the abbot, though it seems possible that an
abbot might appoint a prior and establish a clear sphere of influence within
which the prior would be the authoritative figure. The further reference to
deans, however, reveals that a broader conception of the line of authority is
starting to develop. The abbot might have the power of a feudal lord, but
that power can be diffused either through a prior or through a group of
priors or deans who are not of a very significantly lower grade of authority.
That is, the monastic world does not in Benedict's conception consist of an
abbot who stands far above the monks, since of course the abbot is generally
chosen by and from the monks. However, already in the Rule, can be seen
the early development of a corporate model of structure and organization.

The appointment of the abbot is a case in point. As Benedict puts the
matter, the abbot will often, perhaps even usually, be chosen from among
the cenobites at the relevant monastery. A bishop might occasionally choose
to set in place a "worthy steward" should there be evil ways in place in the
community.[9] Otherwise, Benedict makes it clear that the abbot should be
chosen by the whole community or be chosen by some part of the community that exercises good judgment. In other words, Benedict does not choose
to interfere too greatly in what are already local differences of approach in
the selection of an abbot, unless there are problems in the division which
require that the bishop act from on high. The bishop is clearly the highest
leader, intervening only if there is trouble in the division. The choice of the
abbot is a corporate decision (in the older sense of the word) of the community. The abbot's authority over the community, once selected, is pretty much
absolute, though Benedict offers some cautionary words here: "Once in
office, the abbot must keep constantly in mind the nature of the burden he
has received, and remember to whom he will have *to give an account of his
stewardship*."[10] Benedict further notes that the abbot needs to know divine
law, have several specific virtues, punish with prudence and avoid extremes,
show forethought and consideration in his orders, and keep the Rule in every
particular. In short, Benedict notes, he should "strive to be loved rather than
feared."[11] His advice to abbots concerning how to rule their monasteries
could be written by a modern CEO to her or his managers, particularly the

strictures on prudence, knowledge, and striving to be a model to be loved rather than a master to be feared.

The surviving lives of abbots tend as a genre to present those abbots in a rather hagiographic light (resembling perhaps the halo of perfection found today in biographies, and especially autobiographies, of the captains of industry). Thus, Bede tells us in one of the earliest such hagiographies of the words of Benedict Biscop on his deathbed concerning the choice of a new abbot:

> Wherefore, my brethren, beware, and never choose an abbot on account of his birth, nor from any foreign place; but seek out, according to the rule of Abbot Benedict the Great, and the decrees of our order, with common consent, from amongst your own company, whoever in virtue of life and wisdom of doctrine may be found fittest for this office; and whomsoever you shall, by this unanimous inquiry of Christian charity, prefer and choose, let him be made abbot with the customary blessings, in presence of the bishop.[12]

In Wearmouth and Jarrow, the next abbot was chosen by the community, and as it turned out Ceolfrith was established in the post before Benedict's death some months later. Benedict himself, the founder of the monastery, is for Bede, repeatedly, a venerable and pious man, of noble descent, and dignified and virtuous. In short, Benedict, like his name, is blessed, a paragon of virtue. Intriguingly, during his own abbacy Benedict had established sub-abbots of the two monasteries of Wearmouth and Jarrow, splitting apart his own foundation so that each establishment had an abbot within whose care and control the members of one house continued. Benedict did this because he wanted to continue his own voyages about the world, acquiring religious treasures and especially manuscripts for the monks of the house. Knowing that he would not be close enough as abbot for the monks to trust in his absolute care of them, he invented, and during his lifetime imposed on the monasteries, what management theory today calls a matrix system: each worked on its own, produced its own spiritual results, and answered to Benedict as the superior abbot. Benedict's blessed behavior worked for his own purposes, and for improved care and control of his monks.

Similarly blessed is Bernard of Clairvaux, the paragon of the twelfth century who founded the monastery of Clairvaux and established the ascetic Cistercian paradigm for monastic behavior. He spoke eloquently, often preaching and explaining proper behavior, and he modeled proper ascetic behavior in his own life, taking a life of poverty and fasting and whole-hearted Christian devotion to extremes of piety. As a result, many flocked to his community, and others asked his advice, impressed beyond all utterance by what Butler calls his "wonderful sanctity."[13] He refused various bishoprics and other higher posts, pleading with the pope, in tears, to allow him to continue at Clairvaux with his community there. Nonetheless, his learning and his piety were such that he essentially did make all the decisions for the Christian church in western Europe. Such were his leadership skills, framed within his community and his knowledge base. By the end of his life, 160 Cistercian monasteries had been founded by the monks of Clairvaux and its daughter houses. Moreover, Bernard was influential in drafting and ordering the charter of the newly founded Knights of the Temple, the Templars. His private life was that of a devoted ascetic and mystic; publicly, he gave new life to the Church Militant. Bernard was a CEO from the sidelines, apparently not directly involved but actually serving as the principal mover in developing and influencing the twelfth-century Church.[14] He remained at Clairvaux because he identified so very strongly with its principles and practices, with the community he had established in that beautiful valley. Still, although technically his role was that of abbot, in effect he chose his own over-arching role in a highly bureaucratic structure.

In the world of modern business, it seems best to start with the organizational structure, with the chain of command, since the work varies so much more in the modern day. Study of these suggests that there is, as with the medieval monastery, individual variation. Some companies start with the CEO (the abbot) at the top, who decides what responsibilities to delegate and does so in a straight line to the next executive (the prior), who has a sub-executive (the sub-prior) and so forth down the line. This kind of straight-line chain of command is rare in a large corporation, but it is not impossible. The organization, particularly of the higher echelons, of executive power is generally a mix of company patterns and customs with the CEO's preferences. Often, as with Bill Gates and Bernard of Clairvaux, the real modalities of executive power are not those that appear in the company's formal structure. The CEO enjoys a great deal of flexibility. Bill Gates, for example, famously worked out his own succession plan, decided to become chair of the board and to lead software development, and basically determined his own exit strategy (and to some extent his re-entrance strategy, all based on the fact that he really was the CEO of Microsoft, whatever formal title he took). The more usual line of command involves establishing specific tasks for a group of deans (or priors or executives), bearing in mind what is today called the span of control, the range of work and workers that a given administrator can supervise. Depending on the size of a given company and its products, those deans are organized in bureaucratic structures that follow a number of standard patterns: a hierarchical pattern running down a very clear chain of command, a functional structure (such as a scriptorium in which a leader would establish the specialized tasks of the monks at work on preparing the parchment, writing, illuminating, and binding the codices), a divisional structure organized geographically (as the 160 monasteries founded from Clairvaux would each have their own divisional power but would also answer to the founding monastery), or a matrix structure involving teams of employees to organize and disseminate slightly different products (the Knights Templar perhaps).[15] All of these relatively hierarchical structures can be found in modern corporations, with the matrix structure perhaps the most common in the larger global corporations.

At the same time, despite the framework that looks terribly professional and corporate, and not personal in any way, individuals identify with their workplaces. Corporations encourage this with slogans, health plans, business cards, and a whole host of other ways in which employees are encouraged to immerse themselves in the culture and approach of the company. At the same time, the exigencies of modern life suggest that blind faith in one's employer is hardly wise. Nonetheless, childlike faith in the company still imbues many an employee:

> Workers have willingly offered themselves complete with their personal and family lives to the organization. Like children, they have allowed the organization to determine what is best for them and how they should best be used. They expected no power and that is precisely what they got. Such childlike passivity is fading fast. The divine right of kings or managers no longer exists.[16]

Robert Kelley states here that the time for "childlike passivity" is over, writing in 1985, before the collapse of Enron, before the 2008 destruction of the marketplace brought about by appalling company practices, and before several other débâcles that suggest the continued existence of a human desire to be organized and structured in return for faith and hard work. Clearly, Kelley ought to have been right; equally clearly, he was not. For example, employees of Google today believe passionately in the company slogan to "do no evil," ignoring Google's complicity with censorship in various countries. When Apple was experiencing severe difficulties with its products and structure some years back, the true CEO, Steve Jobs, stepped back into his job and reinvigorated the company, leading his people to a new supremacy in tablet technology. A charismatic CEO can accomplish much, and can earn more.

By the later Middle Ages, many abbots had their own establishments within the monastic enclave, including their own kitchens, their fully appointed accommodations, and their own sense of their continuing importance. Their pursuit of luxury became legendary, to the point that the English abbots offered Henry VIII a ready-made excuse for his abolition of their appurtenances and eventually their monasteries. A modern CEO tends to be recognized first for his stock options, mansion, and foreign-made sports car, and only later for his contribution to the welfare and continued good functioning of his company. Moreover, those of us afflicted with abbatial power and pomp in the form of the modern-day dean or manager will have some fellow feeling for the medieval monk or nun, aware that the abbot was supposed to have been chosen by the community and was supposed to remain part of the community, but aware that this was no longer quite the way things were. In other words, then as now, human nature intervened. Sadly, now we no longer have a Benedictine Rule to rein in abbatial excess, to remind that there will be an accounting, to reinstate the corporate wellbeing of the whole with a well-placed correction. Today we have stock markets, quantitative easing, ineffectual governmental subsidies, and the invisible hand of the marketplace. In other words, our corporations and corporate identities function as well and as poorly as their medieval forerunners.

More intriguingly, fundamental similarities in the modern corporate life and the medieval cenobitic life are developing that offer a deeper parallel between the two eras than existed even a few years ago. In both cases a particular ethos and spiritual mindset suffuses all aspects of the individual's behavior, approach, and function in the corporate world of the monastery or the industry or profession. I refer, of course, to the role that technology plays in the life of every individual in the interlinked world. The massive technological innovations of modern corporate life mean that it takes place at all times and in all places. Emails are sent and answered in the middle of the night, BlackBerrys are on at all times, and text messaging seems to occur almost without the conscious volition of the individual (while eating dinner, holding other conversations, driving). The corporate executive is "on" day and night, focused on the work every minute of every hour. Those not prepared to make this sacrifice – and entering the serious corporate world and remaining there does tend to be described as a sacrifice – are those who cannot join the community and engage in its devotional activities. The kind of privation endured by Bernard of Clairvaux in the pursuit of his spiritual wellbeing for all time comes uncomfortably close to the total devotion and dedication required of the modern executive (and privation is also involved, as very precise codes of behavior, physical fitness, dress, and work patterns are prerequisites of the job). Both are engaged in their work as a constant focus of both mind and heart.

It is not my task here to explore the psychological similarities between the ecstatic joy of the mystic in pursuit of the transcendent and morti-fying the flesh and the exhilarating delight of the executive who has relent-lessly and sleeplessly pursued a deal for the greater good of his corporation. But I suspect that the total dedication to the goal is more similar than is comfortable, given that one works towards eternal delight and the other towards earthly comforts. The human search for something that deserves one's total dedication, one's absolute faith, resolved in the Middle Ages by absolute trust in the Godhead, has not found the same resolution in the modern day. A medieval monk or nun could know that, in return for faithful service and pureness of heart, as an exchange for total dedication, the corporate church would offer absolute security now and in the hereafter. Today that kind of faithful service and wholehearted devotion to the corporation, to Ford, or General Electric or Google, or the Royal Bank of Scotland, does not garner the same absolute comfort. An abbot really could make decisions that would fundamentally alter the spiritual and physical wellbeing of the monks in his care; a CEO, despite the appearance of absolute power and invincibility, generally cannot. Living a life of total dedication has its appeal, its charming simplicity, its faith and its singularity of purpose. Living such a life, however, depends upon absolute faith in the moral and spiritual rectitude of one's abbot; such absolute faith, never all that common, is rarer today. Perhaps that is a shame.

NOTES

1. *Monasteriales Indicia: The Anglo-Saxon Monastic Sign Language*, ed. Debby Banham (Pinner, Middlesex: Anglo-Saxon Books, 1991), §1, pp. 22–23.

2. See *Monasteriales Indicia*, 57.

3. I am grateful to my brother for inspiring this paper; his umbilical relationship with his BlackBerry reminds me that the modern corporation indeed intrudes into every aspect of the modern individual's life. Modern corporate life orders and reorders the life of its minions at will, sometimes without the prudence and care visited upon the medieval abbot by Benedict and by the sure and certain knowledge that the accounting for the abbot would be an eternal one – not one driven by the corporate agenda and the bottom line.

4. Sancti Isidori Episcopi Hispalensis, *De ecclesiasticis officiis*, ed. Christopher M. Lawson, Corpus Christianorum Series Latin cxiii (Turnholt: Brepols, 1989). For convenience, I will be quoting here from the translation, *Isidore of Seville: De Ecclesiasticis Officiis*, trans. Thomas L. Knoebel (New York: Newman Press, 2008).

5. *Isidore of Seville: DEO*, 80–81.

6. *Isidore of Seville: DEO*, 83. Incidentally, Isidore appears to have been right, as yellow vegetables continue to be recommended for singers; apparently they soothe the vocal cords and improve voice production.

7. *Isidore of Seville: DEO*, 85–89.

8. For the Rule of St. Benedict, I am using the readily-available authorized text, despite its shortcomings: *The Rule of St. Benedict in Latin and English with Notes*, ed. Timothy Fry *et al.* (Collegeville, MN: Liturgical Press, 1981). The quotation is from chapter 65 "The Prior of the Monastery," 284–87.

9. *Rule of St. Benedict*, 280–81.
10. *Rule of St. Benedict*, 282–83.
11. *Rule of St. Benedict*, 282–85.
12. Saint Bede, "The lives of the holy abbots of Weremouth and Jarrow: Benedict, Easterwine, Sigfrid and Huetberht," in *The Complete Works of Venerable Bede, in the original Latin, collated with the Manuscripts, and various printed editions, and accompanied by a new English translation of the Historical Works, and a Life of the Author*, ed. and trans. J. A. Giles, Vol. IV (London: Whittaker and Co., 1843), 358–402. The translation is old but serviceable.
13. See Rev. Alban Butler, *The Lives of the Fathers, Martyrs, and Other Principal Saints Compiled from Original Monuments and Authentic Records* (Dublin: James Duffy, 1866; New York: Bartleby.com, 2010), s.v. St. Bernard, Abbot.
14. See Robert S. Hoyt and Stanley Chodorow, *Europe in the Middle Ages*, 3rd edn. (New York: Harcourt Brace Jovanovich, 1976), 447–51.
15. See Stephen P. Robbins and Nancy Langton, *Organizational Behaviour: Concepts, Controversies, Applications* (Toronto: Pearson/Prentice Hall, 2003).
16. See Robert E. Kelley, *The Gold Collar Worker: Harnessing the Brain Power of the New Work Force* (Reading, MA: Addison-Wesley, 1985), 93. Quoted from Randy Hodson and Teresa A. Sullivan, *The Social Organization of Work* (Belmont, CA: Wadsworth/Thomson Learning, 2001), epigraph, 307.

Reincorporating the Medieval: Morality, Chivalry, and Honor in Post-Financial-Meltdown Corporate Revisionism

Kevin Moberly and Brent Moberly

Those who follow such things will have undoubtedly noticed that the Capital One "What's in your Wallet" Viking commercials have undergone a dramatic change since they originally aired. Early versions of the commercials cast the Vikings as a collective, agonistic, and decidedly pre-modern other. Garbed in pelts, wearing horned helmets, and wielding all manner of medieval weaponry, they waited in hordes just beyond the horizon, ready to charge screaming into the fray and ruthlessly visit any unfortunate credit-card purchase with requisite and over-determined medieval violence – that is, any credit-card purchase that was not made from beyond the silvered shield-wall of a Capital One credit card. In more recent commercials, however, the Vikings have acquired a decidedly more domestic mien. Though neither their garb nor their weaponry has changed, they have nevertheless forsworn raiding in favor of more mundane and innocuous pursuits such as babysitting, playing in rock bands, and serving as flight attendants, shoe salesmen, and electricians. The Vikings, as such, have become apt spokesmen for the corporation that once thwarted them at every turn and, arguably, for all of the major banks (including Capital One) whose lending policies were responsible for the global financial crisis of 2007 and 2008. Heavy-handed brutes who cause chaos and destruction at every turn, they are portrayed as well-intentioned and likeable and, if the scenarios featured in the most recent commercials are any indication, well on their way to becoming productive members of society.

A similar shift can be seen in the medieval-themed massively multi-player game, *World of Warcraft*.[1] As Scott Rettberg explains in his 2008 article, "Corporate Ideology in *World of Warcraft*," the commercial success of *World of Warcraft* has always, to some degree, been an outgrowth of the extent to which the game "offers a convincing and detailed simulacrum of the process of becoming successful in capitalist societies."[2] Citing the game's free-market system of auction-houses, the Taylorist, assembly-line-like "grind" that is required to increase reputation, and the hierarchical, quasi-corporate organizational strategies employed by high-end raiding guilds, he argues that "beyond simply portraying capitalism as good, *World of Warcraft* serves as a tool to educate its players in a range of behaviors and skills specific to the situation of conducting business in an economy controlled by corporations."[3] While Rettberg is correct in stating that corporate ideology has always been implicit in the behaviors that the game privileges as good or productive play, *World of Warcraft* officially recognized that this ideology was a viable mode of play in the 2010 *Cataclysm* expansion, when players were given the opportunity to play a race that, before that point, had been almost exclusively identified with the worst excesses of *laissez-faire* corporate capitalism: the diminutive, green-skinned, and unapologetically mercantile goblins. Although the goblins are not significantly different from any of the game's other playable races, they do allow players access to innate and explicitly capitalist racial abilities such as "PACK HOBGOBLIN: Goblins can access their bank vault from anywhere with the help of a trusted friend" and "BEST DEALS ANYWHERE: Wheeling and dealing is second nature to goblins, and they always receive a discount from vendors." Yet the fact that Blizzard Entertainment has acknowledged what had always been a latent (though sometimes only thinly disguised) subtext in the game by making the race accessible to players suggests, as does the shift that has occurred in the way that Vikings are portrayed in the most recent Capital One commercials, that the relationship between the corporate and the medieval is not as simple, straightforward, or adversarial as is traditionally assumed.

Elsewhere, we have explored the ways in which neomedievalist works invoke the medieval to obscure the economics, corporate or otherwise, involved in their production.[4] In this essay, however, we would like to offer an alternative reading. We will examine the resurgence of the medieval as a model for corporate ethics in the wake of the recent financial meltdown and the recession that followed. Accordingly, this essay focuses on how the medieval is invoked and enables the redemption of the corporate in Stieg Larsson's *The Girl with the Dragon Tattoo*.[5] Using Larsson's novel metonymically, we foreground a discursive strategy that, while not new, is enjoying a revival of sorts in the aftermath of the meltdown: a strategy that employs chivalry, honor, and other values traditionally associated with the medieval to argue that what is needed is not a systematic re-evaluation of the role that corporations play and their cost to a society, but a return to a corporate model that, with a nostalgia characteristic of the neomedieval, is constructed as more noble and, therefore, more moral, ethical, and socially responsible than its present incarnations. This essay, as such, is intended to complement our earlier works. Recognizing that all of the texts that we discuss in this article (and indeed the journal in which this article appears) are beholden to, if not are, outright productions of the corporate, this essay hopes to better understand the complex and often contradictory representational strategies through which contemporary media productions (neomedievalist or otherwise) encode what Theodor Adorno and Max Horkheimer argue is the central message of all mass culture: "triumph of invested capital, whose title as absolute master is etched deep into the hearts of the dispossessed in the employment line."[6]

Published in English almost a year before the financial meltdown that crippled the economy of the United States and many other industrialized countries, *The Girl with the Dragon Tattoo* seems uncannily relevant to the events of the crisis and the anxieties that surfaced in its aftermath. Originally titled *Män Som Hatar Kvinnor*, or "Men Who Hate Women," the novel uses the issues of sexual abuse and violence against women as a vehicle to dramatize contemporary anxieties about the threat of corporate power and the perceived inability of the media and other institutions to police or otherwise limit that power. Yet for all of this, *The Girl with the Dragon Tattoo* is not a condemnation of the corporation as an economic, political, and social institution. While *The Girl with the Dragon Tattoo* acknowledges the dangers that corporate abuse poses to society, it does not represent these abuses as endemic and, perhaps, inevitable to the material role that corporations play in late-capitalist economies. Nor does it recognize the degree to which deregulation and similar neo-liberal economic and political policies that began in the Reagan-Thatcher era have allowed corporations to expand beyond national borders and, as Rita Raley argues, beyond the jurisdiction of the nation-state.[7] Instead, the novel offers readers an idealist narrative about the corporate that has become all too familiar in the wake of revelations about the lending and accounting practices that led to the financial crisis and culminated in the investment scandals of Bernie Madoff and others – a narrative that holds the institution of the corporation blameless and instead represents its flaws, excesses, and abuses as an expression and consequence of the character flaws and the corruption of the individuals who are not equal to the almost sacred duties entrusted to them.

The Girl with the Dragon Tattoo might, as such, seem like an odd text with which to begin a discussion about the relationship between the medieval and the corporate. The medievalist impulse, after all, often manifests itself as a reaction against the corporate and the industrial in some of the most canonical works of medievalism. Frodo's last heroic deed, for instance, in J. R. R. Tolkien's *Lord of the Rings* is driving industrialists from the shire. Yet even if one overlooks the degree to which *The Girl with the Dragon Tattoo* is sympathetic to the corporation, it is nevertheless difficult to ignore the fact that the novel is not explicitly a work of fantasy, nor does it contain many of the accoutrements that have come to characterize contemporary medievalism. It does not take place, for instance, in some derivative version of Tolkien's Middle Earth, or even a "long time ago, in a galaxy far, far away." While it emphasizes the difference in climate between the rural north of Sweden and the urban south, neither of these locales is explicitly portrayed as the wilderness, nor do any of the novel's characters embark on a quest to tame them. Similarly, *The Girl with the Dragon Tattoo* does not fetishize the past as simpler or somehow more desirable than the present, but returns again and again to the period immediately following the Second World War and the complex legacy of Sweden's decision to remain neutral during the conflict.

Yet Larsson's novel is nevertheless haunted by the medieval. It is not only peppered with references to Tolkien's trilogy, but explicitly characterizes each of its two protagonists, Lisbeth Salander and Mikael Blomkvist, through allusions to the medieval. This is perhaps most obvious in the case of Salander. A hacker and private investigator, her prominent dragon tattoo is an apt symbol of her Gothic sensibilities and her chaotic and, at times, criminal approach to her work. It is also suggestive of one of the key abilities that makes her so effective at her job: the photographic memory that, Smaug-like, allows her to hoard the treasures she discovers in the course of her investigations. Blomkvist, by contrast, is associated with a very different, though no less recognizable, fixture of the medieval: the knight errant. Embodying the ethics, integrity, and objectivity that many media critics of mainstream media nostalgically associate with the era before twenty-four-hour cable news and the internet, Blomkvist structures almost every aspect of his life, including his work as a financial journalist, in accordance with a strict and unwavering code of behavior. He thus finds himself in a difficult position at the beginning of the novel. Duped into writing an erroneous article about the financial misdealings of investment capitalist Hans-Erik Wennerström, he refuses to reveal the source who fed him the misleading information and is subsequently convicted of libel and sentenced to three months in prison. While this decision might seem strange, especially when readers learn that Blomkvist is aware that he has been set up by Wennerström, it is entirely in keeping with the system of values he outlines in his "controversial" and, appropriately, medieval-titled book, *The Knights Templar: A Cautionary Tale for Financial Reporters*.[8] An exposé, Blomkvist's work describes the degree to which many prominent Scandinavian financial journalists collude with the corporations that they are tasked with monitoring.[9] To Blomkvist, then, these journalists are the contemporary equivalent of the Knights Templar: members of a noble and elite profession who have betrayed their vows to protect the weak and powerless in exchange for the economic and political benefits of financial conspiracy.

Although less explicitly, Larsson also associates the ailing Vanger group with the medieval. A familial concern with roots in nineteenth-century Swedish industrialism and even older, perhaps "twelfth-century" origins, the corporation's management is so convoluted, dysfunctional, and internecine that Blomkvist tells the aging patriarch of the family, Henrik Vanger, that it "sounds medieval in some ways."[10] Yet Blomkvist nevertheless pledges fealty to Henrik Vanger and the Vanger Corporation. Hoping to obtain information about Wennerström's financial misdeeds, he reluctantly agrees to investigate, under the pretense of "help[ing] [...] with the family chronicle," the nearly thirty-year-old mystery surrounding the disappearance of Vanger's favorite niece, Harriet Vanger.[11] In doing so, Blomkvist sets into motion a narrative that might seem more appropriate to a contemporary neomedievalist work than to the sort of island-bound, drawing-room mystery that Vanger and others regard as the normative state of their familial and corporate relations. Indeed, with Blomkvist playing the role of knight, Salander the role of dragon, and both working to understand the circumstances surrounding the disappearance of a young woman who is fetishized as representing the fertile potential of both family and company, Larsson's novel reads almost like a contemporary Scandinavian retelling of the 1996 feature film *Dragonheart*: a film in which an exiled knight joins forces with the last surviving dragon and – through the pretense of rescuing a politically savvy, though otherwise perpetually imperiled maiden – puts an end to a hereditary and corrupt regime.[12]

In *Dragonheart* this corruption is personified by a craven prince who, despite his vows to uphold an ancient, Arthurian "one-code" of honor, inherits and soon exceeds his father's penchant for cruelty and brutality towards the peasantry. In *The Girl with the Dragon Tattoo*, it takes a more financial, though no less brutal, form. On one hand, it is manifested in the character of Martin Vanger, who, as CEO of the Vanger Corporation, not only inherits his father's poor business sense, but also, as Blomkvist and Salander discover, his father's grotesque, criminal pastime: religiously and sexually inspired serial murders of young women. On the other hand, this corruption is manifested in Wennerström whose multi-national economic holdings are composed almost entirely of shell companies for a variety of international criminal enterprises. Using Martin Vanger and Wennerström as representatives, Larsson thus constructs corporate corruption as a quasi-religious, fascist, and blasphemous practice that emerged in the era of post-war industrial capitalism and culminates in the types of corporation that have become synonymous with late-capitalism: corporations that profit from buying and selling other corporations, rather than the production of manufactured goods. Yet although the most pernicious effects of this corruption are social rather than individual, the responsibility for alleviating or addressing them does not lie with the state, which is invariably portrayed as powerless or unwilling to intercede. Instead this responsibility is borne by private individuals who, despite their differences, are nevertheless bound together by their belief and adherence to a neo-chivalric code of honor and who, as a result, can only succeed in purging the corruption by challenging and vanquishing the individuals who embody it on the field of battle.

Thus, just as the death of the corrupt prince and his retinue sets the stage for political reform in *Dragonheart*, the key to restoring the Vanger Corporation to its rightful place at the head of Swedish industry lies not in revising its corporate structure to divest it of its antiquated system of familial governance, but in reforming the Vanger family itself: removing its corrupt members so that its more virtuous members can take their rightful places at the head of the Vanger Corporate board. Although this strategy makes for tidy, proportional endings, it is important to point out that it does not produce justice or systematic reform in either *Dragonheart* or *The Girl with the Dragon Tattoo*. Indeed, although the peasants play a pivotal role in overthrowing the tyrannical government in *Dragonheart*, they are not rewarded with more political power or a more equitable system of political representation, but with what is, arguably, more of the same: a "better" version of the feudal system that demanded their suffering and sacrifice in the first place. Much the same can be said for *The Girl with the Dragon Tattoo*. While Martin Vanger's death and the subsequent revelations about Wennerström's financial misdeeds in the media function to effectively end their respective reigns of terror, these events do not benefit the people who have suffered most: the dozens and dozens of women that Vanger murdered or the countless invisible victims of Wennerström's criminal schemes. Instead, these crimes and the suffering that resulted from them are deliberately covered up, not only by Blomkvist and Salander, who are aware of, but decide not to reveal, the full extent of Vanger's murders, but by the journalistic community as a whole, who invariably use the news about Wennerström's crimes and downfall as an occasion to celebrate the personal triumph of crusading journalists such as Blomkvist. As with the murder of the half-dozen or so peasants who are slaughtered roughly every twenty minutes in *Dragonheart*, everything else is portrayed, quite literally, as the price of doing business: the cost in human lives that must be paid in order to restore the status quo and the people who benefit from it to their former positions of prominence.

The Girl with the Dragon Tattoo, then, hinges upon two potent and interrelated medievalesque fantasies: that the corporate ideal necessarily recalls older feudal ideals, especially in the areas of corporate governance and continuance, and that there exist in such ideals imperatives derived from medieval mores that transcend questions of just profit, loss, and unfettered competition. Though newly dramatized in *The Girl with the Dragon Tattoo*, these twin fantasies are not recent developments; rather, they echo, perhaps unconsciously, attempts by late nineteenth- and early twentieth-century reformers and economists to rationalize, if not constrain, the industrial and economic developments of the period by recourse to what they promoted as more traditional systems of feudal ethics. This strategy is particularly evident in the writings of A. J. Penty and G. D. H. Cole, who rose to prominence in the first quarter of the twentieth century as advocates for the nascent Guild Socialism movement, and those of Alfred Marshall, who was arguably the leading English economist of the time. Though Marshall did concede a cautious sympathy for socialism in general, he was openly skeptical of "ill-considered measures of reform by Utopian schemers" – a category that might well have included Penty and Cole.[13] Nevertheless Marshall advocated, like Penty and Cole, a moral economy regulated by the ideals of the medieval past.

The Guild Socialists located their immediate origins in the Arts and Crafts movement, and they shared that movement's fascination with the medieval as well as its ambivalence towards industrialization, particularly automated means of production.[14] They faulted the Arts and Crafts, however, both for what they considered to be the movement's run-away individualism and as having been co-opted as a "feeder" of luxury. Instead they advocated collective action on behalf of all laborers against, as Penty writes, "that industrial progress 'whose motive is money and whose method is machinery.'"[15] They regarded the contemporary state as complicit in the capitalist alienation of labor, and they proposed as a corrective the establishment of distinct, self-governing "industrial guilds" that would restore workers' control over state and industry.[16] Such industrial guilds were to be, in Penty's words, of the "Medieval or Regulative type," meaning that their concerns would transcend questions of material production to include "the maintenance of Just and Fixed prices and rates and wages, the regulation of machinery and apprenticeship, the upholding of a standard of quality in production [...], and other matters appertaining to the conduct of industry and the personal welfare of its members."[17]

Although Penty's works contain the occasional, strident call for the revival of "our social and industrial past, when there was peasantry on the soil and craftsmen in the workshop, when things produced were beautiful, and when, organized in Guilds, men lived a corporate life, when, in short, England was a true Merrie England," his medievalism was, in practice, nowhere near so absolute, nor was that of his collaborators.[18] While the Guild Socialists condemned industry for its shoddy mass-production and its role in the continued exploitation of its workers, they nevertheless conceded the reality, if not the necessity, of contemporary means of production and instead turned to the medieval for "moral standards" with which to police modern industry.[19] To this extent, the "Guild movement," as Anthony Wright notes, "was never medievalist. It did claim some affinity of spirit with the medieval guild [...] but the theorists of Guild Socialism were concerned to transform the industrial world, not to abolish it."[20] Cole perhaps voices this sentiment most directly in *Guild Socialism Restated* (1920):

> Clearly, we cannot seek to restore the mediæval – that is the communal – spirit in industry by restoring the material conditions of the Middle Ages [...]. If the mediæval system has lessons for us, they are not parrot-lessons of slavish imitation, but lessons of the spirit, by which we may learn how to build up, on the basis of large-scale production and the world-market, a system of industrial organization that appeals to the finest human motives and is capable of developing the tradition of free communal service.[21]

Penty likewise acknowledges that "modern industry differs from Medieval industry," but he insists that such differences "are technical, and no technical difference can involve a difference of moral principles."[22] Industrialism, Penty writes, "grew up in a spiritual vacuum, when all the great traditions were dead."[23] Consequently, its salvation lay in a return to the clear "moral principles" that were understood by the medievals but lost to their more modern counterparts. According to Penty:

> The Medievalists understood what we are only beginning to understand – that there is no such thing as a purely economic solution to the problems of society, since economics are not to be understood as a separate and detached science considered apart from morals. On the contrary, economic issues are primarily moral issues with economic equivalents.[24]

Cole writes:

> In the Middle Ages there were industrial sinners, but they were conscious of sin; for commercial morality and communal morality were the same. Today, commercial morality has made a code of its own, and most of its clauses are flat denials of the principles of communal morality. In the Middle Ages, the motives to which the industrial system made its appeal were motives of free communal service: today, they are motives of greed and fear.[25]

The appeal of the medieval to both Penty and Cole, then, lay in its potential to connect "moral issues with economic equivalents" and thus recast contemporary debates over economic inequality as essentially moral questions. The concept of the "industrial sinner" is compelling to Penty and Cole because it allows them to imagine, as a corrective to what they considered to be the abuses of capitalism, economic actors "conscious of sin," which is to say economic actors empowered by more transcendent moral and ethical concerns.

Though by no means reactionary, Alfred Marshall's medievalism was nevertheless rooted in his ambivalence towards the potential of collectivist causes to address the apparent inequalities of the time while allowing for what he considered to be sufficient freedom of creative, intellectual, and economic expression. As much is evident in his 1907 essay, "The Social Possibilities of Economic Chivalry," which dedicates as much, if not more, attention to the apparent deficiencies of collectivism as it does to its professed subject. Although Marshall opens the essay by expressing concern with, in the words of Hans E. Jenson, "the manner in which real income was used in the economic society of his time" and eventually concedes a "reasonable dissatisfaction, with which every person must regard the existing distribution of wealth," he maintains that these two issues are, at best, only secondary threats to England's overall economic well-being.[26] The true danger, he argues, lies in the "ill-considered measures of Utopian schemers" that would "pervert" justified economic concerns in the promotion of "schemes that claim to be practical, and yet are based on no thorough study of economic realities."[27] Marshall's strident denunciation of "Utopian schemers," however, belies a deeper ambivalence towards collectivist causes, with Marshall himself admitting to a much-qualified socialism later in the essay and even expressing a degree of admiration for the "strenuous and unselfish devotion to social well-being" of those dedicated to collectivist causes.[28] Marshall nevertheless worries, though, that the rise of collectivism and its associated bureaucracy ultimately threatens both the tangible and intangible sources of economic and social progress:

> I am convinced that as soon as collectivist control has spread so far as to considerably narrow the field left for free enterprise, the pressure of bureaucratic methods would impair not only the springs of material wealth, but also many of those higher qualities of human nature, the strengthening of which should be the chief aim of human endeavor.[29]

Here and for the remainder of the essay, Marshall's "higher qualities of human nature" indicates the creative drive that he feels lies at the heart of capitalist enterprise and distinguishes it from a government that "creates

scarcely anything."[30] Marshall's concern for humanity's "higher qualities,"
however, acquires a metaphysical urgency, as Simon Cook observes, in
Marshall's other writings:

> At the deepest level, Marshall's argument with socialism was a meta-
> physical argument concerning the doctrines appropriate to a modern,
> secular and progressive faith [...]. The value of economic competition
> thus acquired a metaphysical justification for Marshall; it was both the
> most recent institutional manifestation of moral freedom, and the key
> economic institution which fostered that creative action which drove
> further progress [...]. The collectivist plans of the socialists, however,
> which sought to replace competition by government planning, led not
> only to inefficiency, but ultimately to 'spiritual death.'[31]

Marshall's ambivalence with collectivism, then, might be said to lie in his
sympathy for its motivations, inasmuch as he identified its motivations as
arising from a creative and commendable altruism, and his concern for
the long-term efficacy of its proposals, both in terms of tangible economic
development and more abstract spiritual effects. For Marshall, writes Cook,
"collectivist doctrines were the product of freedom and spiritual creativity.
Yet in practice such doctrines were likely at present to lead only to 'the
tyranny and the spiritual death of an ironbound socialism.'"[32]

As the title of his essay suggests, Marshall derived his answer to not only
the social and economic disparities of his time, but also (and consequently)
the threat of impending collectivism, from discourses of chivalry reconsti-
tuted in the popular medievalism of the late-Victorian and early-Edwardian
eras, formulating a call for collective, ethical business practice according to
the individualistic, martial standards of an imagined bygone feudal elite.
Thus Marshall writes (in what may perhaps be the earliest mash-up of
fantasy, science fiction, and misplaced classicism):

> If in the Elysian fields a mediæval warrior be now discussing with
> late inhabitants of worlds many billions of miles away from our own
> experiences of his old world, he may hold up his head as he speaks of
> the chivalry of war, the thing that occupied people's imagination most
> in that age [...].
>   But if the talk should turn in the Elysian fields on the elevation of
> life which we have won by the new methods of business, we should not
> hold up our heads as bravely as would the mediæval knight. I want to
> suggest that there is much latent chivalry in business life, and that there
> would be a great deal more of it if we sought it out and honoured it
> as men honoured the mediæval chivalry of war.[33]

As Thomas D. Birch notes, Marshall's call for "economic chivalry" was a call for "improving the quality of all human life both in the 'production of wealth and its use.'"[34] It presupposed that humanity was, though misguided by the allure of material status, inherently altruistic, and it called for workers from all levels of industry to labor unstintingly and cooperatively and to take "delight in doing noble and difficult things because they are noble and difficult."[35] The well-to-do were also to refrain from conspicuous consumption and instead divert those funds to the less fortunate.[36] Likewise, those who were so wealthy as not to have to work were to undertake "solid work for the public weal."[37] Compensation for these efforts would come not as wealth, but in terms that were more symbolic than material, in the form of the "honor" gained through the relative merits of one's endeavors. The rewarding as well as the recognition of honor would be policed not by national or collectivist institutions, but by "public opinion" enlisted by "businessmen" and "economists" to serve as an "informal Court of Honour" charged with judging the relative nobility of various endeavors:

> To distinguish that which is chivalrous and noble from that which is not, is a task that needs care and thought and labor; and to perform this task is a first duty of economists sitting at the feet of business men and learning from them. An endeavor should be made so to guide public opinion that it becomes an informal Court of Honour: that wealth, however large, should be no passport to success if got by chicanery, by manufactured news, by fraudulent dealing, or by malignant destruction of rivals; and that business enterprise which is noble in its aims and in its methods, even if it does not bring with it a large fortune, may receive its due of public admiration and gratitude [...].[38]

Marshall's economic chivalry was, in short, a call for collective action on the individual level without recourse to what he considered to be overreaching and soul-destroying bureaucratic institutions espoused by collectivist causes. If "true socialism," as Marshall puts it, were to be achieved on national and international levels, it would not be through the "iron bounds of mechanical symmetry, which Marx postulated as necessary for his 'International' projects," but through "economic chivalry on the part of the individual," which would, in turn, "stimulate and be stimulated by a similar chivalry by the community as a whole," and so on.[39]

It is difficult to know whether Marshall had Guild Socialism in mind when he wrote "The Social Possibilities of Economic Chivalry." He never identifies any collectivist scheme in particular in the essay, and Guild Socialism only came into its own as a coherent movement in 1915, though much of the movement's immediate inspiration came from Penty's 1906 *The Resto-*

ration of the Guild System.[40] Still, a certain irony emerges when Marshall's "Economic Chivalry" is juxtaposed with the works of the Guild Socialists; whereas the Guild Socialists turn to the medieval to fill a spiritual vacuum left by industrial capitalism, Marshall invokes the medieval as an antidote for a spiritual threat that he felt was inherent in collectivist practice, if not ideology. Although Marshall emphasizes the virtues of "chivalric emulation" rather than the transgressions of Penty and Cole's "industrial sinners," he nevertheless promotes, as do Penty and Cole, medieval precedents of moral and ethical behavior as central to modern reforms, industrial or otherwise.

Neither Guild Socialism nor Marshall's vision of economic chivalry or, for that matter, the optimistic medievalism of late-Victorian and Edwardian England, were to survive past the 1930s. The Guild Socialist movement collapsed after failure of the General Strike of 1926 and is now regarded as little more, as Wright puts it, than "a brief early-century interlude, a current isolated from the mainstream of British socialist development, to be recalled patronizingly or with derision according to taste."[41] As Birch notes, Maynard Keynes would question a key foundation of Marshall's call for economic chivalry in a lecture delivered the same year as Marshall's death – Marshall's enthusiasm for the positive role played by the entrepreneur in *laissez-faire* economics.[42] "The analytical intricacies of [Marshall's] extraordinary engine of analysis" still command, in the words of Theodore Levitt, "the undeviating […] attachment of economists," but his "persistent moralizing" has been "consistently […] ignored" – "his long policy sermon on 'The Social Possibilities of Economic Chivalry'[…] quickly and resolutely forgotten."[43] For its part, the heady medievalism of the period, already inherently nationalistic, would soon be conscripted by the National Socialists to justify the atrocities of the Second World War. It would be replaced by the literary neomedievalism of Tolkien and his followers, which imagined medievalesque realms isolated from the complications of history by their own fantastic and intricate systems of lore, and by the political and economic neomedievalism deployed during the second Bush presidency by neoconservative think tanks and corporate lawyers to justify everything from the torture of terror suspects to the banking chicanery that brought us the Enron and WorldCom scandals, culminating finally in the global financial crisis of 2007 and 2008.[44]

And yet, the popularity of Stieg Larsson's fantasy of a corporate world derived from and ultimately governed by a distinctly medievalesque and neochivalric morality suggests that the ethical medievalism espoused by Penty, Cole, and Marshall might be enjoying a wider resurgence. Marshall's faith in such "informal Court[s] of Honour" may sound naïve to us, but it is worth noting that Marshall's charge that "wealth, however large, should be no passport to success if got by chicanery, by manufactured news, by fraudulent dealing, or by malignant destruction of rivals," etc. nevertheless suggests itself as a fitting coda for *The Girl with the Dragon Tattoo* novel, despite having been written almost a century before Larsson's novel.[45]

In closing, we want to suggest two reasons for this nascent revival of the medieval as an imaginative precedent for the contemporary corporate ideal. The first is historicist, namely that the United States now finds itself in a very similar position to Edwardian England: at, if not slightly past, the apex of its economic potential, with corporations enjoying unprecedented prosperity but with the nation experiencing the widest disparities in income and wealth since the 1920s. In short, current conditions are arguably as fertile for neo-feudal moralists as they were in the time of Marshall and Penty and Cole. The second reason is more cynical (and thus probably more correct): that the medievalesque ethics recently revived by Larsson and espoused by Penty, Cole, and Marshall with their eventual emphasis on individual morality are not (despite the best efforts of Penty and Cole to deploy them as such) calls for collective responsibility, but exactly the opposite. In emphasizing individual "honor" (or lack thereof) as fundamental to corporate ethics, these discourses implicitly discredit historical materialist approaches to corporate malfeasance and instead enable the "bad-actor" fantasy, whereby one or two individuals can be persecuted in lieu of more substantial and collective action against the corporate whole. After all, this is the idealist fantasy that Larsson convinces his readers to accept. He not only represents the troubles of the Vanger Corporation as ultimately stemming from the anti-Semitic and murderous sociopathy passed down from Gottfried to Martin Vanger, but also involves readers in what is perhaps the great subterfuge perpetuated in the novel: Blomkvist and Salander's revision of the history of the Vanger family to conceal the systematic murders of an untold number of innocents for the good of its namesake company.

NOTES

1. *World of Warcraft: Cataclysm Expansion* (PC Version), Blizzard Entertainment, 2010.

2. Scott Rettberg, "Corporate Ideology in *World of Warcraft*," in *Digital Culture, Play, and Identity: A World of Warcraft Reader*, ed. Hilde G. Corneliussen and Jill Walker Rettberg (Cambridge, MA: MIT Press, 2008), 20.

3. Rettberg, "Corporate Ideology," 20.

4. See our "Revising the Future: The Medieval Self and the Sovereign Ethics of Empire in *Star Wars: Knights of the Old Republic*," in *Studies in Medievalism XVI: Medievalism in Technology Old and New*, ed. Karl Fugelso with Carol L. Robinson (Cambridge: D. S. Brewer, 2008), 159–83.

5. Stieg Larsson, *The Girl with the Dragon Tattoo*, trans. Reg Keeland (New York:

Alfred A. Knopf, 2010). All citations from the novel come from this edition. Citations from the original Swedish come from Larsson's *Män Som Hatar Kvinnor* (Stockholm: Månpocket, 2005).

6. Theodor Adorno and Max Horkheimer, "The Culture Industry: Enlightenment as Mass Deception," in *The Dialectics of Enlightenment* (New York: Continuum, 1944, 1972), 124.

7. Rita Raley, "eEmpires," *Cultural Critique* 57 (2004): 122–23.

8. Larsson, *Dragon Tattoo*, 43, 82.

9. Larsson, *Dragon Tattoo*, 82–84.

10. Larsson, *Dragon Tattoo*, 136. The original Swedish is, "Det låter medeltida på något sått" (171). Of the Vanger family's origins, Larsson writes, "The family tree could be traced back to the early sixteenth century, when the name was Vangeersad. According to Vanger the name may have originated from the Dutch van Geerstat; if that was the case, the lineage could be traced as far back as the twelfth century" (135) [Familjeträdet kunde med säkerhet spåras tillbaka tidigt 1500-tal, då familjenamnet hade verit Vangeersad. Enligt Henrik Vanger var det möjligt att namnet härstammade från holländska van Geerstad; om så var fallet kunde släkten spåras ända tillbaka till 1100-talet] (170).

11. Larsson, *Dragon Tattoo*, 124. The original Swedish reads, "[…] hjäpa […] med familjekrönikan" (157).

12. *Dragonheart*, dir. Rob Cohen (Universal Studios, 1996).

13. Alfred Marshall, "The Social Possibilities of Economic Chivalry," *The Economic Journal* 17/65 (1907): 18. As John Maynard Keynes wrote in Marshall's 1924 obituary, Marshall "sympathised with the Labour Movement and with Socialism [...] in every way, except intellectually." See "Alfred Marshall, 1842–1924," *The Economic Journal* 34/135 (1924): 358.

14. For an overview of the origins of the Guild Socialist movement and the chief personalities behind it, see Frances Hutchinson and Brian Burkitt, "The Douglas/New Age Texts in Historical Context," in *The Political Economy of Social Credit and Guild Socialism* (New York: Routledge, 1997), 7–29. On the influence of the Arts and Crafts movement on Penty's architectural practice and its implications for his advocacy of Guild Socialism, see David Thistlewood, "A. J. Penty (1875–1937) and the Legacy of 19th-Century English Domestic Architecture," *Journal of the Society of Architectural Historians* 46/4 (1987): 327–41.

15. Arthur J. Penty, *Post-Industrialism* (London: George Allen and Unwin, 1922), 143. For Penty's critique of the Arts and Crafts movement, see 146–51.

16. For a summary of the Guild Socialist critique of capitalism and the state, see Anthony W. Wright, "Guild Socialism Revisited," *Journal of Contemporary History* 9/1 (1974): 169–70. For an overview of the movement's proposed "industrial guild" system, see 173–74.

17. Arthur J. Penty, *Towards a Christian Sociology* (London: George Allen and Unwin, 1923), 134–35.

18. Penty, *Post-Industrialism*, "Return to the Past," 143.

19. Penty, *Towards a Christian Sociology*, 135.

20. Wright, "Guild Socialism Revisited," 168. Thistlewood likewise writes that, as an architect, Penty was "prompted by the desire to restore conditions that had given rise to medieval buildings, though not by a desire to revert to medieval built forms" (333). Arguably, this approach seems informed by Penty's writings on Guild Socialism as well.

21. G. D. H. Cole, *Guild Socialism Restated* (1920; reprint, New Brunswick, NJ: Transaction, Inc., 1980), 45–46.

22. Penty, *Towards a Christian Sociology*, 135.

23. Penty, "Means and Ends from *Means and Ends*," in *The Gauntlet: A Challenge to the Myth of Progress* (Norfolk, VA: IHS Press, 2003), 41.

24. Penty, *Towards a Christian Sociology*, 101.

25. Cole, *Guild Socialism Restated*, 45.

26. Hans E. Jenson, "Marshall Revisited: A Reply," *Journal of Economic Issues* 19/4 (1985): 971.

27. Marshall, "Economic Chivalry," 12–13. "I do not doubt," writes Marshall about the efforts of the collectivists, "that the paths on which they lead us might probably be strewn with roses for some distance" (12).

28. Marshall, "Economic Chivalry," 17.

29. Marshall, "Economic Chivalry," 17–18.

30. Marshall, "Economic Chivalry," 21.

31. Simon Cook, "Poetry, Faith and Chivalry: Alfred Marshall's Response to Modern Socialism," *History of Economics Review* 47 (Winter 2008): 29.

32. Cook, "Poetry, Faith and Chivalry," 29. Here, Cook quotes from Marshall's 1890 Presidential Address to the Economic Science and Statistics Section of the British Association. See "Some Aspects of Competition (1890)," in *Memorials of Alfred Marshall*, ed. A. C. Pigou (1925; reprint, New York: Augustus M. Kelley Publishers, 1966), 291.

33. Marshall, "Economic Chivalry," 13–14.

34. Thomas D. Birch, "Marshall and Keynes Revisited," *Journal of Economic Issues* 19/1 (1985): 196. Here, Birch quotes Marshall's "Economic Chivalry," 14. Marshall goes on to compare working for the difficulty of the work's sake to the call of "knightly chivalry" on its aspirants to begin "by making [their] own armor" (14).

35. Marshall, "Economic Chivalry," 14.

36. Birch, "Marshall and Keynes," 196.

37. Marshall, "Economic Chivalry," 26–27; Birch, "Marshall and Keynes," 196.

38. Marshall, "Economic Chivalry," 25–26.

39. Marshall, "Economic Chivalry," 27–28.

40. Hutchinson and Burkitt, "Historical Context," 8.

41. Wright, "Guild Socialism Revisited," 166.

42. Birch, "Marshall and Keynes," 198.

43. Theodore Levitt, "Alfred Marshall: Victorian Relevance for Modern Economics," *The Quarterly Journal of Economics* 90/3 (1976): 441.

44. For accounts of literary neomedievalism, see our "Neomedievalism, Hyperrealism, and Simulation" (12–24), as well as the other essays on the subject in *Studies in Medievalism XIX: Defining Neomedievalism(s)*, ed. Karl Fugelso (Cambridge: D. S. Brewer, 2010). For an account of the political and economic neomedievalism of the second Bush presidency, see Bruce Holsinger's *Neomedievalism, Neoconservatism, and the War on Terror* (Chicago: Prickly Paradigm Press, 2007).

45. Marshall, "Economic Chivalry," 29.

Medievalism and Representations of Corporate Identity

KellyAnn Fitzpatrick and Jil Hanifan

Anyone who has popped a quarter into the arcade version of *Gauntlet* from the early 1980s, brought home a console game such as those of Nintendo's *Zelda* series, or renewed a subscription to the currently popular *World of Warcraft* has not only exchanged money for the privilege of playing a game, but has also purchased a commodified representation of the Middle Ages. Many of these games borrow design elements from common understandings of the European Middle Ages, including settings, narratives, clothing, professions, and architecture. These borrowings, however, often make no claims to historical accuracy or realism, and their situation within the processes of the games themselves quite easily characterizes them as instances of neomedievalism as defined by Robinson and Clements.[1] Most of these games have a particular objective – such as fulfilling a quest – and position the player as an adventurer or hero who must use a combination of fighting abilities and magic to kill enemies. Such accomplishments lead to more advanced skills and an increased ability to defeat more powerful enemies, as well as the acquisition of gold – or whatever currency functions within the game – and other useful items such as food, armor, and weapons. In some games, a player can even hone "professional" skills that allow her to develop the ability to craft and sell advanced armor and weapons.

What interests us here are the processes by which players in neomedieval digital games interact with other entities and groups in order to fulfill these game objectives. In addition to the visual tropes listed above, neomedieval digital games also implement social hierarchies and economic arrangements inspired by lexical re-positionings of medievalesque tropes such as guilds, questing groups, and various other incorporated entities. Whether run by artificial intelligence, steered by other "real-world" human beings, or some combination of both, these entities help constitute what Edward Castronova would call the "synthetic" neomedieval world[2] constructed within the game, and also enable and accelerate a player's path towards whatever goals of questing, killing, looting, crafting, role-playing, and social interaction she may have. This essay explores how some of these entities and experiences – guilds, *ad hoc* groups, pre-arranged group quests, opposing factions, raiding parties, etc. – are represented within Blizzard's popular neomedieval MMORPG[3] *World of Warcraft* and two neomedieval single-player role-playing game (RPG) console-game[4] franchises: Bioware's *Dragon Age* and Bethesda's *Elder Scrolls*.[5] Furthermore, just as the emphasis on acquiring, crafting, and trading neomedievally themed objects such as armor, weapons, and gold within the game links the commodified nature of the games themselves with the corporate entities that produce them, they also represent a rich text for neomedieval scholarship.

The creation of medieval spaces and the opportunity to purchase medievally inspired goods did not originate with late twentieth- and early twenty-first-century video games; indeed the creation of these virtual medieval spaces and economies has its roots in a number of earlier cultural practices. The most immediate predecessor that comes to mind is the table-top RPG *Dungeons & Dragons*. Although the mechanics and visual representations involve guidebooks, paper, and pencil rather than images displayed by means of a game console or computer software, *Dungeons & Dragons* functions via the creation of a narrative that employs medievalesque characters and plot.

While the influence of *Dungeons & Dragons* on current video games is widely accepted,[6] critics such as Celia Pearce have made the comparison between Renaissance Faires and MMORPGS such as *World of Warcraft*. Pearce writes:

> The central play mechanic of the MMORPG is what I refer to as social storytelling, or collaborative fiction. The idea is that the story emerges as a direct result of social interaction. As with the Renaissance Faire […] players enter a fully constructed three-dimensional world. Rather than selecting fixed characters, they select particular character roles. These are somewhat generic, but allow players to configure unique characters composed of various traits, which they can evolve over time into a fully developed persona through a system of improvisational collaborative narrative.[7]

A cultural predecessor to the types of neomedieval synthetic worlds discussed above, the Medieval and Renaissance Faire constructs a physical space that purports to represent elements of the Middle Ages. Although these events rarely (if at all) organize themselves around a single controlling narrative, they offer an opportunity for guests to interact with actors who have assumed the roles of various medieval characters and also invite guests to don medieval-inspired "garb," speak in archaic-sounding language, and purchase "medieval" commodities: in essence, producing real-world simulations of the spaces and consumptive practices captured in neomedieval digital games.

It is possible to trace the spatial, shopping, and social practices of Medieval and Renaissance Faires to an even earlier source: the nineteenth-century Medieval Revival, which saw a market place in which consumers could create an imaginary relationship to the medieval through their home decor, bric-à-brac, and, in cases such as Sir Walter Scott's Abbotsford or William Morris's Red House, even the architecture of their homes. Morris himself serves as an exemplary figure of the Medieval Revival. His Red House, which he commissioned from architect Philip Webb, incorporates a number of design elements inspired by medieval architecture, boasts custom stained-glass windows and creates a space visually and literarily linked to the Middle Ages. Morris also made a name for himself through his company's production of decorative items inspired by medieval designs, including stained glass, tapestries, and furniture that offered consumers an alternative to the ostentatious and busy designs then popular in Victorian Britain.[8]

The phenomena of constructing imagined medieval spaces and participating in the consumption and crafting of medieval-themed products, then, can be traced to well before the advent of neomedieval digital games. Notably, earlier iterations of these phenomena have already received extensive critical and scholarly attention within nineteenth-century studies. Morris's medievalism in particular has received considerable scholarly treatment in terms of its interrelationship with his political, economic, and artistic principles,[9] and the Medieval Revival as a whole has alternately been theorized as a reaction to and escape from the industrial revolution and its social and economic repercussions.[10] Although some recent works have defined these earlier forms of medievalism as fundamentally different from neomedieval texts,[11] we would argue that it is possible, while keeping such differences in mind, to view criticism of earlier texts as the groundwork for an analysis of how neomedieval digital games serve as a reaction to and escape from the conditions of contemporary capitalism, globalization, and their social and economic repercussions. Likewise, these earlier texts also demonstrate the use of the Middle Ages as a means of forging group identities and forwarding specific ideologies clothed in medieval costume. The 1839 Eglinton Tournament, for example, in which members of the British aristocracy attempted to stage a medieval tournament complete with jousting and a "Queen of Beauty," was no less an attempt to reinforce the identity of nobility than it was an amusement and diversion.[12] Likewise, Morris's *News from Nowhere* imagines a future in which socialism has overthrown capitalism, yet the world has culturally reverted to a medieval society. The people in this world

forge a social identity that collectively rejects history in favor of the natural-
ized intersection of socialism and medievalism that Morris uses to forward
his own political and social agenda.[13]

As Scott Rettberg has argued, the use of medieval tropes to forward
contemporary agendas is just as relevant in the twenty-first century, as
neomedieval games often cleverly perpetuate the corporate ideologies of the
companies that produce them. He writes, "*World of Warcraft* is both a game
and a simulation that reinforces the values of the Western market-driven
economies. The game offers its players a capitalist fairytale in which anyone
who works hard and strives enough can rise through society's ranks and
acquire great wealth."[14] Furthermore, he argues, the social interaction worked
into the game serves a function of perpetuating this ideology and regulating
related behavior. He notes:

> In a larger sense the game is training a generation of good corporate
> citizens not only to consume well and pay their dues, but also to climb
> the corporate ladder, to lead projects, to achieve sales goals, to earn and
> save, to work hard for better possessions, to play the markets, to win
> respect from their peers and their customers, to direct and encourage
> and cajole their underlings to outperform, and to become better
> employees and perhaps, eventually, effective future CEOs.[15]

The game, he argues, through the advantages and oftentimes necessity of
working with incorporated groups, merely reinforces the values of the corporate entities that have created the games themselves.

There is, indeed, much at stake for corporations in perpetuating themselves and their values through the synthetic worlds they create. First and
foremost, the very existence of most neomedieval digital games is dependent
on for-profit software corporations, in part because the labor and capital
required for their production can often only be found in such companies,[16]
but also because the development of most MMORPGs and console games
is the result of their effort to transpose the considerable commercial and
popular success of games like *Dungeons & Dragons* and *Magic: the Gathering*
into digital products. Secondly, corporate competition among the companies that produce these games results in a diversity of neomedieval synthetic
worlds, both in gameplay experience and commodification strategy.

In terms of MMORPGs such as *World of Warcraft*, consumer access to
the game relies not only on an upfront purchase of software and expansion packs, but also on regular subscriptions, so there is a need to maintain
and improve the existing product. Castronova states that "production does
not stop when the product is finished" in a MMORPG, as these worlds
require continuous upkeep to function and updating via expansion packs

to remain competitive.[17] Indeed, as Aphra Kerr notes, the production model of MMORPGs differs from that of console games: "While the organization of production in the console and PC segments are comparable to the book publishing and film production processes, the production of MMOGs is a more complex process, tending more towards the broadcast model."[18] In other words, because MMORPGs require constant upkeep and frequent improvements of features and rules, periodically new episodes are available as expansion packs at a price, and these new episodes often involve entirely new virtual spaces for gameplay, as well as new character types, rules, or abilities.

While producers of console games such as *Dragon Age* and *Elder Scrolls* also require the same corporate benefits of a plentiful work force and capital, they face different marketing and consumptive concerns that drive their business model and competitiveness. In MMORPGs like *World of Warcraft*, players follow leveling quests, but might prefer other types of play, like dungeons or raiding, and so might avoid questing almost entirely: a business model that allows Blizzard to not only sell the software, but also profit from ongoing player subscriptions. But single-player RPGs rely on a heroic narrative to drive play, and heroic narratives have individual protagonists, escalating tensions and a resolving climax. The essential dilemma confronting the developer of a single-player RPG is narrative closure.[19] Ultimately, the business model of these kinds of games is closer to that of a novel or a film, since once the player completes the final battle and finishes the main story arc, the game is essentially over. So game features that extend gameplay, or present a significantly different gaming experience on replay, become selling points.

Indeed, even among console games, issues such as narrative form and gameplay that emphasize particular aspects that constitute the neomedieval worlds they create become a means of fueling competition for consumers. In regard to Bethesda's *Elder Scrolls* and Bioware's *Dragon Age*, which embody two console franchises in direct competition with each other, both fan forums[20] and industry reviews locate different selling points in narrative interpretation. As one review writes, "Bethesda emphasizes aesthetic presentation and open-ended adventuring, while BioWare and Obsidian have focused on a tighter combat system (hence the rules) and an extendable architecture befitting of the classic *Dungeons & Dragons* experience."[21] As noted above, Bethesda's *Elder Scrolls* franchise presents a huge virtual environment and emphasizes a relatively open-ended game design, while in *Dragon Age: Origins* Bioware has created six different origin stories for characters, which situates the player's character in a specific past with a personal history to encourage replay. Competition thus drives variety, as each model creates a variation on the neomedieval console RPG that attempts to appeal to its own niche market.

Despite the differences among MMORPGs and single-player console

RPGs, most are similar in their incorporation of neomedieval group identities within the games – even if the way these groups are presented varies among game types and titles. *World of Warcraft*, for instance, requires that each player joins one of two opposing factions within the game, the "Alliance" or the "Horde." In addition, players can choose to join a "guild" comprising other players, which provides a support network for completing quests, pooling resources, or simply knowing that, among the thousands of players online, there is a set group that is familiar and welcoming. While players can always form *ad hoc* groups without joining a guild, certain parts of the game – such as dungeons that require cooperative play of five-, ten-, or even twenty-five-player groups – are very difficult to navigate without a reliable and regularly incorporated group such as a guild. Notably, as with most neomedieval texts, the groups produced within these games, even when they adopt names such as "guilds," make no pretensions toward accurate or historic depictions of the guilds and associations of a "real" Middle Ages. Guilds, for example, have very little to do with professions or craft, but instead form a supportive system and hierarchical structure through which larger quests can occur, or even a means of smaller economic exchange away from the auction house.[22]

While, for Rettberg, the neomedieval qualities of these groups help mask a hidden ideological agenda, we would argue that, corporate backing or no, it is a combination of the social interaction and neomedieval culture that draws players to these types of games. As Castronova notes, "Sociality I would argue is what makes digital games a transformative technology as well. The big difference here is not that people feel very immersed, it is that they feel immersed *together*."[23] For Castronova, it is a combination of cultural plenty – in the case of *Warcraft*, a culture fueled by neomedieval myths and incorporated archetypes – and supplemented real-world social interaction that draws players in to synthetic worlds:

> Someone who is lonely in the real world, mostly because they have trouble making first contact, doesn't have to worry in virtual worlds, because people are often thrown together by various missions and quests. Culturally, the real world can be a terribly empty place. Not everyone lives in a community with rich traditions, faiths, and stories that put meaning into everyone's life, whereas in synthetic worlds, everyone is asked to complete quests, fight enemies, and become a hero.[24]

Although the construction of a neomedieval culture that proves socially pleasing for most players often requires behind-the-scenes policing from their parent corporations,[25] and even with such policing in place there is much room for social disaster,[26] such a social component is so important that even in single-player RPG console games this combination of cultural richness and social interaction is necessary to the creation of Rettberg's "capitalist fairytale in which anyone who works hard and strives enough can rise through society's ranks and acquire great wealth." Indeed, games such as *Elder Scrolls* and *Dragon Age* rely on increasingly more complicated systems of Artificial Intelligence (AI) to reproduce the experience of interacting with other entities.[27] *Elder Scrolls,* for instance, establishes "guilds" that serve primarily as sites for side-quests, and a player might elect to join any or all of the five available factions, incorporating these adventures and their interaction with AI-driven characters into the overall game narrative. Likewise, *Dragon Age* uses groups of AI-driven characters called "guilds" or "brotherhoods" as sources for side-quests, but the character's access to these often depends on race or battle type, and the player/character is positioned as an external contractor, as opposed to a full member.

Indeed, if we follow Rettberg's theory that such games replicate corporate behaviors, the range of AI-generated entities in games such as *Elder Scrolls* and *Dragon Age* stand in for the "real" people with whom a player can interact in MMORPGs like *World of Warcraft*, and can therefore be seen as the coworkers, collaborates, superiors, and subordinates found in corporate hierarchical structures. This proves important for players who want the experience of participating in a group – the construction of an incorporated identity – without the necessity of interacting with others in "real" life. As Castronova notes, "As a result, in virtual worlds, you can be a steadfastly individualist person, yet also feel a member of the team, a guild, and a community. In our age of anomie, it is a truly remarkable achievement."[28] In part, then, medievalism is used to perpetuate and imbed corporate identity and capitalist ideology while allowing players to participate in the formation of an incorporated identity and still maintain an individual sense of self.

Whether the other members that help constitute these group identities are driven by AI or a "real" person behind a laptop, what we see more and more are synthetic worlds, created by corporate entities, that construct corporate spaces and identities under the guise of neomedieval tropes; furthermore, these spaces are becoming continually more removed from genuine social interaction. For example, Wizards of the Coast's *Magic: the Gathering* franchise, which originated in 1994 as a neomedieval trading card game in which players would meet – in person – to play, expanded to online play with *Magic: Online*, in which players could compete online against other "real" players through the online medium. While this removed the need for a physical "gathering," it nevertheless required play with other "real" people. With the 2009 introduction of its console game *Duels of the Planeswalkers*, however, a player can now dismiss other "real world" interaction altogether in favor of competing against other "players" powered by an advanced AI.[29]

This move towards completely artificial synthetic reality highlights the importance of studying the use of historically unhinged medieval tropes to re-present and reconfigure medieval attitudes toward groups, work, and community in an increasingly corporate and unceasingly commercial environment. Indeed, while the methods by which medieval-inspired virtual realities are constructed can be traced through over two centuries of carefully documented and studied representations of the Middle Ages – and no other video-game theme can boast such a pedigree – the manufacture of interactive incorporated identities based on artificial entities is something new and not simply yet another neomedieval commodity. Rather, our understanding of these digital games and how they create identities and virtual communities needs to be informed by the rich invention and scholarly analysis of (neo) medievalism.

NOTES

1.   Carol L. Robinson and Pamela Clements, "Living with Neomedievalism," *Studies in Medievalism XVIII: Defining Medievalism(s)* II, ed. Karl Fugelso (Cambridge: D. S. Brewer, 2009), 55–72. As part of their definition of neomedievalism, Robinson and Clements note, "For better or for worse, neomedievalism draws from the Middle Ages (European, but more recently also from non-European sources, such as Japanese). Unlike in postmodernism, however, neomedievalism does not look to the Middle Ages to use, to study, to copy, or even to learn; the perception of the Middle Ages is more filtered, perceptions of perceptions (and of distortions), done without a concern for facts of reality, such as the fact that [Monty Python's] The Knights Who Say 'Ni' never existed. This lack of concern for historical accuracy, however, is not the same as that held in more traditional fantasy works: the difference is a degree of self-awareness and self-reflexivity. Nor is it the same as what we conceive to be medievalism" (62).

2.   Edward Castronova, *Synthetic Worlds: The Business and Culture of Online Gaming* (Chicago: University of Chicago Press, 2005), 3–7.

3.   In a "MMORPG," or "Massively Multiplayer Online Role Playing Game," players assume the role of characters (either pre-set or customized from among pre-set choices) through which they either follow or help construct the game's narrative. The game is played online via computers, in which a substantial number of players inhabit and help construct a virtual environment and the events that occur within it.

4.   A "console game" is designed for an in-home gaming system, such as the Playstation 3 or Xbox 360. While it may have unlimited online capabilities, play in a console game is often limited to one to four players.

5.   For information on the difference in play between traditional console games and MMORPGs, see Laurie N. Taylor, "Platform Dependent: Console and Computer Culture," in *The Players' Realm: Studies on the Culture of Video Games and Gaming*, ed. K. Patrick Williams and Jonas Heide Smith (Jefferson, NC: McFarland & Company, 2007), 223–37.

6. See Jonathan Dovey and Helen W. Kennedy, "From Margin to Center: Biographies of Technicity and the Construction of Hegemonic Games Culture," in *The Players' Realm*, 142–43; Steven Malliet and Gust de Meyer, "The History of the Video Game," in *Handbook of Computer Game Studies*, ed. Joost Raessens and Jeffrey Goldstein (Cambridge, MA: MIT Press, 2005), 24; and T. L. Taylor, *Play Between Worlds* (Cambridge, MA: MIT Press, 2006), 22.

7. Celia Pearce, "Towards a Game Theory of Game," in *First Person: New Media as Story, Performance, and Game*, ed. Noah Wardrip-Fruin and Pat Harrigan (Cambridge, MA: MIT Press, 2004), 148–49.

8. For a good survey of Morris's work, see *William Morris and the Middle Ages: A collection of essays, together with a catalogue of works exhibited at the Whitworth Gallery, 28 September – 8 December 1994*, ed. Joanna Banham and Jennifer Harris (Manchester: Manchester University Press, 1994). Alternately, the William Morris Society has an excellent – if informal – listing of his works at "William Morris: Life and Works," William Morris Society in the United States, www.morrissociety.org/morris

9. See, for instance, Bradley J. MacDonald, *William Morris and the Aesthetic Constitution of Politics* (Lanham, MD: Lexington Books, 1999).

10. See, for instance, Mark Girouard, *The Return to Camelot: Chivalry and the English Gentleman* (New Haven, CT: Yale University Press, 1981); and Alice Chandler, *A Dream of Order: The Medieval Ideal in Nineteenth-Century English Literature* (Lincoln: University Press of Nebraska, 1970).

11. Brent Moberly and Kevin Moberly, "Neomedievalism, Hyperrealism, and Simulation," *Studies in Medievalism XIX: Defining Neomedievalism(s)*, ed. Karl Fugelso (Cambridge: D. S. Brewer, 2010), 26–27. Moberly and Moberly note, "Neomedieval works are, in this sense, very different from the works that define late-nineteenth- and early-to-mid-twentieth-century medievalism. These works were a reaction to burgeoning technologies of capitalism, most notably industrialization […]. The neomedieval, however, does not entirely abandon the medievalist fervor for such concepts as knighthood, chivalry, romance, or quests; instead it commodifies them, extending these privileges to anyone who can afford them. The result is an egalitarian, consumerist version of the medieval in which nobility is measured by one's purchasing power."

12. For an excellent description of the events and context of the Eglinton Tournament, see Girouard, *The Return to Camelot*, 88–110; and Albert D. Pionke, "A Ritual Failure: The Eglinton Tournament, the Victorian Medieval Revival, and Victorian Ritual Culture," *Studies in Medievalism XVI: Medievalism in Technology Old and New*, ed. Karl Fugelso with Carol L. Robinson (Cambridge: D. S. Brewer, 2008), 25–45.

13. William Morris, *News from Nowhere and Other Writings* (1890; repr. London: Penguin, 1993). For excellent readings of Morris's use of the Middle Ages, see Northrop Frye, "The Meeting of Past and Future in William Morris," *Studies in Romanticism* 21.3 (1982): 303–18; and
Michael Holzman, "The Pleasures of William Morris's Twenty-Second Century," *The Journal of Pre-Raphaelite Studies* 4.1 (1983): 26–37.

14. Scott Rettberg, "Corporate Ideology in *World of Warcraft*," in *Digital Culture, Play and Identity: A World of Warcraft Reader*, ed. Hilde G. Corneliussen and Jill Walker Rettberg (Cambridge, MA: MIT Press, 2008), 20.

15. Rettberg, "Corporate Ideology," 20.

16. Castronova, *Synthetic Worlds*, 127.

17. Castronova, *Synthetic Worlds*, 127.

18. Aphra Kerr, *The Business and Culture of Digital Games: Gamework/Gameplay* (London: Sage, 2006), 150.

19. For an overall introduction to narrativity in digital games, see Britta Neitzel, "Narrativity in Computer Games," in *Handbook*, 227–45.

20. See, for instance, the fan-forum topic "Bioware vs. Bethesda: Battle of the Western RPG Giants," *Gamespot*, www.gamespot.com/forums/topic/26571521 (accessed 27 July 2011).

21. Alan Rose, "Metareview – *Neverwinter Nights 2*," *Joystiq*, www.joystiq.com/2006/11/03/metareview-neverwinter-nights-2 (last modified 3 November 2006).

22. For an excellent outline of the internal economy of *World of Warcraft*, see William Sims Bainbridge, *The Warcraft Civilization: Social Science in a Virtual World* (Cambridge, MA: MIT Press, 2010), 137–68.

23. Edward Castronova, *Exodus to the Virtual World: How Online Fun is Changing Reality* (New York: St. Martin's Press, 2007), 36.

24. Castronova, *Exodus to the Virtual World*, 69.

25. See, for instance, Castronova's discussion of the development of anti-harassment policies in synthetic worlds in Castronova, *Exodus to the Virtual World*, 130–32.

26. For illustrations of some of the tentative negative consequences of social groupings in *World of Warcraft*, see Bainbridge, *The Warcraft Civilization*, 131–33.

27. *Elder Scrolls* in particular has received much attention for its development of a "Radiant AI system," which imitates the impact of environment factors and player interaction on the Non-Player Characters (NPCs) with which a player interacts. For more information on this, see Bobby Stein, "Radiant A.I.," *Microsoft*, http://web.archive.org/web/20080621055703/http://www.xbox.com/en-US/games/t/theelderscrollsIVoblivion/20051208-radiantai.htm (accessed 14 July 2011).

28. Castronova, *Exodus to the Virtual World*, 174.

29. See Patrick Buckland, "Duels of the Planeswalkers: All about AI," *Wizards of the Coast*, www.wizards.com/Magic/Magazine/Article.aspx?x=mtg/daily/feature/44 (last updated 22 June 2009).

Knights of the Ownership Society: Economic Inequality and Medievalist Film

Harry Brown

In America's ideal of freedom, citizens find the dignity and security of economic independence, instead of laboring on the edge of subsistence. […] To give every American a stake in the promise and future of our country, we will bring the highest standards to our schools, and build an ownership society. […] By making every citizen an agent of his or her own destiny, we will give our fellow Americans greater freedom from want and fear, and make our society more prosperous and just and equal.[1]

George W. Bush, Second Inaugural Address (2005)

Our journey has never been one of shortcuts or settling for less. It has not been the path for the faint-hearted, for those who prefer leisure over work, or seek only the pleasures of riches and fame. Rather, it has been the risk takers, the doers, the makers of things […] who have carried us up the long, rugged path towards prosperity and freedom. […] They saw America as bigger than the sum of our individual ambitions, greater than all the differences of birth or wealth or faction.[2]

Barack Obama, Inaugural Address (2009)

Disparate Fortunes

Although now more than ever the ideologies personified by Obama and Bush seem to stand in desperate opposition to each other, their differences are almost invisible in their respective inaugural addresses. Both speak of economic opportunity as the nation's fundamental virtue, the guarantee for a just society. Both assure us that prosperity and independence lie within reach of any person willing to work for them, though the path to success may be long and hard. The recent financial crisis, however, has withered hopes for an ownership society, leaving us largely a nation of debtors. Between 2008 and 2010, almost five million American families lost their homes to foreclosure, with another four million families projected to lose their homes between 2010 and 2012.[3]

But even in the wake of recession, American corporate profits have grown at historic rates. They now account for their largest share of the gross domestic product in sixty years, while wages and salaries account for their smallest share in sixty years, as if American corporations inhabit a parallel financial universe where the crisis never occurred.[4] Some companies seem impervious even to the most spectacular disasters. After losing $17 billion following the Deepwater Horizon oil spill in spring 2010, BP returned a substantial profit by the end of the same year.[5] Soon after the disaster, Transocean Limited, owner of the drill platform that exploded and killed eleven workers, rewarded its chief executive with a $200,000 raise and a bonus of $374,000, citing the company's outstanding safety record.[6] Meanwhile, American maritime law stipulated only two years of lost wages, or $60,000, as compensation for the families of the dead oil workers, an injustice Congress moved to correct after the disaster.[7]

The recession and the oil spill represent only the most glaring signs of a deeper undercurrent of economic inequality. Currently, the top 1 percent of Americans hold nearly half of the wealth, while the bottom 40 percent, on average, owe more than they own.[8] In the last twenty years, corporate profits have tripled, while unemployment has nearly doubled.[9] In 1980, a chief executive earned, on average, forty times the salary of a production worker; now an executive earns almost 350 times the salary of a worker.[10] Even as the nation has prospered, poverty has remained steady, with few besides the wealthiest Americans benefiting from economic growth. Although the economy grew fivefold between 1979 and 2008, average income declined for the bottom 90 percent of Americans.[11]

These facts belie the promise of the "ownership society." Nonetheless, the economic independence eulogized by Bush and Obama has become, in spite of the facts, an article of faith. A recent survey by psychologists Michael I. Norton and Dan Ariely shows that Americans underestimate economic inequality in the United States, supposing that the wealthiest 20 percent of Americans hold 60 percent of the nation's wealth, and that the poorest 40 percent hold 10 percent. In fact, the wealthiest 20 percent hold more than 80 percent of the wealth, and the poorest 40 percent hold less than one-third of 1 percent. Respondents also say that they would like to live in a more equitable society, with the wealthiest 20 percent and the poorest

40 percent of Americans holding comparable shares of the wealth. Norton and Ariely conclude, "just as people have erroneous beliefs about the actual level of wealth inequality, they may also hold overly optimistic beliefs about opportunities for social mobility in the United States."[12] In other words, we believe our society to be more just than it is, because we wish it to be so. In fact, we may need to believe it in order to make reality more tolerable.

Meritocracy and the Medieval

Recent medievalist film has emerged as a unique expression of this "overly optimistic" belief about equality in a time of radical inequality. In Antoine Fuqua's *King Arthur* (2004), for example, a Sarmatian nomad's son conscripted into the Roman army repels Saxon invaders and becomes king of a newly unified Britain.[13] In Ridley Scott's *Kingdom of Heaven* (2005), Balian, a French blacksmith's son, becomes the unlikely defender of Christian Jerusalem and the enlightened mediator between Christianity and Islam.[14] In Scott's *Robin Hood* (2010), Robin Longstride, an English foot soldier, steals the identity of a knight, only to prove himself more than worthy of the title in his defense of honest farmers against tyrants.[15] Emblems of Bush's ownership society and Obama's renewed hope for American greatness, they are agents of their "own destiny," who transcend "differences of birth or wealth."

In each film, the medieval milieu serves as a mirror to the present, an implied judgment against the corrupt leaders of our own age who squander enormous wealth and cut dirty deals in betrayal of their own people. *King Arthur* portrays an empire in retreat with abandoned Britons left defenseless against even more vicious foreigners. *Kingdom of Heaven* revises the Third Crusade as an allegory of the modern conflict between Islam and the West, a senseless struggle manufactured by fanatics and warmongers on both sides. In the more populist *Robin Hood*, Scott represents the Crusades as a perpetual and costly war that drives English lords to steal from their people in order to pay war debts. Confronted by injustice, each of the unlikely champions in these films usurps corruption and restores integrity to the realm. Arthur disowns the Roman Empire and forges an alliance with formerly oppressed native Britons, Balian surrenders the gates of Jerusalem but saves its people from pointless slaughter, and Robin starts a democratic revolution when the treacherous King John, insecure in his rule, refuses to recognize the rights of the people.

As medieval legends adapted to modern democratic ideals, the films present a striking pattern. The hero begins as an anonymous plebe and ascends to eminence through honest ambition, loyalty to friends and benevolent patrons, and the sense to seize an opportunity when he finds it. Although initially naïve, he learns quickly, buoyed by charisma and valor. His success over corrupt adversaries suggests that the root of injustice is not structural inequality but rather individual wrongdoing. By demonstrating the potential to transcend "differences of birth or wealth or faction," he legitimates a seemingly unjust social hierarchy as a meritocracy, imperfect and susceptible to abuse, perhaps, but ultimately natural and just.

Although myths of equality properly belong to inequitable societies, medievalist adventure seems an improper vehicle for them. While the republican ideals of Benjamin Franklin and Thomas Jefferson obviously inspire Bush and Obama in their paeans to American meritocracy, their adaptation in *King Arthur*, *Kingdom of Heaven*, and *Robin Hood* seems more surprising. Franklin and Jefferson regarded the democratic experiment, coupled with the practically unlimited availability of land on the frontier, as a means to correct the system that granted a small minority of landowners a vast share of the wealth, while condemning the majority of people to perpetual vassalage. Property would no longer be the means for the few to exercise power over the many, because the many could now hold property for themselves. Franklin extends the promise of economic independence to prospective immigrants in 1782, offering ownership as a guarantee of equality. "Land being cheap," he writes,

> and not likely to be occupied in an age to come, insomuch that the propriety of an hundred acres of fertile soil full of wood may be obtained near the frontiers, in many places, for eight or ten guineas, hearty young labouring men, who understand the husbandry of corn and cattle [...] may easily establish themselves there.

By owning his own farm, a man could escape generations of feudal subjugation: "Multitudes of poor people from England, Ireland, Scotland, and Germany have by this means in a few years become wealthy farmers, who, in their own countries [...] could never have emerged from the poor condition wherein they were born."[16] Jefferson likewise assures a French diplomat in 1781 that the "immensity of land courting the industry of the husbandman" will ensure a more equitable prosperity by curbing the growth of cities and preventing the concentration of wealth among merchants and manufacturers.[17]

For Franklin and Jefferson, the creation of the American republic also awakened a moral conscience that lay dormant in medieval society, when lords and churchmen made decisions for their people, keeping them in a state of intellectual infancy. Industry and "constant employment," Franklin writes, "are great preservatives of the morals and virtue of a nation."[18] Jefferson also reasons that economic dependence "begets subservience and venality, suffocates the germ of virtue, and prepares fit tools for the designs of ambition."[19]

Reflecting on the character of American democratic society in 1840, Alexis de Tocqueville confirms this affinity between economic equality and moral conscience. "When ranks are almost equal in a people," he writes, "each of them can judge the sensations of all the others in a moment." Tocqueville finds that the uncommon sympathy among Americans signals a fundamental break from medieval ways of thinking, which unconsciously valued some classes of human life over others:

> When the chroniclers of the Middle Ages, who all belonged by their birth or their habits to the aristocracy, relate the tragic end of a noble, it is with infinite sorrow; whereas they recount the massacre and tortures of the common people all in one breath and without a frown. […] they did not form a clear idea for themselves of the sufferings of the poor man.

He concludes,

> Feudal institutions rendered one very sensitive to the ills of certain men, but not to the miseries of the human species […] for there is real sympathy only among people who are alike; and in aristocratic centuries one sees those like oneself only in the members of one's caste.[20]

The Culture of Competitive Individualism

Despite Jefferson's wish to curb the growth of manufacturing, most of the nation's wealth in the nineteenth century became concentrated in industry rather than agriculture. Among the first to register the effects of American industrialization, Tocqueville regarded the "small aristocratic societies that certain industries form" an "exception, a monster" to the founding principle of equality. After nearly seventy years of independence, there remain in America "some very opulent men and a very miserable multitude," as in feudal aristocracies of the past. Franklin's promise of economic independence still seemed unrealized to Tocqueville. "The poor have few means of leaving their condition and of becoming rich," he writes, "but the rich constantly become poor." He concludes with a prescient warning that the trend toward economic disparity threatens to undo the entire work of democracy:

> the manufacturing aristocracy that we see rising before our eyes is one of the hardest that has appeared on earth. […] The friends of democracy ought constantly to turn their regard with anxiety in this direction; for if ever permanent inequality of conditions and aristocracy are introduced anew into the world, one can predict that they will enter by this door.[21]

The pattern of economic growth in the second half of the nineteenth century confirmed Tocqueville's fear about "permanent inequality" and new aristocracy. The 1890 census shows half of American families owning nothing and subsisting in wage slavery, while the richest 1 percent held more wealth than all other Americans combined.[22] In *The Incorporation of America*, Alan Trachtenberg attributes this striking level of inequality, much worse than today's, to the creation of corporations, legal entities allowing a large association of shareholders to act as one. Trachtenberg explains that centralized control in business became a great asset, allowing "efficiencies in administration, freedom of negotiation, extensions of control among many companies within single industries, and integrating whole industrial steps, from the extraction of raw materials to processing and marketing within single companies."[23] As companies consolidated into trusts, they became virtual states within states, taking control of entire industries and markets.

Trachtenberg documents the cultural transformation attending the unprecedented accumulation of corporate wealth, particularly in the emergence of a "culture of competitive individualism, of acquisitiveness and segregation," in which wealth itself was a virtue.[24] Andrew Carnegie articulates this ideology most clearly. The "law of competition," he declares, is the law of life: "It is here; we cannot evade it; no substitutes for it have been found; and while the law may be sometimes hard for the individual, it is best for the race, because it insures the survival of the fittest in every department." Economic inequality, Carnegie asserts, is natural and right, no different from the law that enabled the ascent of humanity itself. Competition ensures "wonderful material development" and thus "improved conditions" for all, in spite of its relative winners and losers. "We accept and welcome," he concludes, "great inequality of environment, the concentration of business, industrial and commercial, in the hands of a few, and the law of competition between these, as being not only beneficial, but essential for the future progress of the race."[25] For Carnegie, "great inequality" is no longer the antithesis of meritocracy but rather its inevitable and just result. Democracy is no longer an indictment of the inequalities documented in the 1890 census but rather an apologia for them.

At the same time, Carnegie acknowledges the gulf between the classes as a troubling source of "friction between the employer and the employed, between capital and labor, between rich and poor." Like Franklin, Jefferson, and Tocqueville, he senses that inequality corrodes human sympathies and diminishes national morality. "Rigid castes are formed, and, as usual, mutual ignorance breeds mutual distrust," Carnegie writes. "Each caste is without sympathy for the other, and ready to credit anything disparaging in regard to it."[26] In order to preserve "the ties of brotherhood" between rich and poor, while still allowing for natural competition and inevitable disparity of fortune, Carnegie advocates for philanthropy as modern *noblesse oblige*. Wealthy capitalists, he argues, should dispense a significant portion of their personal wealth to endow parks, museums, universities, and other public institutions. In this way, the robber baronage may become benevolent royalty, with each peer a "trustee to his poorer brethren, bringing to their service his superior wisdom, experience, and ability to administer, doing for them better than they would or could do for themselves."[27] Carnegie proposes to restore class harmony through reinstitution of the feudal trust. Although wealthy donors remain separate and aloof from their "poorer brethren," each caste is obliged to the other, the worker to labor on the economic domains of the capitalist, and the capitalist to spend part of his fortune to protect and cultivate the worker. Feudal Europe became an old model for a new social order, in which the majority of people owned no property and depended for their welfare on the wealthiest men, who might grace them with a minimum wage, a public park, or a look at their art collection. Carnegie's gospel of wealth enshrined this hierarchy as natural law, and philanthropy, in turn, made it conscionable.

Knights of the Ownership Society

Trachtenberg explains that success literature in Carnegie's era registers conflicted attitudes toward inequality in its depiction of the free market as both "a field of just rewards" and "a realm of questionable motives and unbridled appetites," attempting to resolve the tension by portraying scrappy boys overcoming street hoods, grifters, and corrupt capitalists with honest ambition, hard work, and humility.[28] In Horatio Alger's *Ragged Dick*, for example, the bootblack Dick Hunter knows that wealth alone does not signify the value of a person. Success, he learns, comes from "starting in a small way," moving up "by degrees," and, above all, being "strictly honorable in all his dealings."[29]

At the same time, Alger's novel often buttresses the rigid social hierarchy that it appears to defy. Dick often wins by charisma and good looks, signs marking him as more fit than his competitors. "It was easy to see," Alger writes, "that if he was clean and well dressed he would have been decidedly good-looking. Some of his companions were sly, and their faces inspired distrust; but Dick had a frank, straight-forward manner that made him a favorite."[30] Still, his good character pays no dividend until he gains the recognition of a wealthy businessman, Mr. Whitney, who offers him a new suit in exchange for chaperoning his nephew. Dick begins to climb the social ladder not by shining boots and saving pennies but rather by entering into Carnegie's imagined feudal relation between capitalists and their poorer brethren. In addition to bourgeois accoutrement, his patrician

sponsors provide tutoring in morality and manners. In these scenes, Dick's
virtue manifests itself as declarations of gratitude and fealty to his patrons.
When Whitney offers him five dollars as a philanthropic investment in his
future, Dick "shrunk back," telling his benefactor, "I don't like to take it. [...]
I haven't earned it."[31] Before he can conquer, Alger's champion of meritocracy
must be "shrunk" by *noblesse oblige*, demonstrating the friction between the
competing ideals of meritocracy and natural hierarchy.

In the last decade, medievalist film demonstrates the same unresolved
tension. In *King Arthur, Kingdom of Heaven*, and *Robin Hood*, the hero,
like Dick, begins life in squalid struggle, Arthur as a nomad of the steppes,
Balian as a blacksmith's apprentice, and Robin as a brawler. Like Dick, they
are rough and dirty but born to win, destined to forge whole kingdoms with
only a sword and a saddle, awaiting only benevolent patronage. Arthur eventually receives it from the Celtic chieftain Merlin, who sanctions his kingship and his marriage to Guinevere in exchange for his help in defeating the
Saxons. Similarly, King Baldwin of Jerusalem, dying of leprosy, asks Balian
to marry his sister, Princess Sibylla, so that Balian might succeed him as
king. Like Dick, however, Balian shrinks from the offer. Robin also receives
a woman as a philanthropic investment, when Sir Walter Loxley donates his
daughter-in-law, Marian, in exchange for his protection against the royal
tax collectors. Robin seizes the opportunity, already having won his "new
suit" by impersonating Marian's husband, lately killed in France. The films
imagine the Middle Ages as Carnegie and Alger imagined the free market:
occasionally vulnerable to the "questionable motives and unbridled appetites" of venal rulers but ultimately a "field of just rewards" for the right
sort of man, as long as his ambition does not eclipse his fealty to his betters.

While Carnegie might envision industrialized feudalism as the model for
a harmonious relation between justly unequal classes of people, Americans
remain deeply imprinted with the promises of social mobility. As Norton
and Ariely show, we will not admit that the economic contours of American
plutocracy bear any resemblance to those of feudal aristocracy. The rituals
of fealty between Arthur and Merlin, Balian and King Baldwin, and Robin
and Sir Walter do not seem misplaced, but stripped of medievalist decora-
tion these rituals leave us embarrassed and uneasy. Americans recoiled, for
example, when Texas congressman Joe Barton offered a public apology to
BP chief executive Tony Hayward, after President Obama compelled the oil
company to pay reparations. "I'm ashamed of what happened in the White
House yesterday," Barton said. "I think it is a tragedy of the first proportion
that a private corporation can be subjected to what I would characterize as a
shakedown."[32] Although disgusted by Barton's obsequiousness to the corporation that patronizes his state, we felt equally insulted when Hayward failed
to demonstrate reciprocal *noblesse oblige*, churlishly grumbling to reporters

in the midst of the crisis, "I would like my life back."[33] BP chairman Carl Henric-Svanberg sought to strengthen the "ties of brotherhood" between the corporation and its "poorer brethren" with an apology to Americans affected by the spill. "I hear comments sometimes that large oil companies are greedy companies who don't care," he said in a stiff Swedish accent. "But that is not the case in BP. We care about the small people." While Hayward's comment seemed merely selfish, Henric-Svanberg's statement tapped into Americans' deeply repressed anxiety about economic inequality and social class. Justin Taffinder, a New Orleans man, replied angrily, "We're not small people. We're human beings. They're no greater than us. We don't bow down to them. We don't pray to them."[34]

These awkward exchanges between BP and the American public suggest that while many Americans live in the semblance of a feudal relation to transnational corporations, we are sorely wounded when reminded of it. The indignant Taffinder sounds like Dennis, the "anarcho-syndicalist" peasant in *Monty Python and the Holy Grail*, who immediately objects to King Arthur addressing him as an "inferior." When Arthur asserts the sovereignty granted to him by the Lady of the Lake, Dennis retorts, "Strange women lying in ponds distributing swords is no basis for a system of government! Supreme executive power derives from a mandate from the masses, not from some farcical aquatic ceremony!"[35] Comic anachronism broadly serves as the antidote to the gospel of wealth. Wielding Marxist dialectics, Dennis gives comic voice to the "sufferings of the poor man" that Tocqueville finds muted in medieval chronicles. In Mark Twain's *A Connecticut Yankee in King Arthur's Court*, Hank Morgan personifies the "culture of competitive individualism," traveling back to Camelot, where he becomes dictator and wreaks industrial slaughter on the Knights of the Round Table. Terry Gilliam's *The Fisher King* reverses Twain's formula, casting a deranged homeless man as a grail knight questing to steal a cheap trophy from a sophisticate's penthouse.[36] By using anachronism to foreground the parallel inequities of medieval and modern life, these medievalist parodies belie *King Arthur*, *Kingdom of Heaven*, and *Robin Hood*, which employ subtler anachronism in effacing these inequities with the promise of meritocracy.

We find so few working poor in medievalist romance for the same reason that we find so many upwardly mobile knights: economic inequality remains as troubling a dilemma for us as it was for Franklin, Jefferson, Tocqueville, and Carnegie, and we welcome heroes who enable wishful thinking about American meritocracy. While current champions of the free market often invoke the "Founders," Franklin and Jefferson, looking at recent medievalist film, would struggle to understand our enchantment with an age when the great majority of people lived and died in total dependence on a very small class of elites who exercised absolute control over the economy, law, the military, education, and religious belief. Perhaps for the Middle Ages, a mirror to our age, to seem in any way heroic to us, the reality of its abject poverty has to be erased from memory and the medieval world re-imagined as a proto-capitalist playground, where there are no hopeless peasants, only a lot of scruffy lads waiting to become knights.

NOTES

1. George W. Bush, "Second Inaugural Address," Bartleby.com, 20 January 2005, www.bartleby.com/124/pres67.html
2. Barack Hussein Obama, "Inaugural Address," The White House Blog, 21 January 2009, www.whitehouse.gov/blog/inaugural-address
3. Center for Responsible Lending, "The Cost of Bad Lending in the United States," August 2010, www.responsiblelending.org/mortgage-lending/tools-resources/factsheets/united-states.html
4. MarketWatch, "Corporate Share of Pie Most in 60 Years," 29 July 2011, www.marketwatch.com/story/corporate-profits-share-of-pie-most-in-60-years-2011-07–29?dist=countdown
5. BP, "BP Returns to Profit in Third Quarter with Strong Operating Performance," Press Releases, 2 November 2010, www.bp.com/genericarticle.do?categoryId=2012968&contentId=7065828
6. CNN, "Gulf Oil Rig Owner Apologizes for Calling 2010 'Best Year' Ever," 4 April 2011, http://articles.cnn.com/2011–04–04/us/gulf.spill.bonuses_1_piece-of-drill-pipe-oil-spill-oil-rig?_s=PM:US
7. Lindsay Beyerstein, "Will Deepwater Horizon Families Get Their Due?" In These Times, 20 June 2010, www.inthesetimes.com/working/entry/6117/will_deepwater_horizon_families_get_their_due/
8. Economic Policy Institute, "Wealth," The State of Working America, www.stateofworkingamerica.org/articles/view/11
9. Seeking Alpha, "The Big Disconnect: U.S. Corporate Profits Rising with No Job Growth," 26 November 2010, http://seekingalpha.com/article/238799-the-big-disconnect-u-s-corporate-profits-rising-with-no-job-growth
10. AFL-CIO, "2010 Executive Paywatch," Executive Paywatch, www.aflcio.org/corporatewatch/paywatch/ceopay.cfm
11. Economic Policy Institute, "Wealth," The State of Working America, www.stateofworkingamerica.org/articles/view/11
12. Michael I. Norton and Dan Ariely, "Building a Better America – One Wealth Quintile at a Time," *Perspectives on Psychological Science* 6.1 (2011): 9–12.
13. *King Arthur*, dir. Antoine Fuqua (Burbank: Touchstone Pictures, 2004).
14. *Kingdom of Heaven*, dir. Ridley Scott (Los Angeles: Twentieth Century Fox, 2005).
15. *Robin Hood*, dir. Ridley Scott (Los Angeles: Universal Pictures, 2010).
16. Benjamin Franklin, "Information to Those Who Would Remove to America," in *The Autobiography and Other Writings* (New York: Penguin, 1986), 241–42.

17. Thomas Jefferson, *Notes on the State of Virginia* (1787; New York: W. W. Norton, 1982), 164.

18. Franklin, "Information," 243.

19. Jefferson, *Notes*, 165.

20. Alexis de Tocqueville, *Democracy in America*, trans. Harvey C. Mansfield and Delba Winthrop (1840; Chicago: University of Chicago Press, 2000), 536, 538.

21. Tocqueville, *Democracy in America*, 531–32.

22. Alan Trachtenberg, *The Incorporation of America: Culture and Society in the Gilded Age*, 2nd edn. (New York: Hill and Wang, 2007), 99.

23. Trachtenberg, *The Incorporation of America*, 84.

24. Trachtenberg, *The Incorporation of America*, 98.

25. Andrew Carnegie, "Wealth," in *A Documentary History of the United States*, ed. Richard D. Heffner, 7th edn. (New York: Signet, 2002), 203.

26. Carnegie, "Wealth," 202, 203.

27. Carnegie, "Wealth," 207, 208.

28. Trachtenberg, *The Incorporation of America*, 81.

29. Horatio Alger, Jr., *Ragged Dick and Struggling Upward* (1868; New York: Penguin, 1985), 40, 44.

30. Alger, *Ragged Dick*, 4.

31. Alger, *Ragged Dick*, 57.

32. CBS News, "Rep. Joe Barton Apologizes to BP's Tony Hayward for White House 'Shakedown,'" Political Hotsheet, 17 June 2010, www.cbsnews.com/8301–503544_162–20008020-503544.htm

33. "Embattled BP Chief: I Want My Life Back," *The Times*, 31 May 2010, http://business.timesonline.co.uk/tol/business/industry_sectors/natural_resources/article7141137.ece

34. Ben Leach, "Oil Spill: BP Chairman Apologises for Referring to Americans as 'Small People,'" *The Telegraph*, 17 June 2010, www.telegraph.co.uk/finance/newsbysector/energy/oilandgas/7834577/Oil-spill-BP-chairman-apologises-for-referring-to-Americans-as-small-people.html

35. *Monty Python and the Holy Grail*, dir. Terry Gilliam and Terry Jones (London: EMI, 1975).

36. *The Fisher King*, dir. Terry Gilliam (Culver City, CA: TriStar, 1991).

A Corporate Neo-*Beowulf*: Ready or Not, Here We Come

E. L. Risden

Commoditization appears as an issue in some *Beowulf* films – no real surprise there, since it appears in the poem itself – but a particularly interesting instance occurs in director Hal Hartley's *No Such Thing* (2001). A ruthless corporate-media boss can't wait to exploit both the Monster and the girl who finds him: a satiric *Beowulf* story redesigned to sell for a different audience and reconstructed around a new theme. The film suggests that the corporate monster can and will show far more cold-blooded evil than the natural one – neomedievalism turns to critique of corporate culture. While filmmakers have skewered corporate culture before, that doesn't mean they shouldn't do it again, and they have seldom done so in a way so intelligently allusive and literary.

A marvelous and under-appreciated cinematic revision of the Anglo-Saxon epic, placing the *Beowulf* story in near-future New York and Iceland, *No Such Thing* throws particular emphasis on the idea that good and evil are both matters of continual personal and organizational choice. A New York reporter goes to Iceland to learn what happened to her boyfriend, supposedly killed by a monster. She finds the Monster; he probably did kill her boyfriend, but she learns that he suffers from depression, centuries-old exhaustion, and alcoholism, and all he really wants is to die. She returns with him, and the media briefly exploit them both terribly, until she finds the mad scientist who can help the Monster get his wish. The Monster does not inherently do evil because we call him a monster, but the corporation, made up of individuals each with choice and control of his or her actions and opinions, and nominally led by persons of accomplishment and judgment, may repeatedly commit or suborn horrific acts of exploitation, far out-monstering the monster. A company may, as Auden would say, simply sail dully along while the impossible happens: a girl falls from the sky into the sea – or it may, alternatively and worse yet, exploit her.

The satire of *No Such Thing* focuses not on our remnant fear of traditional monsters, but on our numb-headed failure to fear the functional monsters our large and exploitative corporations can become – and on those of us who allow them (by watching them or paying them or simply not resisting them) to do so. They may create commodities not according to constituents'/ customers' needs, but according to (wayward) desires, in some cases desires that they artificially create (e.g., the need for constant, changing, lurid *news* reports, whether they recount anything true or not). Together we *fetishize* (in Marx's term) those commodities by investing them with some magical value, something beyond their contents or usefulness: such news has no use but to draw us back for more news, none of which represents a commitment to anything real or important.[1]

The significance of commoditization[2] marked medieval Germanic literary culture as powerfully as it does ours, if not as pervasively. The concept applies usefully to a consideration of Beowulf as a character, both in his original and contemporary incarnations. From his childhood days as a *kolbìtr* (a Norse term for a "male Cinderella") to his funeral and beyond, Beowulf actively seeks to fill a role that his culture values and rewards: hero. The Anglo-Saxon culture lived and thrived on notions of heroic courage and even more so on gift-giving.[3] Each gift, from lord to thane or thane to lord, strengthens bonds of leadership and service, much as a monetary economy does on manufacture and exchange: each purchase deepens the assumption that a culture must exchange goods to survive; the hero gives and receives gifts, but also in a strong sense lives as a gift: his king employs the hero as a living, applicable commodity, to fight and to win.[4] The hero becomes the commodity that saves his culture from attack: as long as Beowulf remains, the Geats remain. Later incarnations of the *Beowulf* story may also exploit the idea and name of the hero either for thematic purpose or simply for the sake of name recognition to contribute to the salability of a product: thus they to some degree modify and re-commoditize an old commodity. The name Beowulf itself acquires a "magical," value-added status and power, Marx's *fetishistic* power, the same fetishistic power we see Hartley exploit for satirical effect through "The Boss" in *No Such Thing*.

Beowulf as hero-commodity in his own culture participates in the exchange of gifts as commodities of peace and honor, but heroes have their greatest value in the reluctance they create in outsiders to oppose them. Kings or lords, therefore, feel loath to share them. Hygelac makes this point clear to Beowulf by asking him not to go to help the Danes with their monster to begin with and then by wondering if Beowulf has returned from Denmark more Hroðgar's hero than his own. So in some ways our contemporary culture isn't doing something that the epic's own culture didn't already do: we make contracts to limit a commodity's availability to others. With our stars we re-do that voodoo that they did so well, but according to our own sense of commodity. We, too, hoard the hero, then copyright our versions of him, then make him available on the hero market, then immolate him once his value has declined. The process expands to new media and to conform to a wider range of preferences. Audience members want the hero to serve as the commodity they enjoy, the one for which they feel willing to pay. Sellers seek a new magic that transforms the old subject to fit amidst a plethora of additional "similar" products. But corporate medievalism gains a new power when it can pirate the protagonist and repackage him or her, as we see in *No Such Thing*. Sadly, in this case the filmmakers have done so well in the repackaging that none of the reviewers saw what they had made: we end up with a *roman-à-clef*, a *Beowulf* full of interesting making and remaking, but nearly everyone has ignored the key.

Beowulf's death in the poem shows the necessary and ultimate failure of what Marx called "commodity fetishism," the replacement of the person by the commodity; the film places both hero and Monster in the position of fetishized commodity, and their world will happily dispose of both, unaware of what it has lost. Even the best of heroes can't stay young and strong, essentially invincible, forever. The treasure that Beowulf wins by killing the dragon – another valuable literary commodity and a practical one for his survivors – hardly replaces the man, and no new hero will appear sufficient to keep away enemies from the Geats as Beowulf once could. With Beowulf's funeral the Geats dispose of both hero and fetish. They shove the corpse of the dragon over a cliff into the sea, place the treasures on the funeral pyre with their lord, and dump the remnant into his burial mound, "where it now yet dwells, / just as useless to me as it was before" (lines 3167–68). Beowulf has lost his "magic" – his folk lie open to attack – and the treasure has lost its value to his folk, a demystified, devalued mass of metal drained of its fetishistic power by the death of the hero who could have protected it. *No Such Thing* shows that same failure: the monster *is* – he exists as part of the fabric of things – until we fetishize him, or even until he fetishizes himself. Once we have made a transient news item of him, we have lost him, he has lost himself, and the end of the movie suggests that we have thereby lost ourselves as well. The hero shows herself willing to depart with the monster: why stay in a world that values neither of them?

No Such Thing borrows on that old commodity of Beowulf/hero as treasure, as *Beowulf* films generally do. Most film versions stray quickly into their own agendas with barely a nod to the poem – they trade on the fetishistic power of the name, not on the substance of the poem. All also exploit, as did John Gardner in *Grendel*, the monster (either as monster or as idea) as fetish. Each one shows distinct and distinctive commoditizations (e.g., monster as oppressed minority, hero as libidinous adventurer), as does the original (monster as monster, hero as hero). In that sense the Anglo-Saxon culture differed not so completely from our own: they kept commoditization central to their social interaction, as do we, though with different purposes and conceptions of its importance. *No Such Thing* employs no treasure in a physical sense: the Boss locates it temporarily in news items. She addresses her staff so: "There's a world of bad news out there, people. All we need to do is get our hands on the worst of it. Has the President shot himself yet?"

After learning the President has just sold lower Manhattan to a Hollywood movie studio, she continues: "That will fill air time until at least tomorrow afternoon. Maybe by then the President will have done something drastic." For her the frivolous sale of a chunk of New York City doesn't seem drastic: everything has value only as a news commodity, and the magic of its value lies in its outrageousness and lasts for a few days at best.

But Beatrice, our hero, finds a different treasure in her compassion for the Monster, a compassion the world may lose with the Monster's passing, especially if Beatrice passes with him. She removes herself and him from the influence of corporate and even military commoditization. In the Boss's world, and perhaps in ours, that move eliminates them both from existence entirely: they're not real if they don't appear on TV.

The remarkable quality of *No Such Thing* in this context comes from the way it adapts *Beowulf* without using the name, without supplying the denomination of the currency, not allowing the audience its usual fetish – though it does provide another common turn, monster as fetish, more fully than has any other related "product" since *Beowulf* itself. Thus critics and audience fail to bring to consciousness its cultural capital, and they have stayed away from the film in droves. Yet it critiques and satirizes commoditization even as the epic poem does: like the American news director who encourages her young employee boldly to seek it out, we – the audience, *her* audience – insist on commoditizing the Monster, the only choice contemporary consciousness allows us. In our time what else would we do with a monster once we've found it? But, as the film shows us, in destroying the Monster we destroy ourselves – and in this case the notion surpasses cliché. We live by the commodity; the commodity predates us, and we depend on it. When we destroy the commodity, nothing remains for which to live. The Geats destroy the commodity that replaces their hero, thus destroying the symbol of the heroism that held them together – not even the symbolism remains to remind them of heroism past, thus limiting heroism present and future. Out of a tainted sense of honor, perhaps, the Geats remove the guilt (and gilt) on their conscience in a way that we can't, because we are losing the capacity to recognize it. Only the hero of *No Such Thing*, Beatrice, sees the Monster as a being rather than as a passing fetish; for others he represents fodder for a childish system of reporting for public exploitation, something to abuse so we believe we need no longer fear it. With an attention span shorter than the life of a mayfly, we reduce it to a leftover, a fearsome childish imagining that incongruously dared to exist in fact – until we abandon it, as we do all corporate commodities. We reduce the corporation, too, to something that creates readily abandonable commodities; we give it our ear, our eye, our thoughts, our money, our spirit. But we allow no space for the hero in an environment that kills heroism even more readily than it kills monsters: they burn more brightly and so tire us more quickly.

Beatrice – whom her colleagues value mostly because she makes the coffee – appears first as the least likely of heroes. As Beowulf is a *kolbítr*, so she fills the role of a more traditional Cinderella, but in this case with an anti-prince. Beatrice – the name oddly recalls Dante but also calls attention to its etymology, *blessed one* – who has up to that point worked as a receptionist and gofer, gets the assignment to travel to Iceland to find the reputed Monster partly because no one else wants it and partly because the Monster has killed her boyfriend. On screen she appears tiny, mousy, cute. Nearly as soon as she takes up the quest, her plane crashes into the sea, and only she survives, but with her body broken. Her sea-survival replaces Beowulf's early swimming adventures, and she recapitulates his endurance through the horrifying pain she experiences: she must undergo – awake – an unbelievably torturous and painful surgery.

While Beatrice awaits her surgery, "the Boss" visits and reports icily back to New York thus:

> Regarding the Beatrice situation: they say she'll be okay again in time. She might not walk again, though. I'm sure we're gonna have an exclusive on the whole thing. She's worked with me forever … for five months…. She's just a kid. Yeah, yeah, she's pretty, pretty enough anyhow…. Plain, well-adjusted, optimistic – completely out of touch. She'll do whatever we want….

But she won't: Beatrice refuses to believe that audiences want to know what it's like to crash into the sea. The Boss wants the whole story, including "The children: what were the children doing [as the plane fell]?" She even threatens Beatrice that her medical bills won't be covered if she doesn't cooperate and tell her story. Beatrice remains silent, and the Boss goes home: threats don't change the hero's code of honor, but they begin to reshape our idea of the monstrous.

With time Beatrice recovers, and that recovery makes her a hero already to the local folk in Iceland, who meet her as she departs the hospital as though she were a saint. The narrative sequence shows incredible physical courage and determination, though the character must accept her suffering passively:

the heroism appears in acts of will and grit, not of force – not in violent action, but in quiet endurance, a will to persist, to discover and understand what has happened. Beowulf acts similarly when, upon Grendel's attack, he simply grasps the arm of the monster who grasps him: he uses no weapon, nor any aggressive skills of martial attack. Beatrice grasps her Monster by understanding.

When Beatrice resumes her quest, the Icelanders who live near the Monster take her in, get her drunk, and leave her as a sacrifice at the monster's lair, an abandoned American missile site. Jaded, cynical, alcoholic, seemingly immortal, older himself than the human race, the Monster has no interest in their sacrifice, but Beatrice, learning his story, does come to take an interest in his suffering. She sympathizes with his desire to die, and she takes him to New York: she will bring him before the media to make her career (the only fully selfish actions we see on her part occur in that sequence), and in exchange she will find the scientist who, he believes, has the technology to kill him by "proving to him he's a figment of our imagination." Once the Monster arrives in that most commercial of all cities, the media exploit him mercilessly. His promise to hurt no one allows everyone who encounters him, including government scientists interested in what military applications they can learn from him, to torture him mercilessly and with impunity – and they do. Beatrice effects his release and takes him back to Iceland where the scientist, Dr. Artaud (in another brilliant allusion, this one to the "theater of cruelty"), whom she has located, apparently succeeds in taking life from him. As the doctor runs his miracle death-machine, Beatrice stares into the eyes of the Monster, and the screen goes blank. The lingering shot implies the possibility that Beatrice, the viewpoint character – if not all of us with her – dies with him. Heroism dies with the Monster, because it has no more value to its society: people, if we remain, have already moved on to new and equally transient interests. The film also asks whether when we lose our monstrousness, we die, because that is what we find at the core of our being. Without the magical, co-modifying elements of suffering and cruelty, we lack what we need to survive: a horrifying notion, but perhaps true biologically as well as philosophically. The media exploit Beatrice as "hero," the Monster as "monster," anything they can get their hands on for as long as it can attract audience interest. They fetishize their commodities for as long as the public follow their stories, usually a day or two – then the magic dies. Unlike Beowulf, who has value as a commodity as long as he retains life and strength to fight (or reputation sufficient to inhibit invasion), Beatrice and the Monster "exist" at all only so long as the public will pay money to hear or view clips about them.

Our means of delivery of the commodity has moved from oral poem to visual film, but, surprisingly, the message has changed little, adapting only to a different quantum of consciousness: courage has value; compassion has value; both can help us survive – but in our time we also want salable products. Both texts suggest that good and bad mix in us, variably; we must do some things for ourselves, but we do better when we help others as well. Some selfishness can enhance survival; too much destroys us and those around us. Art can still make such points, but probably best, in our time, through satire: in day-to-day terms we still want to believe that big corporations will save us financially – note television's love of stock activity reports. The most powerful satire of cold corporate greed in the film appears in the brilliant (and critically underappreciated) performance of Helen Mirren as the Boss, but the point – dare I say theme – of our financial fixation simmers through the entire film, more subtly, by contrast, in the Monster and Beatrice as corporate outsiders, briefly exploitable, infinitely expendable. And the satirical message contrasts brilliantly with the quiet, visual lyricality and the peculiar, muted, mesmerizing synthetic score that pervade the film.

While one can productively explore the other *Beowulf* films for how they mix tradition and pop culture, I think *No Such Thing* represents the most notable and most polar alternative of the cinematic commoditization process. It most readily recognizes and satirizes, textually and visually, the process of commoditization in which it participates. I think as an audience we weren't quite ready yet for this kind of *Beowulf*: Sarah Polley as a truly gentle hero, and Robert John Burke as a dangerous but intellectual Monster (far more sympathetic than Gardner's Grendel). But it best responds to while least exploiting its original, remaking without clinging and without parodying. And occasionally, ready or not, if we try very hard, we can get from this film what we need. *No Such Thing* lampoons our commoditization fetish, while *Beowulf*, in its own way and for its own time, indulges it to the hilt.

NOTES

1.   See Karl Marx, *Capital*, Vol. 1, Ch. 1, Part 4 (German edition 1867, first English edition 1887, trans. Samuel Moore and Edward Aveling). The text is readily available online in the Marx/Engels Internet Archive at www.marxists.org, 1995, 1999. The (ironic) act of fetishizing places the nominal value of the object in its material nature or in its existence as product without regard to the amount or quality or difficulty of labor that went into its production; thus it represents, for Marx, a misunderstanding of both material and labor.

2.   I prefer this term to the more common *commodification* because I think it more clearly shows the idea that someone has turned the object or subject in question into a commodity. For some interesting reflection on commodity theory and culture see Shane Gunster, *Capitalizing on Culture: Critical Theory for Cultural Studies* (Toronto: University of Toronto Press, 2004). For some useful applications to film studies see especially chapter 2, "Production: The Spectatorship of the Proletariat," in Jonathan Beller's *The Cinematic Mode*

of Production: Attention, Economy and the Society of the Spectacle (Lebanon, NH: University Press of New England, 2006). For studies of economics in cinema, Janet Wasko's *Movies and Money: Financing the American Film Industry* (Norwood, NJ: Ablex, 1982) and *A Concise Handbook of Movie Industry Economics*, ed. Charles C. Moul (New York: Cambridge, 2005) make good places to start.

3.   For discussions of gift-giving see: Charles Donahue, "Potlatch and Charity: Notes on the Heroic in *Beowulf*," in *Anglo-Saxon Poetry: Essays in Appreciation for John McGalliard*, ed. Lewis E. Nicholson and Dolores W. Frese (Notre Dame, IN: University of Notre Dame Press, 1975), 23–40; John M. Hill, "*Beowulf* and Danish Succession: Gift-Giving as an Occasion for Complex Gesture," *Medievalia e Humanistica* 11 (1982): 177–97; Michael J. Enright, "Lady with a Mead-Cup: Ritual, Group Cohesion and Hierarchy in the Germanic Warband," *Frühmittelalterliche Studien* 22 (1988): 170–203; Robert Bjork, "Speech as Gift in *Beowulf*," *Speculum* 69 (1994): 993–1022.

4.   For an interesting expansion on this notion see chapter 4, "The Economy of Honour in *Beowulf*," in John M. Hill's *The Cultural World of Beowulf* (Toronto: University of Toronto Press, 1995), 85–107.

Unsettled Accounts: Corporate Culture and George R. R. Martin's Fetish Medievalism*

Lauryn S. Mayer

> Tyrion owned a fine suit of heavy plate, expertly crafted to fit his misshapen body. Alas, it was safe at Casterly Rock, and he was not. He had had to make do with oddments [...]: mail hauberk and coif, a dead knight's gorget, lobstered greaves and gauntlets, and pointed steel boots. Some of it was ornate, some plain, not a bit of it matched, or fit as it should. [...] Shae stepped back and looked him over: "M'lord looks fearsome." "M'lord looks a dwarf in mismatched armor," Tyrion answered sourly.[1]

From the *Pearl*-poet to the Pre-Raphaelites and beyond, the trope of the knight's farewell to his lady before battle nicely condenses the ideals of courtly love, aristocratic valor, pageantry, and chivalry. To open the battle between the Stark and Lannister forces in *A Game of Thrones*, George R. R. Martin presents us with a relentless attack on the trope. The excellent and costly armor covers a "misshapen," stunted body, and is not even available for use. Tyrion, the leader of one flank, has never been in a battle, and the admiring lady is a whore Tyrion bought from one of his soldiers, whose early promise of a Dulcinea-like transformation ends abruptly as she sells out Tyrion to certain death in a later volume. Moreover, unlike the warlike and noble Starks, the Lannisters' primary means to power is through the accumulation and deployment of wealth. As the epic opens, the Lannisters have risen to power through Cersei Lannister's marriage to the king, Robert Baratheon, and the Lannister clan has been funding the extravagant and careless king in return for key appointments within the court, which in return increase its

---

* I am indebted to Jennifer Logan for her comments on this article.

money and power. Cersei's incestuous relationship with her twin Jaime, in addition, insures that Lannisters will inherit the throne. The Lannisters do not simply use money, but embody it: their unofficial motto is "A Lannister always pays his debts"; Jaime, Cersei, Joffrey, and Tywin are golden-haired and golden-armored, and Tywin is rumored to "shit gold," in an extreme example of creating value. In his multi-volume epic *A Song of Ice and Fire*, Martin weaves together two spheres of matter, or *topoi* – the matter of the corporation and the matter of the medieval – to create a set of texts that form a new kind of medievalism, one now dependent upon narrative structures governing relationships between the corporation and the community.

In order to look at the links among the construction of corporate identity, the constructions of the medieval, and Martin's particular "third path," a cursory look at the change in corporate function, relationships to other institutions, and lifespan is necessary. As Mary Zepernick and others have noted, the earliest identified corporations existed only as temporary and contingent entities, dependent for their existence on the will of the monarch or the state.[2] It was not until the middle of the nineteenth century that the corporations started taking on some of the attributes we now associate with them, and developed into virtually autonomous entities with no limits on their scope, very little regulation on their growth, and the potential for immortality, or at least an existence spanning centuries and generations. In tandem with this development, the relationships among corporations, communities, and the individuals extant in both became increasingly tangled, beginning in the early 1800s, when early corporations began to use laws developed for free slaves to protect their assets, to the 1886 Supreme Court ruling that supported corporations' legal status as persons and, most recently, the 21 January 2010 ruling in *Citizens United v. Federal Election Commission* supporting corporate political advocacy under the First Amendment. What follows is a chimera, in both senses of the word: the corporation, as legally defined individual composed of actual individuals; the corporation, as individual and social participant, but without any of the moral or pragmatic imperatives to fulfill its functions as an individual in society. Noam Chomsky describes the paradox succinctly: "Corporations were given the rights of persons, of immortal persons. But then special kinds of persons. Persons who had no moral conscience. These are a special kind of persons which are designed by law to be concerned only for their stockholders."[3] Robert Monks sums up the problems with this kind of personhood: "The great problem of having corporate citizens is that they aren't like the rest of us. As Baron Thurlow in England is supposed to have said, 'they have no soul to save and they have no body to incarcerate.'"[4] This set of paradoxes has been explored extensively, but I would like to focus on the way in which the corporate chimera frames itself for a society it needs to function, and the corresponding way society frames what it both fears and has grown to see as a necessary economic force. My argument is that cooperation among the corporate, the individual, and society is dependent upon an adoption of fetishism on the part of all three: the corporation, to be recognized and "pass" as an individual within a society, must take on the narratives, tropes, and symbols valued by that society, while rejecting them in its practice as antithetical to its economic agenda; however, the acting limbs in society of a corporation are precisely those individuals who have been acculturated with these narratives, tropes, and symbols, as are the individuals and communities that sustain and depend upon the corporation.[5] Medievalism, as I argue later, provides a fitting habitat for the chimera, being an invocation of an irrevocably lost past that in its inaccessibility opens the space for fantasy. Thus, on both parts, the human elements recognize both the necessarily partial and inadequate nature of this corporate adoption of social being and the inherent impossibility of medievalism and then must attempt to deny and forget this set of recognitions. This is the tragedy of Martin's Tyrion, who, while he recognizes the structure around him as corporate, cannot help thinking and acting as if whores are lovers and his biological relatives are actually a family in the social sense.[6] As Carolyn Dinshaw notes, the fetishist is caught between recognition and need: "the fetishist retains a 'conceptual fiction,' a fiction of nondifferentiation and plenitude, in the face of 'perceptual knowledge': 'I *know*, but even so [...].'"[7]

Compounding this set of conceptual fictions is yet another "fiction of nondifferentiation and plenitude" summoned from the past as both comfort and orthopedic model; Jeremy Rifkin encapsulates this fiction in his micro-history of medieval and early modern Europe:

> We can really begin to take a look at the emergence of the modern age with the enclosure movements of the great European commons in the fourteenth, fifteenth and sixteenth century. Medieval life was a collectively lived life. It was a brutish, nasty affair. But there was a collective responsibility. People belonged to the land; the land did not belong to people. And in this European world, people farmed the land in a collective way, because they saw it as a commons. It belonged to God. And then it was administered by the Church, the aristocracy, and then the local manors, as stewards of God's creation. Beginning with Tudor England, we began to see a phenomenon emerge, and that is the enclosure of the great commons by parliamentary acts in England, and then in Europe. And so, first we began to take the great land masses of the world which were commons and shared, and we reduced those to private property.[8]

This picture of shared responsibility, stewardship, common lands, and common goals would have sounded profoundly strange to William I, who seized huge tracts of southwestern England in 1079 to create the New Forest, subsequently starving out entire villages, to the beneficiaries of monopolies on wool or wine trade, and to the great banking houses of medieval Italy. Granted, there was an exponential increase in enclosure acts between 1710 and 1810, but Rifkin and others are doing their own version of ideological enclosure, stripping the medieval landscape of its complex relationships to private property and profit in order to offer a past that is lost, but still perceived as a retrievable alternative to the chimera. Rifkin's critique depends for its power on another set of tropes, and in his micro-history, the narratives of medievalism are used to create an ideal narrative for the corporation. As previous volumes of *Studies in Medievalism* have discussed extensively, there is no "medievalism" *per se*, rather a number of facets of postmedieval texts, each portraying a particular world and each serving a particular set of agendas: the medieval as crude and brutal past, deployed as a validation and endorsement of providential history and progress; the medieval as the lost past of community, simplicity, and devotion, used as evidence of a perverted *telos* culminating in nihilism, selfish individualism, and decadence; the medieval as an age, again lost, of romance and its assumed values: pageantry, color, chivalry, and courtesy. In all cases, the postmedieval texts that create these worlds are "sealed worlds": while they, of course, do not appear *ex nihilo*, their reliance upon and use of medieval texts, or other medievalist texts, is carefully muted. Character types and plot devices are similar, but the texts will not call attention to deliberate borrowings, as that will break the textual world open and thus endanger its status as site of escape and representation of an accessible and intelligible past. If such deliberate borrowings exist, they are presented for a very narrow audience, as a sophisticated inside joke. Thus, Tolkien's deliberate use of the cup theft and the leaving of weapons outside the mead hall in *The Hobbit* and *The Two Towers* was meant for his fellow Anglo-Saxon scholars, as was the even more esoteric reference to "The Fates of Man" in *The Hobbit*, where Bilbo's tree-climbing excursion was a joking reference to a debate among Inklings Tolkien, C. S. Lewis, and Charles Williams.

On the other end of the scale is what Carol Robinson and Pam Clements have termed "neomedievalism":[9] the medievalist text is a playful, often ironic work of bricolage that deliberately refuses any attempt at a sealed world and argues against access to the past by calling attention to the process of construction; this is not the world of epic, but of satire, comedy, and carnival, the world of *Black Knight*, where Martin Lawrence's character rallies the troops by a grimly humorous reference to the 1991 Rodney King beating at the hands of the Los Angeles Police Department, and *A Knight's Tale*, in which

Nike swooshes appear on armor and in which a tournament opens with face-painted peasants pounding their benches to Queen's "We Will Rock You."

Martin's *Song of Ice and Fire*, however, is doing something new: a medievalism that paradoxically depends for its grip and impact on the recognition/denial dynamic governing corporate/community relationships. The staggering scale of the epic (coming in at 4,839 pages in five volumes, with a sixth on the way), the careful attention to rich and elaborate detail, and the geographic sweep of the texts, complete with maps, invite the reader into a long-term sojourn in the texts. However, the experience of inhabiting this world is unsettling to those looking for a sealed-world escape or a "medieval" experience. Martin draws extensively from both medieval and post-medieval texts and tropes, as does Tolkien, and invites the same comparisons to contemporary culture as does Tolkien. The character of Oberyn Martell, for example, begs for a reading as an attack on Western bigotry, homophobia, and racism. Oberyn's depiction encapsulates a variety of fears, compounded and exaggerated to the point of ludicrousness. The reader first encounters him as a dark-skinned man in a headscarf. Rumors link him with poison and black magic, nymphomania and bisexuality, and the reckless production of bastards framed as "sand snakes." His first request of Tyrion is "for a beautiful blonde woman" he and his paramour can share.[10] In the same manner, Daenary's freeing of the slaves and her naïve assumption that liberation implies regional stability and prosperity echoes both the triumphalist "mission accomplished" rhetoric following the fall of Saddam Hussein, and its bitter aftermath. Martin, however, goes beyond this pattern and makes his way through the volumes gleefully smashing his own and other medievalist texts' attempts at world creation. Of the hundreds of examples, two will have to stand as exemplars. In the third volume (*A Storm of Swords*) the crippled Brandon Stark, his giant servant Hodor, and the Reed siblings, Meera the huntress and Jojen the mystic, are on a northbound quest to try to find a passage through the Wall for Bran's continuing education. They attempt to pass through an abandoned fortress, the Nightfort, a place reputed to be haunted by both the slaughtered and their killers, and passing through an abandoned kitchen, they notice a well in the floor:

> The walls were damp and covered with niter, but none of them could see the water at the bottom, not even Meera with her sharp hunter's eyes. "Maybe it doesn't have a bottom," Bran said uncertainly.
> Hodor peered over the knee-high lip of the well and said "HODOR". The word echoed down the well … Hodor looked startled. Then he laughed and bent to scoop a broken piece of slate off the floor.
> "Hodor, don't," said Bran, but too late. Hodor tossed the slate over the edge. "You shouldn't have done that. You don't know what's down

there. You might have hurt something, or … woken something up."
[…]
Far, far below they heard the sound as the stone found water. It wasn't
a *splash*, not truly. It was more a *gulp* as if whatever was below was
opening a quivering gelid mouth to swallow Hodor's stone. Faint
echoes traveled up the well, and for a moment Bran thought he heard
something moving, thrashing around in the water.[11]

Point for point, this announces itself as a section from Tolkien's *The Fellowship of the Ring*,[12] and is meant to be taken as such; there is no way to read
it otherwise. This deliberate insertion of another text works to destroy both
Martin's and Tolkien's sealed worlds, and goes on to destroy the narrative
trope (awakening of the sleeping danger) itself. As the chapter continues, it
pushes the comparison to the Tolkien trajectory that ends in Gandalf's fall,
beginning with the increasingly loud sounds of an approach and culminating
in what appears to be a borrowed Balrog: "[a] huge black shape heaved
itself up in the darkness and lurched towards the moonlight." The menacing
shape, however, is the obese Samwell Tarly who promptly flops on the floor
and begs for mercy.
      A similar pattern of textual and tropic destruction appears in the trial by
battle between the enormous and brutish Ser Gregor and Oberyn Dorne,
fighting for the innocent Tyrion, accused of Joffrey's murder. Dorne agrees
to fight for Tyrion when he learns that Ser Gregor is the man responsible for
the rape and murder of Oberyn's sister and the slaughter of her children; he
has searched for years for the one responsible and finally, although seemingly
badly outmatched, is driven by his need for justice and revenge. As the battle
continues, Oberyn's only speech to Ser Gregor is the relentless and continual
repetition of these phrases: "You raped her. You murdered her. You killed
her children" – a chant that slowly eats at Ser Gregor's control. Unlike the
redeemed and victorious Inigo Montoya of William Goldman's *The Princess
Bride*, Oberyn's mortal wounding of Ser Gregor and his mantra are both
paid back to him in spades: Gregor grabs Oberyn as Oberyn comes in for
the final killing stroke:

> "Elia of Dorne," they all heard Ser Gregor say. […] "I killed her
> screaming whelp." He thrust his free hand into Oberyn's unprotected
> face, pushing steel fingers into his eyes. "*Then* I raped her." Clegan
> slammed his fist into the Dornishman's mouth, making splinters of
> his teeth. "Then I smashed her fucking head in. Like *this*." […] There
> was a sickening crunch.[13]

Rob Sheffield describes Martin's world as "no country for old hobbits," a world produced for readers who need the promised structure of an escapist text, but who will not invest belief in "Gandalf-ish wisdom or Xena-ish heroes to root for."[14] Martin's medievalism is fetish medievalism, meant for a culture which codes the mechanism of recognition and denial as a guarantor of "the real." This medievalism's imperative is to produce itself as neither whole nor playfully neomedieval, but to refuse any other consolatory framework: a world of the maimed and meretricious, battling it out in mismatched armor.

NOTES

1.   George R. R. Martin, *A Game of Thrones* (New York: Bantam Spectra, 1996), 683.

2.   *The Corporation*, dir. Mark Achbar and Jennifer Abbot (Big Picture Media, 2003).

3.   *The Corporation*.

4.   *The Corporation*.

5.   In the film *The Corporation*, individuals are asked to describe particular corporations; the corporations are invariably anthropomorphized: General Electric is "a kind old man [...] with lots of stories"; Monsanto is "immaculately dressed"; McDonald's is "young, outgoing, enthusiastic" (*The Corporation*).

6.   Tyrion's constant self-condemnation for treating Shae like a lover speaks to his need to believe, and the impossibility of doing so; a post-coital scene typically concludes with a rebuke to himself: "Will you never learn, dwarf? She's a whore, damn you; it's your coin she loves, not your cock." George R. R. Martin, *A Clash of Kings* (New York: Bantam Books, 1999), 69.

7.   Carolyn Dinshaw, *Chaucer's Sexual Poetics* (Madison: University of Wisconsin Press, 1990), 176.

8.   *The Corporation*.

9.   Carol L. Robinson and Pamela Clements, "Living with Neomedievalism," *Studies in Medievalism XVIII: Defining Medievalism(s) II*, ed. Karl Fugelso (Cambridge: D. S. Brewer, 2009), 55–75.

10.   George R. R. Martin, *A Storm of Swords* (New York: Bantam Books, 2000), 522–27.

11.   Martin, *A Storm of Swords*, 763.

12.   "Pippin felt curiously attracted by the well [...]. Moved by a sudden impulse he groped for a loose stone and let it drop. He felt his heart beat many times before there was any sound. Then far below, as if the stone had fallen into deep water in some cavernous place, there came a *plunk*, very distant, but magnified and repeated in the hollow shaft. [...] Nothing more was heard for several minutes, but then there came out of the depths faint knocks." Gandalf ends this scene with: "I do not like it. It may have nothing to do with Peregrin's foolish stone, but probably something has been disturbed that would have been better left quiet." J. R. R. Tolkien, *The Fellowship of the Ring* (1954; New York: Houghton-Mifflin, 2004), 313.

13.   Martin, *A Storm of Swords*, 971–76. As in the earlier example, this is almost an exact echo of the fight between the Count and Inigo Montoya in *The Princess Bride* (New York:

Ballantine Books, 1973), 274–77 – until Martin turns the trope of triumphant vengeance on its head.

14. Rob Sheffield, rev. of *Game of Thrones* (HBO series), *Rolling Stone*, 17 July 2011, www.rollingstone.com/culture/news/game-of-thrones-is-a-genius-fantasy-saga-and-not-just-for-geeks-20110428

Historicizing Neumatic Notation: Medieval Neumes as Cultural Artifacts of Early Modern Times

Eduardo Henrik Aubert

If one of the major tasks of studying medievalism is to provide a basis for the self-critique of modern disciplines dealing with (what they construe as) medieval objects, then medieval musicology constitutes a very promising, and little explored, field of observation.[1] This article will present the results of a study devoted to one of the most fundamental branches of the discipline since its inception: the paleography of early medieval notation. It will do so by moving back to the vast pre-history of the musicological discourse on notation, starting in the sixteenth century and following discursive transformations up to the late nineteenth century.[2]

When medieval musicology was taking shape in the later nineteenth century and its pioneers outlined an approach to neumes, which are the earliest practical medieval notation, they realized that they were not the first to study them. They even made an inventory of their predecessors.[3] However, the very idea of considering these older writers as predecessors meant that the later nineteenth-century musicologists envisaged the discourses with which they were dealing as primitive and very unsuccessful attempts at doing that which they believed only they themselves were managing to accomplish.

As an attempt to counter this problematic approach and to initiate the exploration of the rich corpus of earlier writers who touched upon what we now call neumes, the present article will examine the same sources from a point of view that is, in Foucault's sense of the term, primarily archaeological. That is, instead of positing an unbroken epistemological continuity between early modern writers and the later musicologists in the interpretation of the marks we call neumes, my purpose will be to identify the structural epistemological discontinuities that explain the specificities of the various understandings of neumes before the academic field of musicology came into existence.[4]

If in the past few decades the discussion of neumes has been intense and often taken shape as a theoretical discourse approaching the foundational concepts of musicology itself, it might be profitable to take a step back and understand the musicological interpretation of neumes as one in a series of fundamentally different discourses that have grappled with these visual marks. The archaeology of medieval notation here proposed is the history of a present object whose understanding might be improved by the consideration of how differently this object appeared within discursive formations that are not our own. As I will demonstrate, it is not only a change in the understanding of neumes that can be thus examined, or of things we more generally understand as signs. The transformations are much more radical and involve notions of history and, from a certain point, of the medieval.

Characters

The first modern writer to confront his readers with specimens of what we now know as medieval neumes was Michael Praetorius, in his music encyclopedia *Syntagma musicum* (1614).[5] Dealing with ecclesiastical modes and notation, Praetorius singles out John of Damascus for having created characters (*characteres*) that express the ascending and descending intervals of choral psalmody. It is very difficult, or even impossible, to know what the characters devised by John were, says Praetorius. But Praetorius is sure that they were not the present ones, for he can see in an old missal in Wolfenbüttel that the present characters were not always in use. And so that the reader might know for himself how different some old characters can be from the modern ones, he produces *exempla ad vivum* of both text and (musical) characters from this *vetus quoddam Missale* in Wolfenbüttel. These are the images we might be tempted to refer to as neume facsimiles, but nothing is explained about them. The only discourse that hovers above this striking image is a discourse about the unknowable different.

That the question at stake here is otherness and its unknowability is reinforced by the subsequent development of the text in the same chapter of the *Syntagma musicum*. Just after the *exempla* are given, there is a tract on Hebrew accents that is explicitly conceived of as a digression. Having learned from the texts of Rabbis and grammarians of the old use of accents by the Jews, Praetorius reports having asked a converted Christian about them and being told that modern Jews make no use of them. But he notes that Polish Jews have different melodies from those of German Jews and, despite using accents, pay no attention to them when singing. From this, he concludes, the logic of accents is unknown and must have been so in the past. John of

Damascus's characters, the Hebrew accents, and those unnamed characters taken from the old Wolfenbüttel missal – *our* neumes – are thus a collection of examples of characters from different times and places that cannot be understood. This attitude inhibits, of course, any attempt at writing a history of musical notation.

Praetorius leads us back to the discourses of the late Italian Renaissance and to how they shaped radically different views concerning the history of notation. As Claude Palisca has recently demonstrated, if the debate on music in the early Renaissance was fundamentally informed by Pythagorean, Platonic, and Neoplatonic approaches in which the harmony of numbers rules over the world, the later sixteenth century can be characterized as a period in which those views were increasingly challenged by scholars with an Aristotelian background that places greater importance on empirical observation and rejects the absolute rule of number.[6] These two positions are intimately connected with two different views of history that lie at the heart of the possibility or impossibility of understanding difference in time, and this is where the potentialities of an understanding of neumes came into play.

In Gioseffo Zarlino's influential *Le Istitutioni harmoniche* (1558), references to the history of notation are brief.[7] Zarlino's entire reasoning is based on the duality between the ancients and the moderns. Because of this duality, the past and the present are two separate entities, distinguished and to some measure opposed. When dealing with notation, Zarlino sets himself at a very abstract level of discourse. Every mathematical science, he says, including music, needs demonstration to prove the truth. But the act of demonstration requires a means of making it known to our senses. And that is how mathematicians found (*ritrovaro*) certain signs (*cifere*): points, lines, surfaces, bodies, and numbers. And so did the musicians, who found signs or characters that they called figures or notes. The historical account is inscribed in the logical necessity of things. Impregnated as it is with the early Renaissance abstract and numerical view and expressly leaving aside the discussion of that which does not belong to the *moderni*, this road is not conducive to a history of notation that might in the long run accommodate neumes.

However, Zarlino came under strong criticism by a former student of his, Vincenzo Galilei, the father of Galileo, who rejected Zarlino's overall philosophical position and engaged with empiricist currents. In his *Dialogo della musica antica e moderna* (1581), he states that, by the time of Guido of Arezzo, music was in a state of decay.[8] But, little by little (*à poco à poco*), men started to turn to the arts, and Guido started to reorganize singing. Practical musicians were still using the old Greek characters assigned to the beginning of seven different lines, on which sounds were signified by dots, but Guido used the lines as well as the spaces for the dots, which would be later substituted by the "notes of our time," as developed by Jean de Murs in Paris. Galilei presents a narrative that is based on a principle of successive transformations, which consist in different changes happening across time and is quite different from the polarized model favored by Zarlino. Galilei's processual account of history is also permeated by a fundamental concern with presenting concrete evidence, in the many references to, and reproductions of, notation in old manuscripts, although neumes are still not there.

The epistemological divide goes deeper and touches the very essence of what a sign is. Zarlino's logical account of history is based on the idea that nature and its representation are at peace and that the world is fully transparent to the mind. Zarlino regards the signs created by mathematicians as coextensive (*congiunte*) with the thing, springing from the very matter itself. The central notion of *carattere* employed by Zarlino to designate neumes – and that we already found in Praetorius' *Syntagma musicum* – is a very strong indication of this *episteme*. As *characters*, (our) neumes participate here in a very material understanding of the visual mark, one in which they are on an ontological par with whatever they might indicate, one in which all things are signs and all signs are things. This is the context of a still unfractured "large uniform plain of words and things."[9] This is made very clear by the slightly later *Vocabolario degli Accademici della Crusca* (1612),[10] in which *carattere* is defined as "a sign (*segno*) of anything, printed or written, as the letters of the alphabet or something similar," a definition that insists on material impression, that by itself evokes the notion of sign (*segno*) – also identified with *carattere* in Zarlino's discourse – and that is thus defined by the *Vocabolario degli Accademici della Crusca*: "it is said of that which, as well as offering itself to the senses, indicates something else." The character, or sign, which is materially written and which offers itself to the senses as a thing (*cosa*), is not understandable according to the later notion of a fractured world of signs and things.

Galilei's empiricism, however, depends on the possibility of an estrangement between nature and its representation. Talking about the musical signs of the time of Guido, he characterizes them as "points that have no other being in nature than in the imagination of men." By suggesting the very difference between sign and nature, Galilei paves the way for a concrete study of different signs or sign systems as such, and fosters the breach from which the classical *episteme* of the seventeenth century will be able to develop.

The confrontation of these discourses continued through the first half of the seventeenth century, but it seems that, by 1650, we reach a point at which – as a result of the continuous involvement with the *empiria*, in the footsteps of Galilei – neumes had a chance of becoming visible and intelligible (as different from Praetorius's unintelligible visuality, which is nonetheless evidence for the interest in the *empiria*). The central testimony here is Athanasius Kircher's *Musurgia universalis*, published in 1650. His discourse is highly dependent on Galilei's account of the history of notation, to whose empiricism he adds further manuscripts he himself had seen. In the fifth book of the *Musurgia*, he reports on a copy of an antiphoner from Vallombrosa in which, he says, points were used instead of notes.[11] The interest of this book for the history we are concerned with would be very limited if Kircher had stopped there, but in his seventh book, he comes back to Vallombrosa manuscripts in a much more material and detailed way.[12] The entire passage reads as a reconsideration or correction of what was said in book 5. Instead of the two lines drawn in his visual example, he specifies that there is only one line (*unica tantum linea*) and furthermore that it is traced in red (*rubra*). Nuancing the split point/note, he now talks about certain points and notes (*notas vero mostrant puncta quaedam*). The superposition of the two categories and the very indistinction introduced by '*quaedam*' is a strong indication that Kircher was visualizing the diversity of shapes proper to neumatic writing. By this second look accorded to a manuscript, the *Musurgia* seems to be crossing the barrier of invisibility.

Signs

Until the late eighteenth century, however, neumes remained virtually unknown. All of the music histories from the late seventeenth century until that time completely ignore them. Prinz (1690), Bontempi (1695), Bourdelot (1715), and Malcolm (1721) instead present a very concise history of notation – broadly based on Galilei's and Kircher's foundations – that consists of three basic (evolutionary) steps: alphabetic notation, used by the Greeks and adapted to Latin by Gregory the Great; the points on lines invented by Guido of Arezzo; and what they regarded as "modern notation," which is broadly regarded as equivalent to Jean de Murs' system. This narrative, from our perspective, was vastly sufficient for the ordinary musician. If we look at music dictionaries produced up to 1835, this is the narrative in articles concerning notation, as Brossard (1703), Walther (1732), Gerber (1790–92), Choron and Fayolle (1810–11), and Gathy (1835) do not even mention neumes.

Getting to know neumes required very special contexts and motivations. Three of these contexts – all of them very concretely dealing with the *empiria* of medieval manuscripts – can be identified between the second half of the seventeenth and the third quarter of the eighteenth century: (1) the scholarly output of the French Maurists and some plainchant treatises that were strongly dependent on them; (2) a certain number of German works on church history that were developed in connection with the Protestant universities; and (3) the Spanish interest in Mozarabic liturgy and especially in the old manuscripts of Toledo.

The Maurists were by far the earliest to start uncovering neumes and to try to make them intelligible. The first trace of this interest is to be found in 1641, in the scholarly apparatus of Dom Nicolas-Hugues Ménard's edition of the Gregorian Sacramentary.[13] The bulk of the edition is based on a Missal from St. Eligius, then in the library of Corbie, but the scholarly value of this edition lies in its comparison of the Missal with other sources, carefully discussed in the introduction (with regard to their date and origin) and amply referred to in the volume of commentaries. Collation is, of course, indicative of a rather specific empirical mode, one in which the materiality and specificity of each and every material is carefully examined only to be at a second moment transcended with the establishment of the hypothetical text that is not itself present in any manuscript as such. This is the fundamental dialectic that informs the Maurists' work in general and Ménard's edition in particular.[14] It also illuminates why neumes are to be found in his critical apparatus, which was the first, most empirical, step in the preparation of the edition. In his volume of commentaries, when noting the elements in the Ratoldus Sacramentary that were not kept by his edition, Ménard includes a hymn on the passion of Christ, *Tellus ac aethra*, "which we here put with old notes of chant" (*quem hic ponimus cum antiquis cantus notulis*), with no further commentary.

The same visual example will be taken up by Jean Mabillon himself in 1707.[15] Neumes (*notulae caudatae sed absque lienolis*) are here presented as a stage in notation between alphabetic notation and Guidonian notation. Even though there is no discourse about neumes in either work, the visual reproductions, based on redrawings from the original manuscript, are very telling. Neumes have become associated with a depurated visuality, whose fundamental purpose is the establishment of an orderly system by which evidence can be classified and in which the *form* of neumes is sufficiently intelligible and transparent to refer to their *contents*.

But the Maurists also engaged directly with plainchant and gave much more extensive consideration to neumes in that context. In Pierre-Benoît de Jumilhac's *La science et la pratique du plain-chant*, published in 1673, along with reproductions in an appendix, neumes are part of an account of notation that is extremely elaborate, as it is conceived of as both a historical narrative and a theory of the (musical) sign as unfolded in time.[16] Just like the alphabet, says Jumilhac, all variation of notation in time and space has served to express the same things (the same vowels and consonants for the alphabets and the same sounds and intervals for the "systems"). There is a firmly posited stability of the thing signified, and temporality is an attribute of the sign, not the thing. In this broad construction, the different systems that appear historically are conceived as the sign of the previous system and not as an immediate sign of the sounds. This spiral of signs (i.e., the idea that signs go on changing by themselves without the thing being affected) is what ultimately defines the position that neumes conquer among the Maurists: on the one hand, the dissociation between the stable thing and the spiraling systems of notation makes it possible for the latter to be considered as a historical object and for the many particularities of each system to be identified and classified, but, on the other hand, the cumulative sense of the spiral, i.e., the fact that the newer systems are always more and more distant from the thing, makes the detailed study of secondary or tertiary systems like neumes not a particularly relevant line of enquiry.

The most striking work on neumes among the Maurists comes, however, from the unpublished work of Dom Jacques Leclercq, and most notably from his manuscript plainchant treatises in Bibliothèque Nationale de France MS français 19103, written sometime in the 1660s. Disputing contemporary notions of reform and opposing more specifically the idea that an unstressed penultimate syllable should have only one single note, he provides manuscript evidence in neumatic notation to support his claim, just as some contemporary reformers make reference to neumes but ultimately discard them as, in the words of Nivers, "shadows of notes," as notes that hamper understanding and result in confusion and error.[17] Leclercq bases his approach on a Gradual-Sacramentary from Saint-Denis (Bibliothèque Nationale de France MS latin 9436), whose notation is written "in the most ancient way, used between Saint Gregory and Guido of Arezzo." The most remarkable feature of this portion of the treatise is that Leclercq explains how some of the signs work, according to how many notes they show and in what direction they move. He proposes to be the first person ever to "decipher the notes [...] by comparing them to the extremely old books of the Cathedrals and of the Carthusians," and this is the first formulation of a critical method to read neumatic notation. Although strictly linked to a polemic discourse, Leclercq shows how far the Maurist erudition could have gone in the subject of neumes, and he suggests how important it is to realize that the subject was never regarded as particularly important.

The slightly later works of German church historians who touch upon neumes seem to be operating within the framework of a somewhat different empirical mode. The first source to come up in this context is a dissertation on the singers of the Old and New Testament, written and disputed by Johann Andreas Iussov in Helmstedt in 1708.[18] As it turns out, two-thirds of the dissertation is actually devoted to the early church through the thirteenth century. This provides Iussov with an opportunity to display command of a vast array of sources and, among them, musical sources with neumes. In the times of Gregory the Great, he says, there was no stave, and thus "some notes or characters either simple or composite were associated with the text," with which the ascending and descending intervals of the psalmody were expressed. To support his story, Iussov resorts to a neumed manuscript that he proposes to explain, and his comment is an invaluable statement of method:

> If we had at hand many antiphoners from the time of Guido of Arezzo, then we could gather [colligere] from the newer ones according to which principle the other notes from the old books were later substituted until our own times and thus show [exhibere] the [rhythmical] value and the intervals of the notes.

Collation is not used to arrive at a posited original or to transcend the material evidence as it stands. Its purpose is to precisely understand the otherwise incomprehensible neumatic notation. The neumatic signs thus become objects of investigation in their own right. In contrast to the fundamentally transcendental empiricism of the Maurists – one in which the *empiria* is to be eventually surmounted – Iussov establishes the model and defines the methodology for a sort of immanent empiricism, one in which the *empiria* is that which ought to be eventually understood.

The same attitude informs a number of other works written by German Protestant church historians. One of the earliest is Nicolaus Staphorst's *Historiae Ecclesiae Hamburgensis Diplomatica*, published in five volumes between 1723 and 1731, a vast collection and discussion of sources of the ecclesiastical history of Hamburg. Amid these sources, Staphorst's attention is drawn to an old missal, particularly its calendar, litany, and musical notation in neumes.[19] Quoting the little outside scholarship he could have accessed, including Ménard's reproduction of *Tellus ac aethra*, Staphorst, just as Iussov before him, describes a method, or procedure, for interpreting neumes, one that is ultimately concerned with an understanding of the signs themselves. The basis of this method is comparing the neumes with later versions of the same melodies recorded in more recent notation. Identity between neumes and later versions in more recent notation, however, is never stated, and the signs are not reduced to an old – and improper – form of communicating the present (indeed, timeless) content. Instead, a second source is brought to bear, as he selects two songs (*Lieder*) from a printed psaltery dated before 1471 and notated with neumes on four red lines. Again, there is no claim to fully explain the older source by the newer; they are put side by side, and Staphorst states that the melodies in the later source "have shed some more light on these obscure things" (*etwas mehr Licht in diesen dunklen Dingen gegeben haben*). The neumes are thus not fully enlightened by the more recent and more intelligible source; they retain a measure of opacity and irreducibility. In contrast to what nineteenth-century writers have said, Staphorst's "transcriptions" are not "unsuccessful transcriptions," for they are not transcriptions at all; they are visual approximations of entities that retain their particularity.

Slightly later, in 1745, Johann Ludolf Walther published his *Lexicon Diplomaticum*, in whose 1747 preface Johann Heinrich Jung, secretary of the Prussian monarch, not only praises at length Walther's work with the old notation but also states that, through Walther's explanations, it is impossible for those who appreciate antiquities not to easily understand (*intelligere ac cognoscere*) the old melody and its composition.[20] This is closely related to the purpose in Iussov's dissertation on studying neumes: the old notation should be explained, rather than transcended, for it stands in a close relationship with the melody that it denotes. At the end of the *Lexicon*, whose bulk is devoted to the abbreviations of syllables and words in diplomas and books dating between the eighth and sixteenth century, there are plates of facsimiles. Each plate has a facsimile, a model alphabet derived from it, and the transcription of the text. Among these are to be found some plates with neumes. Following the pattern established by the textual documents, the notation is transcribed in each instance, always indicating time values and providing absolute height for the neumes on lines and melodic direction for those without. Plate 28 lays down the principles of the transcriptions, setting the different signs, classified typologically and chronologically, against their modern equivalents. The fact that Walther only indicated melodic motions in the case of neumes without lines strongly suggests that he is not interested in attaining a chant that can be sung. The understanding and comprehension (*intelligere & cognoscere*) that he seems to seek is of the notation itself: it is the thing as presented (*exhibere*) by the sign that he shows, and not the thing behind or beyond the sign.

The Spanish context behind the interest in neumes was rather different from its French and German counterparts. The reformed monarchy of the Bourbons had become extremely interested in history and made different efforts to preserve – through study, copy, and editing – the medieval manuscripts that came to be seen as repositories of Spanish history. The Church was instrumental in this program, and the monarchy relied on the clerical elite to promote the study of history, instigating the development of what has been termed a Catholic Enlightenment. As far as neumes are concerned, the exploration of sources happened in two stages: the first in the reign of Ferrando VI (1746–59), through the cataloguing efforts of Jesuit Andrés Marcos Burriel;[21] and the second in the reign of Carlos III (1759–88), fundamentally in the liturgical editions of the Mozarabic rite prepared by Francisco António de Lorenzana y Butrón, Cardinal Lorenzana.

Burriel was named director of the Royal Commission of Archives in 1749 and initiated the cataloguing and transcription of the manuscripts conserved in the cathedral archive in Toledo, a vast project that occupied him between

1750 and 1756. The interest in the *empiria* of the old manuscripts gave rise to some of the most astonishing facsimile copies of old notation, all of which were executed by the renowned Toledan calligrapher Francisco Javier de Santiago y Palomares and supervised by Burriel. Neumes were explicitly seen as marks of antiquity, and they were especially important because they attested to the old Use of Toledo, the Mozarabic rite whose legitimacy was being asserted by the Bourbon monarchy and by the clerical establishment in Spain as an equal to the Roman rite. For example, as Burriel clearly indicates in the copy of Toledo MS 35.7, which is a complete facsimile with carefully copied notation, the old notation helps support the antiquity of the Gothic rite.[22] Neumes were very clearly part of a historical and political argument for Burriel, and this is what assured their importance for him. Indeed, Burriel intended to publish editions of the Mozarabic missal and breviary based on the transcriptions he supervised and as indicated in his unpublished "Apuntamientos de algunas ideas para formar las letras," but his relations with the court deteriorated between 1754 and 1756, he eventually had his papers confiscated, and he could not devote himself to the task.

An extension of the previous work (though probably not based on Burriel's manuscript studies) was only to happen some years later, through the efforts of Lorenzana, who supported the edition of the *Missa gothica* while in Mexico in 1770, promoted the lavish *Breviarium gothicum* in 1775, and prepared the *Missale gothicum*, which was published in 1804 after his death. The *Missa gothica seu mozarabica*, whose introduction on the Mozarabic liturgy is written by Lorenzana himself, has a tract on neumes just before the explanation of the Mozarabic mass, and it starts by vertically juxtaposing a chant incipit in modern notation and the corresponding text and music characters "faithfully excerpted" (*excerpta fideliter*) from what he reports to be a ninth-century missal in Toledo.[23] The old music writing, however, is not conceived as a simple sign of antiquity and of prestige attached to the new book; it is to be both understood and transcribed into modern notes (*ut figurae Musicae cognoscantur, simùlque ad Notas nostri temporis eodem valóre reducantur*). In this sense, the enterprise is much closer to the empiricism of the German Protestant authors than to that of the French Benedictines, but it goes a step further than the German tracts on neumes inasmuch as the knowledge of the neumes is not an end in itself, but a means towards the goal of reconstructing the old melodies.

This necessarily entails a very positive attitude towards neumes. In the absence of clefs and measured time, proceeds the tract on neumes in the *Missa gothica*, the singers of the time had an "excellent system of certain signs, with which they could know when the voice should go up and down." At no point is a lack of precision admitted, and the author gives three different kinds of organization from which the pitch can be known: the use of red and blue lines; the distance separating the notes even in the absence of lines; and the oral example given by the master's voice. In what can be seen as the very inversion of previous negative assessments of neumes, the absence of clefs and lines is not a sign of a rough and deformed chant. The neumes are the signs of a melodious and sweet song. However, just as Lorenzana's editions never intended to be more than an improvement of Cisneros's with the aim of conserving (and not reinventing) the liturgy, so the discussion of neumes and the idea that they are precise and even infallible was never pushed as far as basing a project of editing the melodies on the reading of neumatic manuscripts. The task of restoration of a medieval repertory based on medieval manuscripts lay in the nineteenth century, but the writings of the Toledan circle represent what might be the earliest texts in which neumes are put on a par with modern notation.

Arbitrary and Motivated Signs

From the 1760s, and much more clearly in the 1770s, the writing of music history underwent a profound transformation. The nucleus of the change lies in a combined movement consisting of, on the one hand, the development of a firmer and broader framework centered on a new conception of man (and not disembodied musical systems) at the center of musical history and, on the other hand, an erudization of music history in general and of the history of notation in particular.[24] In this transformation, neumes became a necessary part of the general history of notation in the general histories of music. What precisely their place would be, however, remained to be decided as the writing actually happened, since the earliest music histories lacked neumes and no specific model could be adapted from those texts. This context eventually led to a reworking, from the interior, of the comprehension of the musical sign, with reference to the notions of arbitrary or motivated sign. Differently from the Maurists and from the German church historians, for whom the sign was a fixed binary relation based on the notion of representation, the music historians of the late eighteenth century came to formulate the notion of different semiotic rationales, a difference that could also unfold in the evolutionary domain of history. It seems that the introduction of human beings and their historicity in the epistemological horizon broke the closed domain of the representational sign and made authors question how (differently) signs functioned to people in the course of their historical development.

At the origin of this change, there are two very distinctive scholars who had actually first conceived writing a history of music in collaboration: the Italian Jesuit Padre Giovanni Battista Martini (1706–84), and the German Benedictine Martin Gerbert (1720–93), who was Abbot and Prince of Sankt Blasien.

Tragically, neither of them really brought their work to the level of completion we might have expected if Martini had completed his music history
and if Gerbert's library, along with his notes and many medieval manuscripts, had not burned down. Martini is very brief about neumes, limiting
himself to saying that, when "the Points came as vicars of the Letters," they
were extremely varied and confused, "resembling hieroglyphs."[25] Gerbert is
more detailed.[26] Opposing the progress in notation to the decay in music,
Gerbert places neumes between the Greek letters and the staff. Between these
systems, there were, according to him, "notes without lines, superposed to
the texts," which did not determine the quantity of the ascent or descent.
Gerbert's view of neumes is very critical. When he comes to propose an
examination of different facsimiles (*schematibus*) in chronological order, he
characterizes neumes as "truly arbitrary [notes], made of lines, points, traces,
and curves." The negative notion of arbitrariness, here introduced apparently
for the first time to talk about neumes, might have been suggested by the
space created by the opposing movements of music and notation, the former
characterized as involution and the latter as evolution. It should be noted in
passing that neumes are discussed in a specific chapter devoted to the musical
notes of the Middle Ages: Gerbert invents the Middle Ages as a category in
the history of musical notation, and this association remains a major element
in subsequent discourses.

The notion of arbitrariness is picked up and further developed in the
ensuing decades and plays a major role in the subsequent evaluation of
neumatic writing. In 1776, two Englishmen published general histories of
music that, in embracing the entire field of music history, at once: (1) consolidated the newer developments in music historiography initiated by Martini
and Gerbert; and (2) completed the narratives that were only partially carried
out by their predecessors. These books are John Hawkins's *A General History
of the Science and Practice of Music* and Charles Burney's *A General History
of Music*. Both authors subscribe to an evolutionary paradigm, and musical
notation is one of the domains subsumed in this narrative.

Already in his preliminary discourse, Hawkins contrasts the ancient use
of the alphabet and the "more compendious method of notation" developed
nearly half a century before Guido and perfected by him.[27] The point is
developed in chapter 4 of Book I, where the use of the alphabet by the
ancients is criticized as being "a kind of Brachigraphy totally devoid of
analogy or resemblance between the sign and the thing signified."[28] The core
of the matter is the issue of the arbitrariness of the sign, and it is the alleged
non-arbitrariness of the modern system that is valued instead:

There is this remarkable difference between the method of notation
practiced by the ancients and that now in use, that the characters used

by the former were arbitrary, totally destitute of analogy and no way expressive of those essential properties of sound, graveness and acuteness; [...] whereas the modern scale is so adjusted, that those sounds, which in their own nature are comparatively grave or acute, have such a situation in it, as does most precisely distinguish them according to their several degrees of each; so that the graver sounds have the lowest, and the acuter the highest place in our scale.

The account progresses immediately to the stave and to Guido before talking about the "improvements" introduced by Jean de Murs. It is only after having discoursed on modern notation and firmly having developed the notion of its non-arbitrariness as opposed to ancient notation that Hawkins returns in time and talks about neumes, countering the "general opinion that before the time of Guido the only method of notation in use was by the Roman capital and small letters."[29] His position is one of sharp criticism. Taking up the criterion of expressing acuteness or graveness, a fundamental point for the arbitrary/non-arbitrary divide (as we have seen), Hawkins evaluates the "method of notation by irregular points" in the following manner: "the whole contrivance" is "inartificial, productive of error and of very little worth." He adduces further manuscript examples from English libraries only to reinforce the idea that neumes were indeed "barbarous marks." But they are never clearly classified as arbitrary, and some comments on the plates might even indicate otherwise, especially Hawkins's claim that the state of the characters on plate 48 might indicate "the notes are [not] intended to signify anything more than certain inflections of the voice, so nearly approaching to monotony, that the utterance of them may rather be called reading than singing."[30] (Of course, if neumes can be read and if the very manner of writing adiastematic neumes indicates the nature of the vocal delivery intended, neumes may not in fact be arbitrary marks.)

Burney's treatment of notation suggests that he is grappling with the very same problems as his contemporary and compatriot. Neumes are here integrated in the general history of notation, as the general means of notation after the Greeks and before Guido of Arezzo and the advent of the "modern tablature."[31] In spite of the existence of different methods, there were the neumes. But apparently they cannot be treated as a method, exactly because they are arbitrary: "[...] for in the MS specimens which I have seen, the marks placed over the words, in the Middle Ages, previous to the time of Guido, often appear arbitrary, and to have been adopted only in some particular church, convent, or fraternity." Such a statement is in keeping with his contemporaries, and it is further evidence of the centrality of the notion of arbitrariness in the understanding of neumes by eighteenth-century writers. Burney's alleged reason for dealing with them and presenting facsimiles of

neumes is "to convince the reader of the rude state of music in these barbarous ages," and, even though he admits that some examples of neumes might
be intelligible, he treats them as if they are merely exceptions that prove the
rule: "indeed such as can be deciphered may comfort the reader of taste for
the unintelligible state of the rest."

While sharing a strong criticism of neumes (though Burney is much more
inclined than Hawkins to conceive of neumes as arbitrary signs), neither
one manages to come up with a clear position for neumes in the evolutionary narrative that moves from the arbitrariness of ancient notation to
the purposefulness of its modern counterpart. Between those stages of development, there were the Middle Ages – the "barbarous ages" with which
neumes, the "barbarous marks," were closely associated in their eyes – and,
though the authors seem inclined to treat neumes as arbitrary, both men
were fraught with doubt and uncertainty when they actually had to find a
place for neumes in their evolutionary schemes.

It was Johann Nicolaus Forkel, the author of, among other works,
the two-volume *Allgemeine Geschichte der Musik* (1788, 1801), who actually managed to solve the puzzle and pin down the position of neumes in
the evolutionary history of notation. Just like his contemporaries, Forkel
formulated a history of notation that centers on the dichotomy between
the arbitrary and the non-arbitrary sign and that moves from the former
to the latter. Neumes are approached in the second volume of the work.[32]
They are presented as substitutes for the alphabet, coming after the time
of Gregory the Great and before Guido. Neumes without lines are heavily
criticized by Forkel because they show the upward and downward movement of the melody without showing how many degrees it ought to go up
and down. But rough and imperfect as they are, neumes are very clearly
set apart from the old arbitrary use of the alphabet and connected with the
evolutionary chain of the non-arbitrary notation that would eventually gain
enduring value. Even if extremely cumbersome and far too diversified before
the time of Guido, "one can find in them very early vestiges [*Spuren*], which
could have easily led to completion if one had appropriately pursued them
instead of so frequently going in search of new ways [of notating], making
the whole process very long." In other words, while former authors would
either regard neumes as arbitrary signs or have trouble deciding about their
arbitrariness, Forkel, without lessening his harsh evaluation of neumes, very
clearly presents them as non-arbitrary and fixes them at the very early stages
of what would become modern notation. This formulation would be fundamental for the nineteenth-century engagement with neumes, but it would
take some time before it gained roots and became widely accepted.

Symptoms

François-Joseph Fétis was the pre-eminent European authority on neumes in the second quarter of the nineteenth century. Given his renown, he felt quite comfortable asserting that, in 1845, after thirty-eight years of study, "the success of my undertaking is such that I have managed to arrive at the complete solution of all the problems posed by these notations."[33] In the late 1840s and early 1850s, however, his studies of neumes became the object of extremely harsh criticism and the focus of a major epistemological break that brought about the first formulation of the musicological interpretation of neumatic notation.

Fétis's first surviving comprehensive treatment of neumes is a section called "The Middle Ages: musical notation," in the 1835 "Philosophical Summary of the History of Music," which opens the first edition of his extremely influential *Biographie universelle des musiciens*.[34] In these few pages, an entirely novel conception is put forward, for he at once envisages neumes as a specific historical problem, one that is meant to be solved in its own right irrespective of the earlier or later history of musical notation, and ties it to a particular interpretation of history by associating it with a specific period, the Middle Ages. Neumes are not just a chain in the overall evolution of notation, and, as a result, they cannot be explained only by reference to an internally motivated chain of developments. Whereas alphabetic notation was characteristic of the Greek and Roman worlds, the northern Europeans developed their own systems of notation. For Fétis, there had been three such systems: the Celtic, which he claims must have been entirely original to the Celts and does not seem to have penetrated southern Europe, and the Saxon and Lombardic systems, which he identifies with the neumes that became the usual notations in Europe after the barbarian invasions. In this system, Saxon and Lombardic are the two groups that account for the different notations found in medieval European manuscripts. They share a common ancient origin, having developed under the influence of the East long before the barbarian invasions and exhibiting many common features. Placing neumes under the aegis of a germanized – and also, albeit remotely, orientalized – medieval period is not negative for Fétis, as it had been since Gerbert and then Burney and Hawkins had applied the notion of the "Middle Ages" to the history of notation. Indeed, tacitly distancing himself from the little interest these authors accorded to neumatic writing, Fétis affirms that "one is dealing here with one of the most interesting and less known facts of music history."

This novel view of history is coupled with a changed attitude towards the problem of the sign. Fétis takes up the notion of arbitrariness and applies it unwaveringly to the interpretation of neumes. But here the idea that neumes are arbitrary does not mean that they are uncertain. Much to the contrary, it signifies that they are a precise and fully codified sign system, designating the thing signified with utter exactitude through a convention. This is the crux of Fétis's argument and the core of the debate that leads to an epistemological shift around the year 1850. Fétis proposed that both branches of neumatic notation express absolute tonal value, and, in two plates illustrating each of these branches, he distinguishes between the various isolated signs that indicate the degrees of the diatonic scale and the ligated ones that also express specific absolute heights. This is a structured system that can be read with certainty provided one knows what the structuring convention is, i.e., provided one is in possession of the arbitrary link between significant and signifier.

The belief in an absolute tonal value of neumes expressed by means of an arbitrary system of signs defines the task of the interpreter as a decipherer in search of a key, a position compared by many writers from the 1840s through 1860s to that of Champollion in his decipherment of hieroglyphic writing, although apparently not evoked by Fétis himself. Fétis met his fiercest opponent in Théodore Nisard, who wrote a series of extremely critical articles in the late 1840s and early 1850s upholding the restoration project and defending a new course for the study of neumes. In his most comprehensive study on neumes, which appeared in five parts from 1848 through 1850 in the *Revue archéologique*, Nisard does not explain all of his views on the interpretation of neumes, putting off a full development of them.[35] But he very clearly champions a different approach that eventually countered Fétis's. Even though a few elements might be taken to be arbitrary – and Nisard talks about *notes de convention* – his understanding of what he terms an "ideographic system" is that of an essentially motivated one. Here one begins to see the gradual but steady penetration of Forkel's notion that neumes are motivated signs. Some ornaments, for example, were said to be indicated "by the very form of neumes," and the notion of an essential and necessary relation between the sign and the thing lies at the heart of what Nisard terms a *sémiologie neumatique*.

The term *sémiologie* itself is highly meaningful here. At the time, *sémiologie*, or *séméiologie* (a relatively novel word), had a strictly medical sense, referring to the study of the signs and symptoms of a disease.[36] *Sémiologie* denotes a study in which the sign (or symptom) is caused by the thing of which it is a sign (the disease) and its proper interpretation can lead back to the discovery of the thing. It posits a necessary causal nexus between the two elements. The allusion to the medical field is no coincidence, and Nisard's text is a very early testimony of a structural transference of the practice of medical sem(e)iology to other domains of knowledge, which, according to Carlo Ginzburg, would amount in the 1870s to "the silent emergence of an epistemological model [...] in the humanities."[37] The field of knowledge was no longer populated by metaphorical signs, but by metonymical traces, or symptoms. Placing neumes under the auspices of the strongly connoted term *sémiologie* thus amounts to a reversion of the arbitrary system envisaged by Fétis: the neumatic shapes become the symptoms of the music.

This understanding of neumes came to be the dominant discourse of late nineteenth-century scholarship, and it received a very influential formulation in the works of Charles Edmond de Coussemaker. He is the crucial link between, on the one hand, the polemics of the late 1840s and early 1850s and, on the other hand, the subsequent structuring of the musicological approach to neumatic notation. It is through his re-elaboration of his contemporaries' ideas that the epistemological attitude to the sign subsumed in Nisard's expression *sémiologie neumatique* became the touchstone of future research. In his 1841 monograph on Hucbald, Coussemaker discussed neumes, and even though he explicitly avowed agreement with Fétis, he still regarded them as somewhat imperfect.[38] Coussemaker believed, however, that neumes, differently from Hucbald's tonal system, contained in themselves the conditions for improvement that would lead to the modern notation. The advantage of neumes over Hucbald's notation is formulated in the following terms: "What distinguishes neumes and make them superior to the use of letters for notation is that they speak to the eye at the same time as to the intelligence by the upper or lower position occupied by each sign." The formulation establishes a difference between, on the one hand, signs that speak only to the intelligence and, on the other hand, those that speak to the eyes, a language that appears to contrast the immediacy of sight to the mediation of thought, thus evoking the fundamental problem of the direct (or motivated) and indirect (or arbitrary, or conventional) sign relations.

In 1852, Coussemaker discussed neumes at greater length in his influential *Histoire de l'harmonie au Moyen Age*, and, from the vantage point acquired by the particularly fertile exchanges of the preceding five to seven years, he was able to offer a developed systematization of the semiological outlook on neumes that was already hinted at in his *Mémoire sur Hucbald* when he blatantly refused to embrace Fétis's dominant view that neumes were an arbitrary system of signs.[39] The tonal interpretation of neumes, which Coussemaker saw as possible, even if difficult and not always completely clear, is the foremost concern. The basis of the analysis is Coussemaker's extremely influential theory that neumes derived from prosodic accents that could normally be ascribed an exact value in context, since almost all intervals were either seconds or thirds. Coussemaker goes on to discuss rhythm and ornament and states that neumes express both, putting the question under the aegis of the general problem of *la séméiologie neumatique*. This intimately connects Coussemaker to Nisard's *sémiologie neumatique* and consecrates the advent of an enquiry that will be deeply interested in the close study of the shapes of neumes: as symptoms of melody, these forms are causally linked to the Gregorian phrase whose restoration is the ultimate goal of research. But, being symptomatic, they are not easily legible: they deserve close study and prolonged examinations and comparisons. It was a matter of science – a science yet to be established.

The interest in medieval neumes, which reached a sort of climatic moment between 1845 and 1855, would continue to be extremely important in the second half of the century. The project of restoring Gregorian chant acquired a whole new dimension as it came to its first potentially practical results with editions that claimed to be truly Gregorian and contained the repertory of the Mass and Office. The most important of these was the Gradual issued by the bishops of Reims and Cambrai in 1851, claiming to derive its authority from the Montpellier manuscript discovered by Fétis.[40] This first major ecclesiastical attempt at restoration set the scene for a profound and renewed engagement with the neumed manuscripts and for different attempts by individuals and institutions to improve the results of the Reims and Cambrai commission. The investigations of medieval neumes rapidly grew in number and further developed the potentialities of the fundamental framework developed around the 1850s and associated with the expression *sémiologie neumatique*.

This framework still had all the language of certainty and of definitive answers in the different works published by Félix Raillard between the 1850s and the 1880s. In his *Explication des neumes*, from 1852, in a very Fétisian tone, he would say, having worked in order to improve the results of the Reims and Cambrai edition, "I derive rules of interpretation that are certain and easy."[41] Neumes are fundamental for him not, however, because of tonal value. He accepted, as became the norm from the mid-nineteenth century on, that the value of neumes did not lie in tonal indications. Rather, having defined the four necessary components of restoration (finding the number of notes for each syllable, establishing their tonal value, determining the appropriate time length of each note, and indicating the mode of execution, i.e., dynamics, pauses, and ornaments), Raillard admits that the first two had already been accomplished by the edition of Reims and Cambrai – it is the latter two that, in Raillard's view, need attention and this is where neumes are of fundamental assistance.

Raillard is perfectly representative of the epistemological framework that emerged in the middle of the century. For him, it is the form of neumes that reveals the nature of the melody: neumes are "the faithful image of the voice effects they represent," and it is by "the form itself of neumes" that one can derive rhythm, pauses, and ornaments. And this is how he tries to tackle the interpretation of signs that had been a matter of dispute, such as the *quilisma*. This is a very clear statement that neumes and chant are not superimposed arbitrarily, but are rather two inherently articulated things, the first (neumes) being the direct consequence of the second (chant), which makes it possible, given the causal relationship, to move back in the opposite direction and deduce the cause (chant) from its direct effect (neumes).

Raillard's contemporaries were not as thorough as he was in the exposition of the principles of restoration (and, as we shall see presently, his model of scholarship would be superseded in the last quarter of the century), but they were in agreement with his basic principles: a shift of attention from the tonal to the rhythmic and expressive contents of neumes; and a belief in the careful study of a large number of sources with the purpose of revealing the traces of chant that are inscribed in the very form of neumes.

The 1850s were marked by a proliferation of small *mémoirs* on the restoration of chant, most of which were either preparations to or comments on editions of chant, and they helped anchor the new scholarly outlook on neumes in the general debate, pursuing and strengthening the overall revision stemming from the criticism of Fétis's proposals. This outlook, however, would not be exactly revised, but more properly strengthened and structured through the musicological works that started appearing in the 1880s from scholars in the Abbaye Saint-Pierre de Solesmes, which, through the impulse of founder Dom Guéranger, was to become the central headquarters of the restoration enterprise.[42]

The culmination of this process is observable in the works of the two pioneer "neume scholars" of the Solesmes school – Dom Joseph Pothier and Dom André Mocquereau. With these two scholars, the symptomatic reading of neumes penetrates deeper. There is no simple key to neumes; there are only traces. And these traces are very concrete and palpable, for neumes are anything but conventional, and they not only reveal the chant, as consequent traces that allow one to reconstruct the causal chant, but they also reveal the very nature of a chant that was intrinsically different from modern music. This notion is here efficiently applied for the first time to dispute any understanding of neumes as fundamentally deficient for not showing precise pitch, and this is also a trace to be interpreted and understood in its relation to the thing that caused it. Mocquereau elaborated at length on the notion of neumes (which were based on accents) as images that spring naturally from the melody itself:

> But what pertains to our thesis is to demonstrate that grammatical accents, from which all neumatic and modern notations will derive, are not signs adapted by convention to the music of language, but shapes arising naturally out of oratorical melody, drawn in its image

(at least regarding the melody of words considered in themselves) and thus admirably appropriate to their role and to their signification.[43]

According to Mocquereau, accents were applied to oratorical speech, whose inflections were only those of heightened discourse, not those of fully-fledged music. Thus, the fact that accents, i.e., neumes, were applied to music must be interpreted as indicating "the previous existence of a very simple melodic state, intermediary between speech and music and whose sounds could be transmitted through the simplicity of oratorical accentuation."[44] This state is associated by him with liturgical psalmody, an explanation that allows him to envisage a "harmonious adaptation" (*convenance harmonieuse*) between the music and the notation. It was thus the transformation in the form of chants and their growth in number that eventually led to a change in notation, and ultimately to the advent of diastemacy, a principle that is also interpreted as natural: "at the origin of musical notation [for him, diastematic notation, neumatic notation being oratorical, and not musical, notation] just as at the origin of languages, of writing, of the arts and the sciences, nature precedes convention and appears as the first master of man."[45]

Thus, the fact that accents, i.e., neumes, were applied to music must be interpreted as indicating the existence of a simpler state of chant. If neumes are the natural and concrete traces of a certain condition of chant, nothing in them can either be interpreted as a defect or an imperfection (this would ultimately presuppose that neumes do not refer strictly to a concrete cause in the past) or be regarded as an immediately transparent and rapidly legible indication (it is the process of generation of the sign through chant that has to be understood first). This is how the study of neumes came to amount to an ontology in the making: as neumes are traces and as these traces are different from our own, they necessarily involve essentially different musical processes and musical beings than ours.

Conclusion

As the preceding considerations show, the criticism of earlier views of neumes cannot be structured as though all of these discourses stood on the same ground. The fundamental presuppositions – and the very notion of what a sign is – have suffered clear breaks along the way, and criticism would have to work itself up from this basic and structural level of discourse. But this also invites current scholars working with neumes to develop a sharper awareness of their own discourses and of how their scholarly production is affected by the frequently tacit notions that underlie their research.

NOTES

1. Among the exceptions, see Annette Kreuziger-Herr, *Ein Traum vom Mittelalter: Die Wiederentdeckung mittelalterlicher Musik in der Neuzeit* (Köln: Böhlau Verlag, 2003). See also Kreuziger-Herr, "Imagining Medieval Music: A Short History," *Studies in Medievalism XIV: Correspondences: Medievalism in Scholarship and the Arts*, ed. Tom Shippey with Martin Arnold (associate editor) (Cambridge: D. S. Brewer, 2005), 81–109.

2. This article introduces some of the arguments and materials in a book manuscript I am currently preparing, *The Modern Life of Medieval Neumes*. Because of this, bibliographic references have been kept to a minimum. When, in the present article, there are many quotes from the same work, I have, whenever possible, given one single reference for each work, mentioning the pages from which all the following quotations come.

3. The first such list is to be found in François-Joseph Fétis, "Préface historique d'une dissertation inédite sur les notations musicales du Moyen Âge, et particulièrement sur celle de la prose de Montpellier," *Revue de la musique religieuse, populaire et classique* 1 (1845): 266–79 (266–72).

4. On Foucault's notion of archaeology, see especially Arnold I. Davidson, "Archaeology, Genealogy, Ethics," in *Foucault: A Critical Reader*, ed. David Couzens Hoy (New York: Basil Blackwell, 1986), 221–33.

5. Michael Praetorius, *Syntagma musicum*, 3 vols. (Wolfenbüttel, 1614–20), 1, 11–14.

6. Claude V. Palisca, *Music and Ideas in the Sixteenth and Seventeenth Centuries* (Chicago and Urbana: University of Illinois Press, 2006).

7. Gioseffo Zarlino, *Le Istitutioni harmoniche* (Venice: Francesco Senese, 1558), 121 and 172–73.

8. Vincenzo Galilei, *Dialogo della musica antica e moderna* (Florence: Giorgio Marescotti, 1581), 36.

9. Michel Foucault, *Les mots et les choses: une archéologie des sciences humaines* (Paris: Gallimard, 1966), 55.

10. *Vocabolario degli Accademici della Crusca* (Venice, 1612), accessed online at http://vocabolario.signum.sns.it/_s_index2.html

11. Athanasius Kircher, *Musurgia universalis* (Rome: Typographia Haeredum Francisci Corbelletti, 1650), 215.

12. Kircher, *Musurgia universalis*, 555.

13. *Divi Gregorii Papae Liber Sacramentorum*, ed. Nicholas-Hugues Ménard, 2 vols. (Paris: Claudii Sonnii & Dionysii Bechet, 1641–42).

14. Gabrielle Bickendorff, "Die Geschichte und ihre Bilder vom Mittelalter: zur 'longue durée' visueller Überlieferung," in *Visualisierung und Imagination: Materielle Relikte des Mittelalters in bildlichen Darstellungen der Neuzeit und Moderne*, ed. Bernd Carqué, Daniela Mondini, and Matthias Noell, 2 vols. (Göttingen: Wallstein, 2006), 103–52 (137–40).

15. Jean Mabillon, *Annales Ordinis Sancti Benedicti*, 4 vols. (Luca: Leonardo Venturini, 1739), 4, 632–33.

16. Pierre-Benoît de Jumilhac, *La science et la pratique du plain-chant* (Paris: Billaine, 1673), 68–71.

17. Gabriel-Guillaume Nivers, *Dissertation sur le chant grégorien* (Paris, 1683), 43–45; Jean Lebeuf, *De l'état des sciences, dans l'étendue de la monarchie française, sous Charlemagne*

(Paris: Jacques Guérin, 1734), 62; Jean Lebeuf, *Traité historique et pratique sur le chant ecclésiastique* (Paris: J. B. Herissant & Jean Th. Herissant, 1741), 2; Léonard Poisson, *Traité théorique et pratique du plain-chant, appelé grégorien* (Paris: P. N. Lottin & J. H. Butard, 1750), 42–43.

18. Johann Andreas Iussov, *De cantoribus ecclesiae Veteri et Novi Testamenti* (Helmstedt: Litteris Hammianis, 1708), 1, 19–22 and 40–41.

19. Nicolaus Staphorst, *Historiae Ecclesiae Hamburgensis Diplomatica*, 5 vols. (Hamburg: Theodor Christoph Felginern, 1723–31), 1, 337–41.

20. Johann Ludolf Walther, *Lexicon Diplomaticum* (Göttingen: Johann Peter & Johann Wilhelm Schmidt, 1747).

21. On Burriel's enterprise, see Susan Boynton, "A Lost Mozarabic Liturgical Manuscript Rediscovered: New York, Hispanic Society of America, B2916, olim Toledo, Biblioteca Capitular, 33.2," *Traditio* 57 (2002): 189–219; Susan Boynton, "Reconsidering the Toledo Codex of the Cantigas de Santa Maria in the Eighteenth Century," in *Quomodo Cantabimus Canticum? Studies in Honor of Edward H. Roesner*, ed. David Butler Cannata, Gabriela Ilnitchi Currie, Rena Charnin Mueller, and John Louis Nádas (Middleton, WI: American Institute of Musicology, 2008), 209–22. In this article (p. 220, n.8), the author announces a forthcoming monograph under the title of *Silent Music: Medieval Ritual and the Construction of History in Eighteenth-Century Spain.*

22. José Janini and José Serrano, *Manuscritos litúrgicos de la Biblioteca Nacional* (Madrid: Dirección General de Archivos y Bibliotecas, 1969), 168.

23. *Missa gothica, seu mozarabica*, ed. Francisco Antonio Lorenzana and Francisco Fabián y Fuero (Los Ángeles: Typis Seminarii Palafoxiani, 1770), 69–72.

24. See Georg G. Iggers, "The European Context of Eighteenth-Century German Enlightenment Historiography," in *Aufklärung und Geschichte: Studien zur deutschen Geshichtswissenschaft im 18. Jahrhundert*, ed. Hans Erich Bödeker, Georg G. Iggers, Jonathan B. Knudsen, and Peter H. Reill (Göttingen: Vandenhoeck & Ruprecht, 1986), 225–45.

25. Giovanni Battista Martini, *Storia della musica*, 3 vols. (Bologna: Istituto delle Scienze, 1761–81), 1, 183.

26. Martin Gerbert, *De cantu et musica sacra*, 2 vols. (Sankt Blasien, 1774), 1, 47–60.

27. John Hawkins, *A General History of the Science and Practice of Music*, 5 vols. (London: T. Payne & Son, 1776), 1, xvii.

28. Hawkins, *A General History*, 1, 16–18.

29. Hawkins, *A General History*, 1, 379.

30. Hawkins, *A General History*, 1, xxx.

31. Charles Burney, *A General History of Music*, 4 vols. (London: for the author, 1776–89), 1, 437–38.

32. Johann Nicolaus Forkel, *Allgemeine Geschichte der Musik*, 2 vols. (Leipzig: Schwickertschen Verlage, 1788–1801), 2, 348–50.

33. Fétis, "Préface historique," 275.

34. François-Joseph Fétis, "Résumé philosophique de l'histoire de la musique," *Biographie universelle des musiciens*, 5 vols. (Paris: H. Fournier, 1835–44), 1, xxxvii–ccliv (clx–clxvi).

35. Théodore Nisard, "Étude sur les anciennes notations musicales de l'Europe," *Revue archéologique* 5 (1848–49): 701–20; 6 (1849–50): 101–14, 461–75, 749–64; 7 (1850–51): 129–43.

36. See John Deely, "The Word 'Semiotics': Formation and Origins," *Semiotica* 146 (2003): 1–49.

37. Carlo Ginzburg, "Clues: Roots of an Evidential Paradigm," in *Myths, Emblems, Signs* (London: Hutchinson Radius, 1990), pp. 96–125 (96).

38. Charles Edmond Henri de Coussemaker, *Mémoire sur Hucbald moine de St. Amand et ses traités de musique* (Paris, 1841), 115 and 147–59.

39. Charles Edmond Henri de Coussemaker, *Histoire de l'harmonie au Moyen Age* (Paris: Victor Didron, 1852).

40. On this, see Karl Gustav Fellerer, "Zur Choral-Restoration im Frankreich um die Mitte des 19. Jahrhunderts," *Kirchenmusikalisches Jahrbuch* 58–59 (1974–75): 135–47.

41. Félix Raillard, *Explication des neumes ou anciens signes de notation musicale pour servir à la restoration complète du chant grégorien* (Paris: E. Repos, 1852).

42. See Pierre Combe, *Histoire de la restoration du chant gregorien d'apres des documents inedits: Solesmes et l'edition Vaticane* (Solesmes: Abbaye de Solesmes, 1969).

43. André Mocquereau, "Origine et classement des différentes écritures neumatiques: 1. Notation oratoire ou chironomique, 2. Notation musicale ou diastématique," *Paléographie Musicale* 1 (1889): 96–160 (97).

44. Mocquereau, "Origine et classement," 103.

45. Mocquereau, "Origine et classement," 159.

Hereward the Dane and the English, But Not the Saxon: Kingsley's Racial Anglo-Saxonism

Michael R. Kightley

Charles Kingsley belongs to that particular class of nineteenth-century gentleman who was extraordinarily famous in his own time, but who has since faded into relative obscurity. When he is now remembered, it tends to be for his children's book *The Water-Babies*, or for his controversial debate with John Henry Newman.[1] What is rarely remembered is that Kingsley held the Regius Chair of Modern History at Cambridge for nine years, starting in 1860.[2] "Modern History" meant post-classical, and so in these years, Kingsley engaged directly in the discourse of medieval English and Old North studies, producing a significant work of early medieval history: a series of lectures on the interactions between the Germanic tribes and the Roman Empire, which was subsequently published in 1864 under the title *The Roman and the Teuton*.[3] In the same period, he also produced an equally important work of historiography: a Conquest-era romance about the English resistance fighter Hereward the Wake. This potent position as popular fiction writer, with one foot nonetheless firmly grounded in the discourse of medieval studies, establishes him as a perfect example of what Allen J. Frantzen calls a "gatekeeper" of medieval knowledge, someone who selectively filters and transmits this knowledge to popular audiences.[4] One of the most important aspects of this gatekeeping comes in terms of his racial medievalism, and more specifically, his racial Anglo-Saxonism. This article has, therefore, two main focuses: first, the influence of medieval studies on Kingsley's theorizations of the English race, and second, his transmission of this racial thinking to broader audiences via *The Roman and the Teuton* and *Hereward the Wake: "Last of the English."*[5]

Both of these texts originate, at least in part, in Kingsley's awareness of, and involvement in, the discourses of Anglo-Saxon studies, Germanic studies, and philology. A close relationship with the noted philologist F. Max Müller, who eventually wrote a preface to a later edition of *The Roman and the Teuton*,[6] placed him in contact with these discourses even before he assumed his Cambridge chair. According to Susan Chitty,

> [h]e had recently been moving in historical circles at Oxford, since Max Müller, Taylorian Professor of Modern European Languages, had married his niece [...]. The young couple had borrowed the rectory for their honeymoon and through Müller Kingsley met [Leopold von] Ranke and many distinguished Germans.[7]

Between Ranke, author of *Geschichten der romanischen und germanischen Völker von 1494 bis 1514* (*History of the Roman and Germanic Peoples from 1494 to 1514*), and Müller, author of *Lectures on the Science of Language*, Kingsley's access to philological and historical discourses would have been extensive. As Clare A. Simmons has observed, Müller was pivotal in popularizing the growing belief in Britain that the "Science of Language" was a valid means of proving an essentialist view of the virtues of the English character.[8] To borrow Simmons's words, Müller "argued that languages are not mixed; that is, one language may assimilate vocabulary from another, but in net effect, languages replace each other rather than merging," and, moreover, that philology was "used to suggest that the American historical concept of 'Manifest Destiny' was applicable to the European situation, and that the Germanic-speaking races, and notably the English speakers, were destined to rule the world."[9] Even though Kingsley probably disagreed with some of these assertions, Müller's ability to connect philology to racial development would have nonetheless offered Kingsley an intellectually sanctioned validation for pursuing his desire to develop his own theory of the evolution of the English race.

Perhaps the most important discourse for the development of Kingsley's racial Anglo-Saxonism was the considerable body of Anglo-Saxon histories, a body whose growth had been sparked by the work of Sharon Turner at the beginning of the century. This article will demonstrate that Kingsley's involvement with these histories was extensive and involved. For example, Kingsley wrote a letter about his course on Early English Literature at Queen's College[10] which indicates he was familiar with the French historian Augustin Thierry's work on the Norman Conquest,[11] while *Hereward* refers to the works of Francis Palgrave (e.g., on the effect of William's construction of fortresses in England (2:125)) and of E. A. Freeman (e.g., on "the facts of Godwin's life" (1:9)). Moreover, *Hereward* is dedicated to the antiquarian Thomas Wright, who Kingsley asserts "first disinterred" the historical Hereward "when scarcely a hand or foot of him was left standing out from beneath the dust of ages."[12] While Freeman's work was certainly influential on Kingsley, Freeman's voluminous text *The History of the Norman Conquest of England* was not completed until after the first editions of *Hereward* and *The Roman and the Teuton*,[13] so this article will focus on the histories published earlier in the century, most particularly Turner's *The History of the Anglo-Saxons* (1799–1805), and to a limited extent Francis Palgrave's *History of the Anglo-Saxons* (1831) and John Mitchell Kemble's *The Saxons in England* (1849). Kingsley not only knew these and other such histories[14] but also conceived his theories in direct response to them, particularly his theories about the origin and nature of the English race, and of the "Teutonic" races in general.

It should be noted that the bare fact that Kingsley engaged directly with these texts does not mean his understanding of them or of the Anglo-Saxon period was beyond reproach. For example, when you consider that the afore-mentioned letter recommends Edward Bulwer-Lytton's romance *Harold: The Last of the Saxon Kings* as a valid historical teaching text,[15] it would be overly optimistic to suggest that Kingsley's familiarity with Anglo-Saxon literature and criticism made him much more than a well-read generalist; even Müller's preface to *The Roman and the Teuton* reveals his awareness of Kingsley's limi-tations as a historian, full as it is with qualifications and reservations about his friend's work.[16] At the same time, however, this limitation did not signifi-cantly hinder Kingsley's willingness, even eagerness, to contribute to the field and to its growing discourse on race.

Discourses are, of course, never discrete, and so Kingsley's theories were contributing not only to the discourse of Anglo-Saxon studies, but also to any number of overlapping discursive fields, perhaps the most important of which was the political. Simmons's analysis of Müller's repeated pleas for British support of Germany in the 1870 Franco-Prussian War[17] gives some sense of how politically loaded discussions of the Teutonic race could be. This war broke out after the publication of *Hereward* and *The Roman and the Teuton*, but it had been very long in the coming. Even more immediate to Kingsley's thinking of the mid-1860s would have been the concern around the Schleswig-Holstein question, which grew throughout the middle of the nineteenth century and culminated in the two Schleswig Wars of 1848–51 and 1864.[18] The "question" revolved around the problem of determining Danish and German national loyalties in a region of conflicting linguistic and racial identities. Was, to choose just one example, a German-speaking individual in Holstein actually a Dane because that duchy happened to be under the rule of the King of Denmark? The implications of such questions of identity were not isolated within Denmark and the German Confedera-tion; they also held significant ramifications for the English, particularly in the minds of Anglo-Saxon scholars.[19] As T. A. Shippey indicates, "[a] critical point in making the connection is that the ancestral homeland of the Angles, or English, is thought to lie in the district of Angeln in southern Schleswig, i.e. now just to the south of the Danish-German border."[20] The identities of the inhabitants of Schleswig and Holstein, therefore, were intimately connected to the identities of the original Anglo-Saxons and by extension the modern English as well, making the "question" a racially-charged quagmire of politics and scholarship for many English thinkers. The racial origins of the English were up for question and Kingsley chose to put forth an answer.[21]

The Spirit of Odin the Goer

Hereward the Wake: Last of the English first appeared in serial form in *Good Words* throughout the course of 1865, followed by publication as a book in 1866,[22] right in the midst of Kingsley's tenure at Cambridge and shortly after the publication of *The Roman and the Teuton*. The lectures on which this latter text was based were popular among the undergraduates at Cambridge, but the response to their publication from the academic community at large was far from universally positive, including a particularly harsh review from Freeman. Following a challenge to Kingsley's merits for his post, Freeman states that "Mr. Kingsley once could, and still can by an effort, write good sense and good English, but there are pages and pages of these lectures which are simply rant and nonsense – history, in short, brought down to the lowest level of the sensation novelist."[23] It is not hard to imagine how such criticisms could have strongly encouraged Kingsley to channel his considerable narrative powers into striving for accurate historical detail in *Hereward*. Kingsley makes clear his desire for an air of historicity in the opening pages of the novel by making an offhand reference to John Lothrop Motley's history *The Rise of the Dutch Republic*; he then follows this reference up a few pages later by providing a translation of the Anglo-Saxon Chronicle's brief account of the first arrival of the Danes in 787 (1:5). Kingsley's initial description of Hereward makes this attempt at historical credibility explicit: "I have, in this story, followed facts as strictly as I could, altering none which I found, and inventing little more than was needed to give the story coherence, or to illustrate the manners of the time" (1:17).

Regardless of his truth claims, Kingsley's *Hereward* is, unsurprisingly, full of embellishments upon his sources, and it is in these embellishments that his racial theories have the most room to flourish.[24] To be precise, I would suggest that his novel is one of the most concerted attempts in the nineteenth century to demonstrate the glories of the Danish influence on Englishness. This attempt requires Kingsley to take a somewhat complex, if not sophisticated, view of his hero's identity: first, Kingsley is emphatic that

Hereward's racial heritage is not Anglo-Saxon but Anglo-Dane, and second, as the subtitle proudly declares, Hereward is put forth as a symbol of English national identity. The interplay between these different levels of identity provides a structural framework for the narrative that is introduced in the prelude and the opening chapter and eventually resolved in the concluding chapter.

The prelude to *Hereward* opens with an explanation for why lowlanders rarely get the same praise in literature as do highlanders, partly in response, as Andrew Wawn has pointed out, to Walter Scott's representation in *Waverley* of "the seductive regional spirit of the Scottish highlands."[25] Kingsley's response culminates in an encomium on the indomitable courage of those dwelling in the lowland Danelaw at the time of the Conquest:

> When the men of Wessex, the once conquering, and even to the last the most civilized, race of Britain, fell at Hastings once and for all, and struck no second blow, then the men of the Danelagh disdained to yield to the Norman invader. For seven long years they held their own, not knowing, like true Englishmen, when they were beaten; and fought on desperate, till there were none left to fight. (1:4)

The lowland versus highland binary that Kingsley constructs in the opening pages quickly shifts, therefore, to a Wessex (or generally Anglo-Saxon) versus Anglo-Dane paradigm, with the Norman thrown in as spice. We have here the first suggestion in the novel that Kingsley does not abide by the traditional use of "Anglo-Saxon" as an all-inclusive umbrella term for the English of the period; for Kingsley, the Anglo-Dane is potently distinct, sufficiently so to challenge the Anglo-Saxon for what it means to be "true Englishmen." The damning by faint praise of the Anglo-Saxon resistance to William in this passage is made explicit shortly thereafter, when Kingsley suggests that "[f]or a while [the Anglo-Saxons] had been lords of all England. The Anglo-Saxon race was wearing out. The men of Wessex, priest-ridden, and enslaved by their own aristocracy, quailed before the free Norsemen" (1:6–7). Note here that while "the Anglo-Saxon" seems to be a fairly stable identity, particularly early in Kingsley's novel, the notion of Anglo-Danishness is blurred by numerous other terms, including "the Norsemen." For Kingsley, the Anglo-Saxon was localized at this stage in England, epitomized in Wessex, and limited by that localization, while "Anglo-Dane" was able to draw upon the traditions of a much wider cultural geography, from Iceland and Greenland, to Norway, Sweden, and Denmark, and even to the Varangians at Constantinople.

This racialized rhetoric in the first half of the prelude lays the groundwork for the by then unsurprising revelation in the second half that Hereward's family is Anglo-Dane. Familial racial identity is not simply a matter of biology in *Hereward*, however; it is also a matter of politics. Kingsley draws on the historical enmity between the houses of Godwin and Leofric, here Hereward's father, as a way of personalizing the broader racial divide that he has put forth. Kingsley informs his readers that Godwin, "though married to a Danish princess, and acknowledging his Danish connection [...], constituted himself (with a sound patriotic instinct) the champion of the men of Wessex, and the house of Cerdic," first of the West Saxon kings (1:10). While Kingsley does express respect for Godwin elsewhere, his reference to the earl's "sound patriotic instinct" is somewhat tongue in cheek, since it is followed by a reference to the possibility that Godwin had Alfred, son of Ethelred, murdered to further his own agenda. Leofric, on the other hand, "though bearing a Saxon name, seems to have been the champion of the Danish party" (1:9). Kingsley goes out of his way in the first chapter to have a messenger recount a scene in which the self-serving nature of Godwin and the righteous self-sacrifice of Leofric are demonstrated, when Leofric feels the need to oppose his own son's misdeeds in open court, which leads directly to Hereward's outlawry (1:49–54).[26] The messenger's tale demonstrates the function of Godwin and Leofric, and their respective families, in the novel: by focusing on these two houses, Kingsley narrows his depiction of the Saxon-Dane tensions sufficiently for narrative to encompass them. But the tension between them does more than that – the fact that Kingsley's descriptions of the two both begin with qualifiers ("though married to a Danish princess," "though bearing a Saxon name") is not insignificant. Kingsley emphasizes that each earl seems to have reasons to belong to the other's camp, and, therefore, that self-determination must play at least some role in their political and racial stances. Each earl is motivated by at least two conflicting racial loyalties and, it appears, is unable or unwilling to reconcile them.

Kingsley actually spends much of the prelude presenting a case that Hereward was Earl Leofric's son, which is based on little historical evidence. History aside, if Hereward was the son of Leofric, then it is easier for Kingsley to accomplish one of his primary objectives in the early chapters: to situate the young hero within a Danish or Viking set of cultural expectations. With this relationship established in the prelude, Kingsley is able to have Hereward take Leofric's unlikely association with Anglo-Danishness even further. Hereward himself emphasizes this racial identity multiple times in his first scene in the novel (1:35), but it is later in the chapter that he expresses his identification with his Viking heritage most clearly. As one of the most intriguing treatments of race in nineteenth-century medievalism, it is worth quoting at length. Hereward, having learned that he has been outlawed, considers the options that remain to him:

Where would he go? Where would he not go? For the spirit of Odin
the Goer, the spirit which has sent his children round the world, was
strong within him. He would go to Ireland, to the Ostmen, or Irish
Danes, at Dublin, Waterford, or Cork, and marry some beautiful
Irish Princess with gray eyes, and raven locks, and saffron smock, and
great gold bracelets from her native hills. No; he would go off to the
Orkneys, and join Bruce and Ranald, and the Vikings of the northern
seas, and all the hot blood which had found even Norway too hot to
hold it; he would sail through witch-whales and icebergs to Iceland
and Greenland, and the sunny lands which they said lay even beyond,
across the all but unknown ocean. Or he would go up the Baltic to
the Jomsburg Vikings, and fight against Lett and Esthonian heathen,
and pierce inland, perhaps, through Puleyn and the bison forests, to
the land from whence came the magic swords and the old Persian
coins which he had seen so often in the halls of his forefathers. No; he
would go south, to the land of sun and wine; and see the magicians of
Cordova and Seville; and beard Mussulman hounds worshipping their
Mahomets; and perhaps bring home an Emir's daughter,
          "With more gay gold about her middle,
          Than would buy half Northumberlee."
Or he would go up the Straits, and on to Constantinople and the
great Kaiser of the Greeks, and join the Varanger Guard, and perhaps,
like Harold Hardraade in his own days, after being cast to the lion for
carrying off a fair Greek lady, tear out the monster's tongue with his
own hands, and show the Easterns what a Viking's son could do.
                                                    (1:61–62)

Before engaging the specific details of the passage, it is worth looking at it
as a whole. Hereward is here attempting to map the scope of the Viking
world from the settlements on Greenland to the Varangian Guard. Despite
Hereward's awareness of the national and ethnic differences between the
groups that this scope encompasses, he genuinely believes that there is something, called "Viking" in his vocabulary, that unifies them. This belief is
quite similar to Benedict Anderson's conception of "imagined communities":
Hereward and those he includes in his definition of Vikingness "will never
know most of their fellow-members, meet them, or even hear of them, yet
in the minds of each lives the image of their communion."[27] This bond,
while insubstantial and "imagined," is very real, particularly for the romantic
Hereward, who has been regaled with stories of the Vikings throughout his
childhood (1:65–66). Interestingly, as Hereward is defining the breadth of
the Viking world, he is also wiping clear his own identity – he is replacing
his identity as resident of Bourne and England, and the limitations thereof,

with the broad, almost unlimited, potential that comes along with a racial
identity as encompassing as "Viking." In this way, Hereward takes his father's
alignment with the Anglo-Danish party over the Anglo-Saxons even further;
in fact, Hereward takes the Saxon versus Dane debate to an entirely different
order of magnitude. While Leofric merely aligns himself politically within a
broader English nation, Hereward redefines the question onto the international stage. Whereas in England the Saxons and Danes were two distinct
ethnic groups but were also still unified within one kingdom, in Hereward's
imagined community Anglo-Saxons are merely one group against which the
Vikings have pushed. Hereward's choice to define himself racially as Viking
is, therefore, also a choice to define the Anglo-Saxon as other.

Saxons are certainly not the only foreign races in Hereward's world-view;
as encompassing as "Viking" is for Hereward, it is emphatically not all-
encompassing. While even the rumors of the settlements in North America
are sufficient to include them in Hereward's definition of the Viking community, Hereward nonetheless incorporates into his definition some representations of otherness, including the "Easterns." This label certainly includes
the Christians of the eastern empire, but Hereward focuses particularly on
the "Mussulman hounds worshipping their Mahomets." It is not coinci-
dental that Hereward chooses Muslims to serve as the outer limit of the
Viking world. Kingsley may very well have been aware of the prosperous
trade relationships between Viking Age Norsemen and Muslims. Moreover,
Hereward's focus on Islam as marking the boundary of the Viking world
resonates well with his fascination with the heroes of romance, in which the
encounter with the Muslim is an easily recognizable motif. Intriguingly, the
blanket definition of the romance other as Muslim actually mirrors Hereward's blanket definition of the Scandinavian cultures as uniformly Viking.

The "Easterns" are not the only foreigners used in Hereward's act of racial
self-definition. His first impulse, after all, is to find "some Irish princess"
to marry. The inclusion of this desire is anomalous in the otherwise logical
structure of Hereward's thought progression. Hereward begins his definition
close to home, with the Norsemen in nearby Ireland, and then expands his
definition outwards from there in steps, each time adding another, larger
layer to the sphere of the Viking world, and eventually reaching the full
expansion of that sphere with his description of the Eastern others. Simple
enough, except that in the center of these concentric circles dwells the Irish
princess, an other very near the core of Hereward's racial schema. There is,
however, a connection between Hereward's depictions of the Irish princess
and the Muslim – each is an expression of sexual desire. After all, the focal
point of Hereward's description of the Mussulmen is his intention to "bring
home an Emir's daughter." The question becomes, then, what effect these
two foreign women, not to mention the "fair Greek lady," have on Here-

ward's racial self-definition. The fact that both the Irish princess and the emir's daughter are described in terms of wealth certainly resonates with the Viking spirit of wild freedom to take what one desires, to plunder, raid, and carry off women, but it is more than that: the fact that Hereward expresses desire for specifically foreign rather than Viking women indicates that the young hero has gendered his understanding of race. The Viking is the masculine, adventurous and exploratory, full of "the spirit of Odin the Goer," while the foreign is the feminine, the valuable prize to be seized.

This gendering of race is not isolated to this passage. It is actually a theory that Kingsley had held since at least as early as 1849, when he lectured on it as part of a course on Early English Literature to, intriguingly, women at Queen's College, "which Maurice and other professors at King's [College] had established [...] primarily for the examining and training of governesses. Kingsley was ready to share in the unpopular task because he believed in the higher education of women."[28] Kingsley had to give up the course, but some of his ideas are preserved in a letter he sent informing his replacement of what he had covered. In it he refers to the Anglo-Saxons as a "female race" who "required impregnation by the great male race, – the Norse."[29] Here again, we see the definition of the various Scandinavian races with a single blanket term, this time "Norse" rather than "Viking." And again we see the sexualized imagery that characterizes Kingsley's descriptions of the Norse/Viking interactions with racial otherness. Here, even more explicitly than with the Irish princess and the emir's daughter, the Anglo-Saxon is passive and dormant, awaiting contact with the masculine energy of the Norse. Kingsley encourages his successor to:

> Give them a lecture on the rise of our Norse forefathers – give them something from the Voluspa and Edda. Show hem [sic] the peculiar wild, mournful, gigantic objective imagination of the men, and its marriage with the Saxon subjectivity (as I fancy) to produce a ballad school. Remember two things. The Norse are the great *creators*, all through – and all the ballads came from the North of England and the Lowlands of Scotland, *i.e.*, from half Norse blood.

Kingsley is probably drawing here on Bulwer-Lytton's *Harold*, which includes a "ballad of the Norse, which had, in its more careless composition, a character quite distinct from the artificial poetry of the Saxons."[30] Bulwer-Lytton goes on to claim in a footnote that the influence of such Norse ballads on the "early national muse" of the English "may be traced [to] the minstrelsy of our borders, and the Scottish Lowlands," especially under the rule of Canute. The correspondences between these arguments are not, of course, absolute, but they are suggestive enough to think that Kingsley was reflecting on Bulwer-

Lytton's argument, especially since he refers to "Bulwer's Harold" earlier in the same letter. "Wild" is not far from "careless," and "superficial" could be a rein-terpretation of "artificial." More significant, however, is the sense that both writers have of border culture: places where direct communication between two cultures can take place, where, in this case, Norse and Saxon experience an everyday, routine contact with each other, rather than the more ethereal or even imaginary notion of the other that an insulated community might hold. It is not hard to see how Kingsley may have been able to reimagine such a border culture as a "marriage" between genders, where the two certainly do become one, but still nevertheless clearly remain two.

The gendered construction of the relationship between the Saxons and the Danes in Kingsley's letter is clearly problematic. On the one hand, it is a symbiotic relationship, since neither race can produce the desired literature on its own. Symbiotic relationships are not always equal, however, and in this case it is clear that Kingsley agrees with Hereward in valuing the Danish significantly over the Saxon. The richness of the string of adjectives in King-sley's characterization of the Norse contrasts with the rather ambiguous description of the Saxons. The Norse's imagination is vital and directed to the external object, whereas the Saxon is subjective, inward-looking. Perhaps most potent of all is the fact that Kingsley goes on to describe the Norse as "the great *creators*, all through." So, masculine energy is the creative, active force, whereas the feminine is the passive canvas awaiting that creative force. With this in mind, it becomes clear why Kingsley is so insistent that Here-ward is Anglo-Dane and not Anglo-Saxon – after all, Hereward is the heroi-cally creative force that will influence the ready and waiting Saxons.

Kingsley's conception of the Saxons may be even more interesting than that of the Danes. We have already seen that Kingsley felt that at the time of the Conquest "[t]he Anglo-Saxon race was wearing out. The men of Wessex, priest-ridden," were "enslaved by their own aristocracy" (*Hereward* 1:6–7). Kingsley is here echoing, directly or indirectly, Palgrave's representation of the Danish raids on England and the racial tensions that ensued:

> It is certain that [the Danes] must have recollected their kindred with the Anglo-Saxons; but this circumstance rather heightened than miti-gated their ferocity. They considered the English, for this familiar name now began to be in use, as apostates and recreants from the warlike virtues of their ancestors. They viewed them as cowards – who, contemning the banquet of Valhalla, had yielded up its joys, for the song of the Priest and the mummery of the Quire.[31]

The priesthood is something that is eating the Saxons apart from the inside and draining, as Palgrave makes clear, "the warlike virtues of their ancestors."

Likewise, Kingsley's phrase "priest-ridden" evokes images of infestation and rot. While Kingsley is engaging here in typical anti-Papist rhetoric, these two passages also engage in the discourse that E. G. Stanley explores in *The Search for Anglo-Saxon Paganism*. As Stanley writes, in the wake of Jakob Grimm's influence on the field, "the assumption is made, explicitly or implicitly, that whatever was not touched by Christianity, whatever remained purely Germanic, purely pagan, was more original and more glorious."[32] By the time of the Viking raids, let alone by Hereward's day, then, the Anglo-Saxon had been far too Christianized (or, more properly, Roman Catholicized), rotted out by "the mummery of the Quire." Note that the solution, a return to one's pagan origins, is one of the first thoughts to strike Hereward, when he conceives of himself as infused with "the spirit of Odin the Goer." But this solution is problematically presentist. While the Anglo-Saxons may very well have romanticized their pagan heritage, as Kingsley's Hereward does, the quasi-holy war nature of Palgrave's characterization of the Viking raids is absurd enough to demonstrate how keenly critics of the time, including Kingsley, desired to reclaim their pagan origins.

"Civilized" and "Nomadic" Races

Robert Sirabian points to the difficulty in unraveling the "tensions" and "oppositions" in Kingsley's representation of Anglo-Saxon history in *Hereward*, questioning whether Kingsley sees this history as linear or cyclical, as "a justification of progress" or "a check against the problems associated with progress."[33] I would suggest that one way of beginning to resolve this difficulty is to realize that Kingsley's "priest-ridden" Anglo-Saxons are merely one manifestation of a recurring concern with degeneration throughout Kingsley's writings, *The Water-Babies* being the most famous example. Moreover, this concern about degeneration was no mere theoretical fancy for Kingsley, but was rather a motivating political force. Kingsley was an active lobbyist for sanitary reform and, as Michael Banton suggests, behind this work was his belief "that poor health contributed to the degradation of races."[34] Since degeneration posed this real and dire threat, the progress of humanity was for Kingsley as much about resisting devolution as it was about evolving, and the best cautionary tale was offered, of course, by the once greatest of civilizations, Rome. Lecture II of *The Roman and the Teuton*, "The Dying Empire," takes such degeneration as its topic, beginning with an extended description of the degenerate status of Roman society in the second half of the fourth century:

> The only powers really recognised were force and cunning. The only aim was personal enjoyment [...]. The palace was a sink of corruption,

where eunuchs, concubines, spies, informers, freedmen, adventurers, struggled in the basest plots, each for his share of the public plunder.[35]

The title of *The Roman and the Teuton* makes it clear that it is to the Teutonic that one must look for an alternative to this Roman degeneracy. In order to construct this opposition, Kingsley draws on an important image in the Anglo-Saxonism of the time: the Teuton as forest-dweller. Kingsley tells a fairy tale of innocent forest children (allegorically, the Teutons) who find their way to the garden of trolls (the Romans) and are progressively corrupted by the luxury within; these children defeat the trolls and then fight amongst themselves for possession of the garden. The demonizing of the Romans in this narrative is clear: not only are they at fault for their own vices, but they are also responsible for the loss of the innocence of the hitherto pure Teutons. The story does not, however, end there; Kingsley refers back to the image of the Teutons as forest-dwellers in later chapters. This forest-dwelling image is certainly not Kingsley's alone; he is engaging in a well-established tradition in the Anglo-Saxonist criticism of the time. Freeman referred to the "German forest" and the "Scandinavian rock,"[36] for example, while Palgrave refers to the Germanic tradition as "a fruit of the old oak" that "the Germans brought with them from their forests,"[37] and so forth. The primitivism of this forest imagery presents the Germanic people as existing outside of the corruptions of civilized life – free, wild, and vital, much like Hereward's notion of the Vikings – in order that their initial purity may be established. Some may have fallen to the temptations of the trolls' garden, but the original and fundamental spirit of the people remains that of the forest. One of the recurrent themes of Kingsley's medievalism is an attempt to foster this original spirit.

I would suggest that this forest-dweller versus civilized man discourse draws heavily upon Sharon Turner's notion of "the two great classes of mankind": what he calls the "civilized" and the "nomadic" races.[38] Turner argues that a people has one of two impulses – either the desire to remain stationary or the desire to wander – and that these impulses have led, throughout history, to a number of racial divergences. Turner goes to some pains to emphasize that, in general, the evolutionary pathway of a nomadic race was not at all inferior to that of the civilized: in some of the nomadic races, he argues, "the alteration was a deteriorating process, declining successively into abso-lute barbarism. But in more, it became rather peculiarity, than perversion."[39] Turner goes on to describe the nature of the civilized races, specifically how they "exercised mind in frequent and refined thought" and thereby came to the various governmental, religious, and artistic advances that mark their societies.[40] "But these civilized nations, notwithstanding all their improve-ments, and from the operation of some, have degenerated into sensuality;

into the debasing vices, and to effeminate frivolities."[41] Civilization, then, is gendered female, or to be more precise it takes on a feminine nature as it degrades into vice. Turner's descriptions of the nomadic races are, not surprisingly, significantly more masculine: "[y]et amid these habits, a fearless and enterprising spirit, and a personal dignity and highminded temper were nourished; and the hardy and manly virtues became pleasing habits."[42] While it is notable that the masculine is described in terms of virtue, in contrast to the feminine vices above, Turner does complicate such a simplistic reading. His theory quickly throws a wrench into the otherwise direct civilized/feminine versus nomadic/masculine binary by arguing that the "life of constant activity" of the nomads meant that "the female virtues were called perpetually into action; and their uses were felt to be so important, that the fair sex obtained among all the tribes of ancient Germany a rank, an estimation, and an attachment, which were unknown in all the civilised world of antiquity."[43] The nomadic lifestyle, therefore, despite its "hardy and manly" qualities, also fosters the best aspects of the feminine and, perhaps more importantly, fosters an increased societal respect for its values. Turner's theory, then, is that while the civilized is associated primarily with the female and the nomadic primarily with the masculine, the civilized society encourages the *vices* peculiar to femininity while the masculine lifestyle of nomadic society cultivates its *virtues*.

Turner's theory of the "two great classes of mankind" clearly helps to situate Kingsley's *The Roman and the Teuton* within the nineteenth-century understanding of the Empire and the Germanic tribes. There is, however, a potential logical problem when one attempts to apply these critical works to Kingsley's representation of Hereward's aggressive self-definition as Anglo-Dane rather than Anglo-Saxon. Specifically, if Turner and Kingsley both present the Germanic/Teutonic tribes as the vital and the masculine that opposes the corrupt effeminacy of the Romans, how then does the Saxon come to be the "female race," awaiting "impregnation" by the Norse? The question is related to a persistent problem in Anglo-Saxon studies: the difficulty in differentiating late Anglo-Saxon culture from its early Germanic roots. The answer can therefore be found in the cultural changes that occurred in the centuries separating the proto-Germanic, "forest-dwelling," "nomadic" Teutons, and the more mature (chronologically, not morally), "civilized" Saxons of the Viking Age. Herein lies one of the key differences between the words "Teuton" and "Saxon" in Kingsley's imagination. "Teuton," for Kingsley, evokes the notion of purity and potential, whereas the "Saxon" was one instance of a failure, if only in the long term, to live up to that potential. The late Saxon world in Bulwer-Lytton's *Harold* is represented in part by "an ancient Roman fountain, that now served to water the swine";[44] the Saxons, inheritors of Roman civilization, were unable to resist the corrupt side of becoming a civilized race, instead straying further and further from their Teutonic roots. In the opening lines of *Hereward*, Kingsley expresses such degeneration in evolutionary terms:

> In the savage struggle for life, none but the strongest, healthiest, cunningest, have a chance of living, prospering, and propagating their race. In the civilized state, on the contrary, the weakliest and the silliest, protected by law, religion, and humanity, have their chance likewise, and transmit to their offspring their own weakliness and silliness. (1:2)

The Darwinian influence is obvious here. For Kingsley, civilization has removed from Anglo-Saxon culture the hardening trials of life in the Teutonic forest; instead of the natural selection for the manly virtues that is inherent to the Northern races, civilization provides an artificial selection for the feminine vices, and hence the possibility of the early, masculine Germanic settlers of England degenerating into the feminized and "priest-ridden men of Wessex."

Marriage, Synthesis, and Racial Regeneration

Kingsley's theorizations on gendering and the degeneration of races are related to Muscular Christianity, a term that came to be intertwined with his name. In a sermon at Cambridge in 1865, after expressing strong reservations about the meaning and utility of the term, he explains it by comparison to early Church history. He defines persecution-era Christianity in terms of "all that is loveliest in the ideal female character," namely "gentleness, patience, resignation, self-sacrifice and self-devotion."[45] But, as is the pattern in Kingsley's view of history, this exclusive focus on the feminine characteristics caused "grave defects [...] to appear in what was really too narrow a conception of the human character," this time namely cunning, falsity, intrigue, cowardice, querulousness, passion and cruelty.[46] The solution to such degeneration was "chivalry," which "asserted the possibility of consecrating the whole manhood, and not merely a few faculties thereof, to God."[47] He emphasizes worldly rather than abstract virtues, some of which are overtly masculine, such as martial excellence. The key word in the above quotation, however, is "whole"; for Kingsley, Muscular Christianity is not a claim for the preeminence of the masculine or manly virtues, but rather an assertion of the need for a balance – or in other words, a marriage – between the masculine and feminine virtues.

This view of the ideal Christian character as a marriage of masculine and feminine characteristics was one of the issues that infused Kingsley's all-too-public and all-too-vitriolic debate with John Henry Newman. In the

January 1864 edition of *Macmillan's Magazine*, Kingsley published a review of volumes seven and eight of his friend and in-law James Anthony Froude's *History of England: From the Fall of Wolsey to the Death of Elizabeth*. Midway through his review, at the culmination of a claim about the "deep demor-alization which had been brought on Europe"[48] by belief in papal authority, Kingsley sets his sights on the Catholic Church's approach to truth:

> Truth, for its own sake, had never been a virtue with the Roman clergy. Father Newman informs us that it need not, and on the whole ought not to be; that cunning is the weapon which Heaven has given to the saints wherewith to withstand the brute male force of the wicked world which marries and is given in marriage.[49]

The merits of his claims aside – Kingsley came out much the worse in the ensuing debates – Kingsley's selection of marriage as a key bone of contention is quite telling. Chitty has argued that lurking behind Kingsley's attack was, on the one hand, a distaste for what he saw as Newman's effeminacy and, on the other hand, a related distaste for the celibacy of Rome's priests;[50] Kingsley felt that this effeminate celibacy was an attack on the masculine contribu-tions to Christianity made possible through marriage. Chitty points to an 1851 letter in which Kingsley claims that "the cardinal point" of Christian belief is "the terrible question of 'Celibacy versus Marriage' [...], your views of which must logically influence your views of everything afterwards."[51] This assertion proved to be true at least for Kingsley himself, whose belief in the centrality of marriage to proper Christian life was still influencing his argu-ments over a dozen years later, not only in his debate with Newman but also shortly thereafter in his *Hereward*.

Kingsley spends a considerable amount of time in *Hereward* examining the effects of marriage on his hero, in part because Hereward actually has two marriages: he abandons his first wife, Torfrida, and the outlaw life they have been forced into, in order to marry his second wife, Alftruda, and to return to civilized life under Norman rule. Needless to say, this abandon-ment of Torfrida has both religious and legal implications, though Kingsley's criticisms of the Church shine through when he is quick to point out that such issues would have been glossed over with ease: "doubtless, Holy Church contrived that it should happen without sin, if it conduced to her own interest" (2:274). This corruption in the Church mirrors Hereward's personal "sin," which for Kingsley is definitely one of degeneration. Despite writing an encomium on outlawry merely two chapters before, Kingsley describes how the outlaw life threatens to draw Hereward's band, and Hereward and Torfrida in particular, into degeneration:

Away from law, from self-restraint, from refinement, from elegance, from the very sound of a church-going bell, they were sinking gradually down to the level of the coarse men and women whom they saw; the worse and not the better parts of both their characters were getting the upper hand; and it was but too possible that after a while the hero might sink into the ruffian, the lady into a slattern and a shrew. (2:224)

Note that Hereward and Torfrida are becoming much more like the "forest-children" of *The Roman and the Teuton*, minus the innocence, of course, which sets the stage for an encounter with the temptations of civilization. This temptation manifests itself in the letters of Alftruda, which catalyze Hereward's degeneration into a "ruffian." She tempts Hereward with the greener-grass alternative to the difficult life of a forest outlaw. After all, Hereward's choice is not only about two women; it is also a choice between the hardy, nomadic, male, forest life of remaining English, and the elegant, refined, civilized, female life of betraying his race in favor of succumbing to Norman rule. Neither option is perfect, certainly, but the former is merely a challenge to Hereward and Torfrida's moral convictions (though admittedly one that tries them sorely), while the latter is a life of corruption and further degeneration.

As the case is, Hereward chooses against his racial, religious, and moral obligations. His marriage with Alftruda proves a disaster, culminating in his imprisonment. But the physical imprisonment is only a shadow of his emotional and racial submission to those he vowed to resist. When Hereward's jailer is surprised at his willingness to fight against the remaining English resistance under Waltheof in exchange for his freedom, Hereward completes his long degeneration: "[w]hy not against him? He is but bringing more misery on England. Tell that to William. Tell him that if he sets me free, I will be the first to attack Waltheof, or whom he will. There are no English left to fight against" (2:282). The indifference of the opening question indicates how far he has fallen, which is quickly reinforced by his casual reference to doing whatever William "will"; this devaluation of freedom resounds all the more strongly since "personal independence" is presented in the text as "the peculiar mark, and peculiar strength, of the English character" (2:195) and especially of its Anglo-Danish component. The most significant aspect of these lines, however, is the fact that they are performative. Hereward, as the subtitle of the novel indicates, is the "last of the English," but when he ceases to define himself as English, when he devalues the sense of freedom that is inherent to Kingsley's sense of Englishness, then there truly are "no English left."

While the union of Hereward and Alftruda leads Hereward to degenerate, to borrow Turner's words, "into the debasing vices, and to effeminate frivolities," it is important to reemphasize that Kingsley did not think ill of marriage or of women – quite the opposite. Alftruda's effect on Hereward is only representative of the civilized race's potential *long-term* effects on the nomadic race with which it bonds. As the case is, vital to Kingsley's theory of the "marriage" of races is his belief that such a marriage is actually able to *reverse* racial degeneration, at least initially and for a certain period of time. Here, again, he was probably drawing on Turner, who describes the process in general terms:

> Their mental progress, from all these causes, has been usually checked into that limited and stationary knowledge, soon becoming comparative ignorance, into which, even the cultivation and social comforts of civilization have hitherto invariably sunk; and from which the irruptions, spirit, and agencies of the Nomadic tribes, or the newer kingdoms which they have founded, have repeatedly rescued the human race.[52]

Perhaps most notable about this argument is its all-encompassing inevitability and applicability. The very settled nature of the civilized nations, with their "stationary knowledge," leads "invariably" to sinking into corruption. Meanwhile, the wild "irruptions" of the nomadic nations leads "repeatedly" to them rescuing, ironically via invasion, their civilized neighbors.

Note that Turner is not talking about specific races or historical events, but about the "human race"; this universality in Turner's model is a function of its cyclicality. After the nomadic race has reinvigorated the civilized, there may be a period of idyllic union, but eventually the hybrid race, being settled, begins to become susceptible to the dangers of "stationary thought." Turner's model for the interaction between the races can, therefore, be effectively conceived of as a Hegelian dialectic. If the civilized race is the thesis, then the nomadic race is the antithesis: both are lacking, each in certain complementary ways. Only by coming together in synthesis are these deficiencies overcome. Moreover, no synthesis of races is complete; on the contrary, it eventually requires another reinvigorating synthesis. Races, then, like the dialectic, are in continual motion; the difference is that, unlike the dialectical schema, Turner's model for race defines this motion not as progress but rather as cyclical maintenance, the repeated mending of the degeneration inherent to civilization.

These notions apply well to Kingsley's constructions of race: his Teutons are obviously the antithesis to his Romans. Likewise, his Norse are the antithesis to his Saxons, producing a synthesis in the Anglo-Saxons and Anglo-Danes of the pre-Conquest era. This synthesis, and particularly its Anglo-Saxon manifestation, however, eventually requires a new antithesis, namely William and his Normans. This need for repeated regeneration is partially due to the incomplete integration of the races during their "marriage." For example, Kingsley attributes the beginning of the degeneration process in Teutonized Rome to the tensions between the pagan Teutons and the still predominantly Roman clergy:

> this very difference of race exposed the clergy to great temptations. They were the only civilized men left, west of Constantinople. They looked on the Teuton not as a man, but as a child; to be ruled; to be petted when he did right, punished when he did wrong.[53]

The cause of the degeneration, therefore, is that the synthesis between these two races was not entirely complete: there were remnants of the tension between thesis and antithesis. Herein lies the reason for the tension between Anglo-Saxon and Anglo-Dane in *Hereward*. The Danes partially reinvigorated the Saxons, but not completely; something of the original Saxon rot survived and then spread, leading eventually to the need for further regeneration from the Normans.

Just as Hereward's marriage to Alftruda symbolically reenacted the encounter between the Germanic tribes and the Romans, likewise his earlier marriage to Torfrida closely parallels the Norman Conquest of England. Torfrida is from St. Omer, a town in modern-day northern France, though at the time under the influence of Count Baldwin of Flanders; Kingsley gives little attention to her father but indicates that her mother was a Provençal. Torfrida, then, while not Norman, is definitely continental and at least partially French. Because of this cultural difference, their courtship is not without difficulties; despite her love for Hereward, Torfrida fears the implications of his lack of courtly manners:

> Gradually she found out that the sneers which she had heard at English barbarians were not altogether without ground. Not only had her lover's life been passed among half brutal and wild adventurers, but, like the rest of his nation, he had never felt the influence of that classic civilization without which good manners seem, even to this day, almost beyond the reach of the western races. (1:205)

So Kingsley is careful to emphasize that Hereward is entirely untouched by "classic civilization," that Torfrida will be marrying a barbarian who has never truly been out of the metaphorical forest. Conversely, Kingsley makes Torfrida's extensive contact with civilization equally clear, specifically through her access to her uncle, the Abbot of St. Bertin, and to his private library, which leads her to a "deep and sincere longing – as one soul in ten thousand has – after knowledge for its own sake" (1:171). Moreover, the dark side of civilization is present in this desire for knowledge, since she delves into the works of classical and medieval sorcery, and even learns much from her Lapp nurse, who is "skilled in all the sorceries for which the Lapps were famed throughout the North" (1:168).

Both Hereward and Torfrida, then, are characterized by the virtues and the weaknesses of their respective racial classes (in Turner's words) or genders (in Kingsley's). Despite its Odd Couple nature, however, the marriage turns out remarkably well. Each seems to mute, if not cure, the racial weaknesses in the other. She "as much awed him by her learning, as by the new world of higher and purer morality, which was opened for the first time to the wandering Viking" (1:206–7). The choice of "wandering" here clearly connects Kingsley's thinking to Turner's classification of his race as "nomadic." Hereward, "for his part, drank it all in," and Kingsley is quick to ensure that this receptiveness is gendered: "but the spell was on him – a far surer, as well as purer spell than any love-potion of which foolish Torfrida had ever dreamed – the only spell which can really civilize man – that of woman's tact, and woman's purity" (1:207). Here again is the feminine, civilizing force, but it is not the only teaching force in the relationship; after all, even as Torfrida is teaching Hereward, he is unconsciously teaching her the "foolish" nature of her dabblings in sorcery. This lesson may seem insignificant in comparison to "the new world of higher and purer morality" to which she exposes him, but it is a lesson which later yields the greatest victory to the resistance at Ely, when her demonstration of Christian faith counters the spells of William's witch. Andrew Wawn asserts that Kingsley found it "emotionally as well as intellectually hard to regard the Conquest as a beneficial fusion of the best elements of Anglo-Danish and Norman tradition."[54] It may indeed have been difficult for Kingsley, but clearly he did come to feel that the marriage between the Anglo-Danish, wandering, male Hereward, and the French, civilized, female Torfrida was one that counteracted the weaknesses endemic to both of their races.

Not only does this marriage allow Hereward and Torfrida to overcome their racial flaws, it also allows them to become something new, something, from Kingsley's perspective, greater than either of them had previously been. When he hears the tale of the battle of Hastings, Hereward's declarations of racial affinities culminate in a sudden, tearful expression of respect for his familial foes, the Godwinssons: "Honor to the Godwinssons! Honor to the southern men! Honor to all true English hearts! Why was I not there, to go with them to Valhalla?" (1:269). This outburst indicates a progression in Hereward's thinking: he still sees a distinction between the Anglo-Saxons and the Anglo-Danes, but he now sees this distinction as secondary to their community under the term "English." Hereward realizes that as important as his familial and racial loyalties to the Anglo-Danes may be, his loyalty to England as a whole must take precedence, particularly in times of crisis. This realization is strong enough that it even imprints itself on Torfrida, who, in response to her husband's tears, "whether from a woman's sentiment of pity, or from a woman's instinctive abhorrence of villany [sic] and wrong, had become there and then an Englishwoman of the English, as she proved by strange deeds and sufferings for many a year" (1:269). Torfrida, then, performs the ultimate act of racial self-definition, literally metamorphosing herself into the Englishness that she admires in her husband. Kingsley's choice of the phrase "Englishwoman of the English," rather than "of England," is significant: she is joining the community of individuals, not simply adopting a new geographical home.[55]

The History of Men and Women, and of Nothing Else

Kingsley believed passionately that "[t]he history of the masses cannot be written"[56] and, therefore, that the best way to access historical truth is through understanding the great individuals of the time.[57] He adopts this argument as the thesis of his inaugural lecture at Cambridge:

> If they wish to understand History, they must first try to understand men and women. For History is the history of men and women, and of nothing else; and he who knows men and women thoroughly will best understand the past work of the world [...]. He [the great individual] may appeal to the meanest, or to the loftiest motives. He may be a fox or an eagle; a Borgia, or a Hildebrand; a Talleyrand, or a Napoleon; a Mary Stuart, or an Elizabeth: but however base, however noble, the power which he exercises is the same in essence. He makes History, because he understands men. And you, if you would understand History, must understand men.[58]

Note that the great individual does not make "history," as in "the history of men and women," but rather "History." This capital letter is the difference between the "history of the masses" and that of the great individuals. "History" is actively made, while "history" is merely passively lived, and only the great individuals are capable of both. This difference is affirmed most strongly by Kingsley's selection of biographies, and preferably autobiographies, as the most constructive source by far of historical information.[59]

It is actually the flipside of this belief that concerns us here: it seems to me that Kingsley felt not only that the individual is the best access point for understanding a historical community, but also that the community can itself be personified in the individual, that the very identity markers that characterize an individual can be applied equally effectively to the characteri-zation of races. This "race as individual" approach explains, for example, the differences between Turner's and Kingsley's otherwise similar ideas. After all, Kingsley would not have been satisfied with Turner's comparatively abstract description of races as settled or nomadic, preferring notions like "male" or "female," which offer a much more personalized, substantial, and vivid meta-phor for conceptualizing racial communities. This "race as individual" theory can also be seen in Kingsley's firm belief in the notion of races having ages. "Races," he argues in his lecture on "The Forest Children," "like individuals, it has been often said, may have their childhood, their youth, their manhood, their old age, and natural death. It is but a theory – perhaps nothing more. But at least, our race had its childhood."[60] As Kingsley indicates, this is not his theory alone. The very first paragraph of Kemble's study of Anglo-Saxon England, for instance, defines his subject as "the history of the childhood of our own age, – the explanation of its manhood."[61] But Kingsley takes this concept considerably further than most; Banton suggests, for example, that Kingsley felt that the age of a race was related to the "tasks" which it "had been called by God to accomplish."[62] For Kingsley this concept is much more a simple metaphor for the past's relationship with the present. While lecturing on the defeat of Valens by the Goths in 378, Kingsley returns to his image of the Goths as forest-children:

> The Teuton had at last tried his strength against the Roman. The wild forest-child had found himself suddenly at death-grips with the Enchanter whom he had feared, and almost worshipped, for so long; and behold, to his own wonder, he was no more a child, but grown into a man, and the stronger, if not the cunninger of the two.[63]

The Teutons, therefore, were a child race, while the Romans were adult, and more importantly, the interactions between them are defined by the power dynamics of that age difference. In the same way that the child both emulates and struggles with the adult, so too does Kingsley's Teuton with the Roman. Furthermore, the age of a race is apparently not a static condition, since the child is growing into adulthood. Most significant, however, is the fact that age is yet another way of theorizing the interactions between races; the vital youthfulness of the Teutons is part of what allows them to reinvigorate the Romans, who have grown frail and morally infirm.

Generations of the English: The Ending of Hereward

The final chapter of *Hereward* takes place nearly eighty years after Hereward's death, so it is in the final lines of the previous chapter that Kingsley eulogizes his hero and the freedom that he embodied:

> [T]hey knew not that the Wake was alive for evermore: that only his husk and shell lay mouldering there in Crowland choir; that above them, and around them, and in them, destined to raise them out of that bitter bondage, and mould them into a great nation, and the parents of still greater nations in lands as yet unknown, brooded the immortal spirit of the Wake, now purged from all earthly dross – even the spirit of Freedom, which can never die. (2:317)

Kingsley, therefore, asserts that Hereward's legacy lies in his ability to elevate "Freedom," which is naturally bound to the limitations of "all earthly dross," to the level of undying "spirit"; it is this spirit that will drive the English to fulfill their destiny of becoming "the parents of still greater nations." Freedom will be transmitted to future generations, and not just generations of individuals but also of nations. This passage, then, implants Hereward into the imperial enterprise, even suggesting him as one of its grandfathers. This conception of the spread of English influence as generational in structure is the final way in which Kingsley invokes the "race as individual" analogy. As discussed above, Kingsley saw races as possessing gender, age, and the ability to marry; here we have that third term taken to its logical conclusion, the ability of races to birth other races.

The propagation of races is a central concern of the final chapter of *Hereward*. Kingsley begins with a summary of the history of "Crowland Minster" after Hereward's death. The summary leads into a discussion about the recent coronation of Henry II; this discussion takes place between Hereward's granddaughter Torfrida and her husband Richard of Rulos, who had begun to drain the Deeping Fen. The now old Richard indicates that he can finally rest in peace now that "he sees an English king head the English people," since he believes that Henry unites the virtues of the Normans and the pre-Conquest English (2:322). But Richard himself embodies something else, something that looks forward rather than back to the conflicts of the past. The novel ends with Torfrida deciding on a new epitaph for her grandfather Hereward's tomb: "[h]ere lies the last of the old English" (2:323). She then selects one for her aging husband: "[h]ere lies the first of the new English; who, by the inspiration of God, began to drain the Fens." Richard, then, is the first of an entirely new race, specifically the child of the marriage of the Normans and the old English; he represents the first of the "still greater nations" that the old English will parent. His most famous act, draining the fens, is symbolic of this combined lineage. This closing chapter forms a framing structure with the prelude to *Hereward*, "Of the Fens," which established a connection between the Fenland and the nature of the Anglo-Danes who dwelled on it, a connection reinforced by the use of the wetlands as a defense for the Anglo-Danish resistance. By beginning to drain the fens, then, Richard is integrating Anglo-Danishness into a unified English identity.

Perhaps the most significant effect of the frame structure of *Hereward* is to emphasize the overarching movement in the book with regard to race in England. The frame serves to juxtapose the image of competing racial groups depicted in the first chapter with the united English of the end of the novel. The fens work, in effect, to situate the Hereward story in the broader narrative of the ethnogenesis of the English people. This grand narrative that Kingsley constructs can be summarized as follows. Long before the Conquest, the Danes, the Saxons and the Normans were young and separate, each with strengths (especially the Danes) and weaknesses (especially the Saxons); the weaknesses became more pronounced as time passed, resulting inevitably in racial degeneration; the Conquest, while a horrible crime against the sovereignty of England, allowed the races to bond in a regenerative marriage; and eventually this marriage yielded (and continues to yield) fruit through the generation of a pure, united English that possesses the strengths of each of its parents (especially the Danish) and whose long arm reaches bountifully across the world.

This grand narrative is, as with much of Kingsley's racial thinking, at the same time both sophisticated and problematic in nature. As Hereward's youthful fantasies illustrate, Kingsley's depictions of the racial tensions of pre-Conquest England demonstrate an awareness of the vast difficulties, on both the political and interpersonal levels, of progressing out of a period of invasion and colonization into one of cooperative coexistence. Kingsley makes clear that Hereward was a member of a variety of different, overlapping communities, and, moreover, that his loyalties to these groups could be in direct conflict. Kingsley is addressing an issue that remains an important focus of study for medievalists: in Patrick J. Geary's words, "individuals could simultaneously hold several identities, seeing themselves as part of larger confederations as well as smaller groups."[64] While Geary is referring to barbarian interactions with Rome, the notion applies equally well to the England of the beginning of *Hereward*, in which Kingsley points to a labyrinth of national, racial, religious, and familial communal ties. Hereward's actions in the first few chapters make clear that self-definition is the decisive factor in resolving such conflicts: it is Hereward's conscious, even if overly romantic, decision to imagine himself as Viking that makes him a member

of that identity group before all the others. The complexities of this relatively sophisticated view of pre-Conquest England's identity issues are not,
however, compatible with the end goal of Kingsley's grand narrative. The
sum total of *Hereward* presents diversity as problematic disunity, fracturing
English strength rather than tempering it; it is through the elimination, or at
least reduction, of racial difference that the single, unified, English identity
is achieved. Self-definition still exists, as Torfrida's conversion to Englishness
demonstrates (notably in the *first* half of the novel), but the options become
more and more limited as the novel comes to a close: English or other.

The movement of *Hereward* is, therefore, from complexity to simplicity.
The key question that Kingsley either avoids or does not see the need to ask
is, of course, that of what is lost in this progression towards unity: what is lost
when the fens are drained? This primacy of racial unity over difference runs
deeper than Kingsley's overt grand narrative – it is intrinsic to the assumptions behind his theories of race. Any theory of racial qualities involves a
certain amount of essentialism, but Kingsley's belief that the individual is a
valid model for the race takes this further. It suggests that there is an archetype for each race, by asserting, at least in principle, that the range and depth
of an entire race can be embodied in a single individual. While Kingsley's
intentions behind this theory were simply to facilitate the conceptualization
of race through the use of a microcosm, the effect is nonetheless the same.
The over-simplified microcosm has the ability to blot out the nuances and
variations within the macrocosm, a problem that plagues Kingsley's emphasis
on reading history through the lens of its exceptional individuals. The great
individual approach not only devalues the importance of the communal
masses to history but also recruits historiography to write out those masses,
and the differences they embody, in favor of the individual. The fact that this
individual is, by the very definition of the theory, *extra*ordinary and therefore
specifically unrepresentative of the community is an irony that Kingsley's
work leaves unexplored.

In 1903, Louis Cazamian suggested that Kingsley "gives a definitive view of
the most vital aims and ideals of his time, under the guise of fiction."[65] While
this may be slightly overstating the case, the influence and reach of Kingsley's
voice in the nineteenth-century discourse of race should not be underestimated. The impact of his fiction is, perhaps, best illustrated by the fact that
the plight of Tom in *The Water-Babies* contributed to the drafting, less than
a year later, of the Chimney Sweepers Regulation Act, which prohibited the
use of children as chimney sweeps.[66] Wawn addresses the influence of *Hereward* itself, pointing out that "[c]onstant repackagings and reprintings in
both presentation and pocket editions kept the work before the public gaze,
as did its many years of service as a School Certificate text."[67] Moreover, as
Chadwick argues, the impact of his lectures was also considerable:

He held a steady audience of 100 undergraduates or more, far larger than any of his predecessors had achieved, or indeed any of his contemporary professors in other faculties. Some of the young men came no doubt because they were interested in Kingsley, not because they were interested in history. But the one might lead to the other.[68]

This audience increased dramatically, of course, once these lectures were published in book form. Chadwick's emphasis on the interest in Kingsley himself is key; his personal fame gave Kingsley an appeal to audiences that were otherwise uninterested in Anglo-Saxon scholarship. P. G. Scott characterizes Kingsley "as a popularizer rather than a discoverer, a transmitter of facts to which the public was making an inadequate response."[69] While I would suggest that Kingsley was also a discoverer, Kingsley's position was a potent one either way: he was able to bring the racial thinking of the early Anglo-Saxon histories into greater contact with the varied discourses of evolution, social activism, and contemporary fiction. The histories of such prominent scholars as Turner, Palgrave, and Kemble captured significant audiences in their own right, but these audiences were nevertheless limited; Kingsley's audiences, on the other hand, were likely much larger and certainly more diverse. His popularity allowed him to re-transmit the racial ideas of those histories to a veritable cross-section of society, from scholars, to popular-fiction readers, to social activists, to congregations. He was, in short, one of Frantzen's "gatekeepers," much like William Morris and J. R. R. Tolkien would be over the subsequent century, individuals who preside over the "process of filtering, of admitting into discussion some aspects of the past and prohibiting others."[70] Kingsley sifted through the histories of the Anglo-Saxons and the racial ideas therein, disregarded some, modified others, and swallowed some whole; his engagement with these ideas, both directly in his own history, *The Roman and the Teuton*, and indirectly in his fictions and other writings, marks him – and by extension the histories he transmitted – as vital to the racial debates of the period.

NOTES

1. Kingsley openly attacked Newman and the Roman Catholic Church at large, charging them with deceit and distortion of the truth; the controversy resulted in Newman producing his famous 1864 *Apologia Pro Vita Sua*.

2. Kingsley was admittedly not the first choice for the post; Lord Palmerston first offered the position to J. W. Blakesley, vicar of Ware and once fellow and tutor at Trinity College. See Owen Chadwick, "Kingsley's Chair," *Theology* 76 (1975): 2–8 (2). Chadwick points out that Kingsley's credentials were not overwhelming, consisting primarily of *Alex-*

andria and Her Schools (1854), a collection of essays that he had delivered at Edinburgh, but Chadwick also argues that challenges to Kingsley's qualifications are "anachronistic" (8), since Oxbridge professorships had not yet been fully professionalized, and, furthermore, that many of these challenges "arose, not from any knowledge of better possibilities, but from the hindsight that Kingsley's tenure of the chair was not in all respects a success" (5). Making a slightly contradictory but nonetheless important point, Chadwick suggests that the proof is in the metaphorical pudding, since "Kingsley did far more for history in Cambridge than his contemporary [Goldwin Smith] did in Oxford" (8), specifically the production of a significant, if controversial, work of history, namely *The Roman and the Teuton.*

3. Charles Kingsley, *The Roman and the Teuton: A Series of Lectures Delivered before the University of Cambridge* (Cambridge: Macmillan, 1864).

4. Allen J. Frantzen, *Desire for Origins: New Language, Old English, and Teaching the Tradition* (New Brunswick, NJ: Rutgers University Press, 1990), 124.

5. Charles Kingsley, *Hereward the Wake: "Last of the English,"* vols. 3–4 of *The Novels and Poems of Charles Kingsley* (New York: Taylor, 1899); originally published in 1866. Volume and page references are to the 1899 edition.

6. Max Müller, preface to *The Roman and the Teuton*, by Charles Kingsley, new edn. (London: Macmillan, 1889), v–xxix.

7. Susan Chitty, *The Beast and the Monk: A Life of Charles Kingsley* (London: Hodder, 1974), 204.

8. Clare A. Simmons, "Anglo-Saxonism, the Future, and the Franco-Prussian War," *Studies in Medievalism VII: Medievalism in England II*, ed. Leslie J. Workman and Kathleen Verduin (Cambridge: D. S. Brewer, 1995), 131–42 (132).

9. Simmons, "Anglo-Saxonism, the Future, and the Franco-Prussian War," 133. Simmons also points to Reginald Horsman's important analysis of Anglo-Saxonism in America, *Race and Manifest Destiny: The Origins of American Racial Anglo-Saxonism* (Cambridge, MA: Harvard University Press, 1981)

10. A London school founded in 1848 by F. D. Maurice for the education of women.

11. Frances Kingsley, ed., *Charles Kingsley: His Letters and Memories of His Life*, 4th edn., 2 vols. (London: King, 1877).

12. Kingsley is presumably referring to Wright's 1846 "Adventures of Hereward the Saxon," in *Essays on Subjects Connected with the Literature, Popular Superstitions, and History of England in the Middle Ages*, vol. 2 (London: Smith, 1846), 91–120; this text was previously published in two sections, "Adventures of Hereward the Saxon," *Ainsworth's Magazine* (1845): 437–41, 512–18, and "The Last Adventures of Hereward, the Saxon," *The New Monthly Magazine* 74 (1845): 402–5. Kingsley claims in his dedication that Wright has taught him how to reconstruct the Hereward story, and this is probably not an exaggeration: Wright's version includes references to some of his key sources for the Hereward story, specifically the *Gesta Herewardi*, the Peterborough Chronicle (91n. in the 1846 edition), and the account of Geoffrey Gaimar (119n.). The central importance of the first and third of these sources to Kingsley's own version of the story indicates that Kingsley may have begun his research by following these leads.

13. More analysis of Freeman's influence on Kingsley is, however, certainly needed, but it is beyond the scope of this article.

14. Prominent among these other histories would be Wright's *The Celt, the Roman, and*

the Saxon: A History of the Early Inhabitants of Britain (London: Hall, 1852). While Kingsley was almost certainly familiar with this text, given his admitted debt to Wright's version of the Hereward story, it was not nearly as influential on his racial thinking as were the other histories mentioned above. This is probably due to the fact that Wright's text focuses almost entirely on material culture and on archaeological evidence, avoiding broader ethnographical or racial theorizations; in Wright's own words, his purpose was simply "to supply the want of a manual of British archæology" (viii). Kingsley does seem to draw on Wright's text for certain details, but he had to turn elsewhere for larger ideas on race.

15. Edward Bulwer-Lytton, *Harold: The Last of the Saxon Kings*, 3rd edn., 2 vols. (New York: Scribner's, 1903); originally published in 1848. Page references are to the third edition. Bulwer-Lytton aggressively asserts the historicity of his *Harold*: "I consulted the original authorities of the time with a care as scrupulous, as if intending to write, not a fiction but a history. And having formed the best judgment I could of the events and characters of the age, I adhered faithfully to what, as an Historian, I should have held to be the true course and true causes of the great political events, and the essential attributes of the principal agents" (1:xiv). The confidence that allows Bulwer-Lytton to claim knowledge of "the true course," "true causes," and "essential attributes" of events eight centuries before his time demonstrates clearly the faith held by some in the power of narrative to access historical fact.

16. Müller's analysis of his friend's work is at times remarkably blunt: "I am not so blinded by my friendship for Kingsley as to say that these lectures are throughout what academical lectures ought to be. [...] They do not profess to contain the results of long continued original research. They are not based on a critical appreciation of the authorities which had to be consulted. They are not well arranged, systematic or complete" (Preface, x–xi).

17. Simmons, "Anglo-Saxonism, the Future, and the Franco-Prussian War," 134–35.

18. T. A. Shippey rightly states that "summarising the Schleswig-Holstein question is notoriously impossible," but he nevertheless does an admirable job: "one may perhaps say that the root of the matter was that the king of Denmark ruled the two duchies of Schleswig (or Slesvig) and Holstein (or Holsten), but not as king of Denmark. One may also say, very roughly, and across the evidence of decades of referenda, boundary shift and 'ethnic cleansing,' that Slesvig (to use the Danish form) was on the whole Danish-speaking, and Holstein (in the German form) German-speaking. Large numbers of German-speakers, therefore were also quasi-Danes. [...] The matter was settled in 1864 by the Austro-Prussian invasion of the two duchies and forcible take-over of both Holstein and Slesvig, including large areas ancestrally and linguistically Danish, a take-over reversed only in 1920, after World War I, and to become at least open to negotiation again in 1945, after World War II." See T. A. Shippey's Introduction to *Beowulf: The Critical Heritage*, ed. T. A. Shippey and Andreas Haarder (London: Routledge, 1998), 1–74 (17–18).

19. For British responses to the situation in Schleswig-Holstein, see Andrew Wawn's *The Vikings and the Victorians: Inventing the Old North in Nineteenth-Century Britain* (Cambridge: D. S. Brewer, 2000), 232–34, and Keith A. P. Sandiford's *Great Britain and the Schleswig-Holstein Question 1848–64: A Study in Diplomacy, Politics, and Public Opinion* (Toronto: University of Toronto Press, 1975).

20. Shippey, Introduction to *Beowulf: The Critical Heritage*, 17.

21. For more on the relationship between the Schleswig-Holstein question and *Here-*

ward, see Andrew Wawn's "Hereward, the Danelaw and the Victorians," in *Vikings and the Danelaw: Select Papers from the Proceedings of the Thirteenth Viking Congress, Nottingham and York, 21–30 August 1997*, ed. James Graham-Campbell *et al.* (Oxford: Oxbow Books, 2001), 357–68 (364).

22. For this project, I have decided to use the book version rather than the serial, because it more fully engages historical discourse, particularly in terms of his footnoting. In his summary of these two versions, Larry K. Uffelman points out that in the conversion from serial to book, "[a]lthough Kingsley did occasionally simplify historical material in the novel, he added more than he subtracted. For instance, he deleted six footnotes, but added thirty-five others." See "Kingsley's *Hereward the Wake*: From Serial to Book," *Victorians Institute Journal* 14 (1986): 147–56 (150).

23. Quoted in Chitty, *The Beast and the Monk*, 249. See Catherine Hall's "Men and Their Histories: Civilizing Subjects," *History Workshop Journal* 52.2 (2001): 49–66, for further analysis of the reception of Kingsley's lectures, specifically the scathing response of Edward Spencer Beesly, Professor of Modern History at University College, London.

24. The most important of Kingsley's many sources are the twelfth-century Latin prose *Gesta Herewardi*, the closely related *Liber Eliensis*, and Geoffrey Gaimar's Anglo-Norman verse *L'Estoire des Engles*.

25. Wawn, "Hereward, the Danelaw and the Victorians," 364.

26. There is a rather effective moment in which one of Leofric's retainers speaks to him in "broad Danish," while Harold Godwinsson is speaking to King Edward in French (1:53–54). The association of the Godwins with the Norman Edward is used as an indication of their, and more generally the Saxons', degradation.

27. Benedict Anderson, *Imagined Communities: Reflections on the Origin and Spread of Nationalism*, rev. edn. (London: Verso, 1991), 6.

28. Margaret Farrand Thorp, *Charles Kingsley 1819–1875* (Princeton, NJ: Princeton University Press, 1937), 65.

29. Frances Kingsley, ed., *Letters and Memories*, 1:201.

30. Bulwer-Lytton, *Harold*, 1:10.

31. Francis Palgrave, *History of the Anglo-Saxons* (London: Murray, 1842), 105; originally published in 1831.

32. E. G. Stanley, *The Search for Anglo-Saxon Paganism* (Cambridge: D. S. Brewer, 1975), 8.

33. Robert Sirabian, "Anglo-Saxonism and Charles Kingsley's *Hereward the Wake: Last of the English*," *The Year's Work in Medievalism* 18 (2003): 77–90 (78).

34. Michael Banton, "Kingsley's Racial Philosophy," *Theology* 76 (1975): 22–30 (24).

35. Kingsley, *The Roman and the Teuton*, 18–19.

36. Quoted in W. R. W. Stephens, *The Life and Letters of Edward A. Freeman*, 2 vols. (London: Macmillan, 1895), 1:120.

37. Palgrave, *History of the Anglo-Saxons*, 253.

38. Sharon Turner, *The History of the Anglo-Saxons*, 4th edn., 3 vols. (London: Longman, 1823), 1:9; first edition published 1799–1805. Volume and page references are to the fourth edition.

39. Turner, *The History of the Anglo-Saxons*, 1:8.

40. Turner, *The History of the Anglo-Saxons*, 1:10.

41. Turner, *The History of the Anglo-Saxons*, 1:11.

42. Turner, *The History of the Anglo-Saxons*, 1:15.

43. Turner, *The History of the Anglo-Saxons*, 1:15–16.

44. Bulwer-Lytton, *Harold*, 1:5.

45. Frances Kingsley, ed., *Letters and Memories*, 2:212.

46. Frances Kingsley, ed., *Letters and Memories*, 2:212.

47. Frances Kingsley, ed., *Letters and Memories*, 2:213.

48. Charles Kingsley, "Froude's History of England, Vols. VII & VIII," *Macmillan's Magazine* 9 (1863–64): 211–24 (216–17).

49. Kingsley, "Froude's History of England," 217.

50. Chitty, *The Beast and the Monk*, 236.

51. Frances Kingsley, ed., *Letters and Memories*, 1:255.

52. Turner, *The History of the Anglo-Saxons*, 1:11–12.

53. Kingsley, *The Roman and the Teuton*, 221.

54. Wawn, "Hereward, the Danelaw and the Victorians," 366.

55. This distinction would probably have been quite conscious on Kingsley's part, since it is one that Bulwer-Lytton discusses in his *Harold*, specifically in reference to the practice of the Norman nobility to call themselves not "Counts or Dukes of Normandy, but of the Normans" (1:17n.). Bulwer-Lytton goes on to indicate that a parallel practice continued with the Anglo-Norman kings until Richard I.

56. Kingsley, *The Roman and the Teuton*, 231.

57. Edward Spencer Beesly took Kingsley to task on this point, asking, "how would contemporary history look if written by an Irish peasant or a Spitalfields weaver?" (quoted in Hall, "Men and Their Histories," 63). Kingsley may actually have been very interested in such a history since it was not the value of the perspective of the masses that he questioned, but rather their ability to write and to create history. Both Kingsley and Beesly had arguments from influential Anglo-Saxonists that could support their positions. Turner would have come down on Kingsley's side, having argued that "when great political exigencies evolve, which threaten to shake the foundations of civil society, they are usually as much distinguished by the rise of sublime characters, with genius and ability sufficient to check the progress of the evil" (*The History of the Anglo-Saxons*, 1:473). Kemble, however, argues that "[c]ould we place ourselves above the exaggerations of partizans, who hold it a point of honour to prove certain events to be indiscriminately right or indiscriminately wrong, we should probably find that the course of human affairs had been one steady and very gradual progression; the reputation of individual men would perhaps be shorn of part of its lustre"; see John M. Kemble, *The Saxons in England: A History of the English Commonwealth till the Norman Conquest*, 2 vols. (London: Longman, 1849), 2:450.

58. Kingsley, *The Roman and the Teuton*, xi–xii.

59. Kingsley, *The Roman and the Teuton*, xii.

60. Kingsley, *The Roman and the Teuton*, 6.

61. Kemble, *The Saxons in England*, 1:v.

62. Banton, "Kingsley's Racial Philosophy," 24.

63. Kingsley, *The Roman and the Teuton*, 81.

64. Patrick J. Geary, *The Myth of Nations: The Medieval Origins of Europe* (Princeton, NJ: Princeton University Press, 2002), 84.

65. Louis Cazamian, *The Social Novel in England 1350–1850: Dickens, Disraeli, Mrs. Gaskell, Kingsley*, trans. Martin Fido (London: Routledge, 1973); originally published in 1903.

66. Chitty, *The Beast and the Monk*, 222.

67. Wawn, "Hereward, the Danelaw and the Victorians," 360, referencing J. A. Balfour's 1895 *Notes on Hereward the Wake*.

68. Chadwick, "Kingsley's Chair," 8.

69. P. G. Scott, "Kingsley as Novelist," *Theology* 76 (1975): 8–15 (11).

70. Frantzen, *Desire for Origins*, 124.

From Romance to Ritual: Jessie L. Weston's Gawain

Helen Brookman

> Behind Romance, lies Folk-lore, behind Folk-lore lie the fragments of forgotten Faiths: the outward expression has changed, but the essential elements remain the same.
>
> Jessie L. Weston[1]

Jessie L. Weston at the Fin-de-Siècle

Jessie Laidlay Weston (1850–1928), an oft-maligned figure of controversy, is best known for her influential study that blended folklore and Arthurian myth, *From Ritual to Romance* (1920). Weston was also an active scholar, prolific translator, and popularizer of Arthurian texts. Her translations and other studies have received little modern scholarly attention, yet they reveal across their entirety a coherent medievalizing project that sought to shift popular opinion about many of the keystones of Arthurian studies. This project became centered on one of the most debated figures in Arthurian romance: Sir Gawain. The purpose of this article is to draw the focus away from *From Ritual to Romance*, and back to Weston's earlier works in the last years of the nineteenth century and the early years of the twentieth: the studies with which she made her scholarly reputation. By examining Weston's popularizing translations alongside her more scholarly works, it will use her fascination with Sir Gawain to consider how she sought to reinterpret the literature of the Middle Ages, and to promote a particular vision of the legendary past.[2]

Although Jessie L. Weston's career began in the late Victorian period, spanned over thirty years, and produced scores of publications, her reputation has been fixed in a modernist moment in 1920. The ideas she set forth in *From Ritual to Romance* had a significant impact in the field of Arthurian studies, with much twentieth-century criticism responding to her work. Whether any present-day scholars agree with her view of the ritual roots of the Grail myth and the centrality of motifs representing sexuality and regeneration (and "Who does?" asks Norris J. Lacy),[3] they often still feel the need to raise and respond to her work. With the exception of James Frazer's *The Golden Bough*, no scholarly work of the period is so well remembered and discussed.

Yet the work is a misleading text by which to judge the whole of Weston's diverse and idiosyncratic career. Following T. S. Eliot's statement in the first note to "The Wasteland" that "Miss Weston's book will elucidate the difficulties of the poem much better than my notes can do," Eliot scholars – starting with Ezra Pound and encouraged by later comments made by Eliot himself – sought to distance Weston's work from Eliot's poem.[4] It contains mysterious references to a source who was "supposedly an initiate of [modern-day] occult rituals" and these elements have been overemphasized.[5] Weston's recent critics have sought to remove her work from the shadows of old critical debates, to allow us to consider it in a new, historical light. They have discussed their "quest" to establish Weston's biography and, as no personal papers or photographs seem to exist and archives tell us next to nothing about her upbringing or education, admitted the necessity of focusing instead on her scholarly output.[6]

Yet Weston's translations are often judged only by how useful they are to modern medievalists, particularly students; they are out of copyright and therefore available in online versions and reprints. Lacy states that Weston's style of translation in texts such as *Parzival, Morien*, and *Sir Gawain and the Green Knight* is "even for its time […] so stilted and archaic as to be almost unreadable." "It strikes us now," he states, "as almost comical."[7] However, Weston's choice of archaic language surely suggests a deliberate usage particular to the translation of "ancient" literature in this period. Translation is a mode of re-creation and imagination that yields as much to analysis as poetry or prose.

This article has no interest in critiquing the accuracy of Weston's translations or highlighting her errors. Equally, it does not intend to rehabilitate Weston's scholarship, defend it in terms of the current field of Arthurian studies, or seek to determine the rights or wrongs of Weston's views. Rather, in the mode of modern medievalism studies, its purpose is to explore her scholarship on its own terms by taking a fresh look at her earlier material, and to understand how it formed a response to the medieval past. From this critical perspective, it will draw the focus back from Weston the controversial, modernist, anthropologist author of *From Ritual to Romance*, to consider Weston at the *fin-de-siècle*: as translator; textual scholar; folklorist; interpreter and popularizer of Arthurian literature; a writer in dialogue with Tennyson and Malory and the *Gawain*-poet as much as fellow Arthurianists. It will examine how her renderings of medieval texts reflected her often deeply ideological understanding of Arthurian literature.

Translation and Publication

Jessie Weston published her first scholarly work at the age of forty-four. She had received a cosmopolitan education, having shown at an early age, "abundant proof of exceptional intellectual powers."[8] She attended school in Brighton, and later a conservatory in Hildesheim, Germany and the Crystal Palace School of Art. Remarkably, even for the daughter of an aspirational tea-broker, she then studied in Paris with the French medievalist Gaston Paris. His teaching influenced Weston's approach to Arthurian literature and he remained her mentor until his death in 1903. Weston followed Paris in belonging to the Celticist or Insular school, believing that Arthurian literature had evolved from a tradition of popular tales originating within the British Isles, in opposition to the Continental or Inventionist school, whose primarily German scholars had dominated the study of Arthurian literature and legend for much of the nineteenth century. With no extant texts surviving earlier than those of the twelfth-century Chrétien de Troyes (whom the European scholars therefore believed was the creative originator of Arthurian material), the search for earlier evidence of the Arthurian tales roamed into the fields of mythology, anthropology, and folklore studies.

Weston began to publish in the 1890s, after the death of her father.[9] Attending the Bayreuth festival in 1892 with her friend Alfred Nutt, she openly "deplored the fact that the English public knew so little of the sources on which Wagner's operas were based."[10] Nutt was the son of the publisher David Nutt and a scholar of folklore, and he duly proposed that if she translated Wolfram von Eschenbach's *Parzival*, one of the sources for Wagner's *Parsifal* (1882), he would print it. Two years later, her 2400-line verse translation was published, marking the beginning of her prolific publishing career.[11] Her readers were the many people to whom Alfred Nutt hoped to sell books; primed on Wagner and Tennyson, they wanted to know more about the literature, but were unable to read it in the original languages. Over the following decades, Weston produced works for Nutt under three publishing series, each with slightly different aims and audiences. She translated Arthurian texts from a variety of medieval European languages and produced studies and surveys on the treatment of Romance figures in the various traditions and cycles. This article will return to this prolific period shortly, to explore these publications in detail.

During the first decades of the twentieth century, Weston also regularly contributed articles and reviews to journals, including *Folklore*, the *Athenæum*, *Modern Philology*, *Romania*, the *Revue Celtique*, and *Quest*, a new journal on mythological and Arthurian themes that was established in 1910. In the same year, Alfred Nutt died. Weston described herself in a published appreciation of his life as "one who for upwards of twenty years had been closely connected with Alfred Nutt in those studies in which he took so deep and unselfish an interest."[12] Her new attachment was to the American publisher Houghton Mifflin, who published two anthologies of her translations of Middle English literature.[13] From her focused folklore works for Nutt, Weston had moved to broad international publication.

Meanwhile, in scholarly circles at home, she refined the theories that she had been developing since the turn of the century. She developed her interest in comparative religion, an overarching term for a variety of studies in the early twentieth century, including the anthropological writings of the "Cambridge ritualists," such as Jane Harrison's *Themis*, or the theosophist and "secret wisdom tradition" beliefs of G. R. S. Mead and the Quest Society. Her continuing thoughts on the Grail myth were developed in *The Quest of the Holy Grail* (1913) and ultimately in *From Ritual to Romance* in 1920.

Weston became known as an authority in the British and international academic communities, and beyond: among college students and the reading public. Following the success of *From Ritual to Romance*, Weston enjoyed some formal recognition to match her reputation.[14] She died in 1928, at the age of seventy-eight, shortly after contributing an article on "Legendary Cycles of the Middle Ages" to the formidable *Cambridge Medieval History*.[15] The last decade of the nineteenth century and the first of the twentieth formed a key stage in Weston's career, as she established herself in Arthurian studies. Yet the translations and studies that Weston published were not only the space in which she developed her controversial theories; together, they formed a project in which she sought to shift radically both popular and scholarly opinion.

Nutt's approach to folklore – "daring to use modern folk-tales in elucidation of mediæval romance," as Weston put it – influenced her approach from the start.[16] He founded the Folklore Society in 1878, and in 1890 became the publisher of the journal *Folklore*, to which Weston contributed frequently. Her study *The Legend of Sir Gawain* was published in 1897 in Alfred Nutt's "Grimm Library," a series Janet Grayson describes as an "ambitious effort intended for serious students of romance and myth."[17] Nutt wished to explore the farthest reaches of folklore with new scholarship, by covering topics from *An Irish Precursor of Dante* to *Pre- and Proto-Historic Finns, Both Eastern and Western*; he sought to define the series by naming it in veneration of the nineteenth-century founding fathers of folklore studies. Weston's work appeared alongside that of distinguished scholars such as the German Celticist Kuno Meyer, and Eleanor Hull, a co-founder of the Irish Texts Society.[18] It was in this context that Weston published three other scholarly studies, *The Legend of Sir Lancelot du Lac* (1901), *The Three Days' Tournament* (1902), and *The Legend of Sir Perceval* (1906, 1909). Weston described *The Legend of Sir Gawain* as "the careful sifting of the stories connected with the individual knights; the attempt to discover what was the *original* form of each legend."[19] Weston deemed textual scholarship to be a noble task with a very solid goal; she wrote in *The Legend of Sir Gawain* of the day "when all the leading MSS. of the cycle have been carefully edited, and all the romances dissected and compared, [when] we shall find that the original Arthur saga is very simple in form."[20] One reviewer found this work:

> a gallant and learned attempt to disentangle the original Gawain myth from the general body of romance with which it has become complicated [...] these detailed studies, carried out with the fine scholarship shown by Miss Weston, are invaluable in clearing the path for the final survey of the tangled woods of Arthurian legend.[21]

The second of Nutt's publishing series to which Weston contributed had more populist aims. The series, "Arthurian Romances Unrepresented in Malory's *Morte D'Arthur*," allowed her to develop her career as a translator, delving into a variety of medieval European languages to produce accessible texts of previously obscure romances. The series included *Sir Gawain and the Green Knight* (1898) from Middle English; *Tristan and Iseult* (1899) from the Middle High German of Gottfried von Strassburg; *Guingamor, Lanval, Tyolet, Le Bisclaveret* (1900) from the Anglo-Norman of Marie de France; *Morien* (1901) from Middle Dutch; *Sir Cleges and Sir Libeaus Desconus* (1902) from Middle English; *Sir Gawain at the Grail Castle* (1903) from three sources: the French continuation of Chrétien that she believed to be by Wauchier de Denain, the French *Prose Lancelot* or *Vulgate Cycle*, and Heinrich von dem Türlin's Middle High German *Diu Crône*; and later *Sir Gawain and the Lady of Lys* (1907) from "Wauchier."[22] The series sought to reach beyond the most popular manifestations of Arthurian myth in late Victorian and Edwardian culture, which were primarily based on Malory's *Morte Darthur* and Tennyson's *Idylls of the King*.

The texts were visually designed on the themes of contemporary Arthuriana. Pocket-sized, beautifully bound, and highly collectable, the books had hard-board covers, all bearing the same wood-cut imprint with block colors and gold detail. The image shows a crowned knight in a long gold brocade coat, riding out on a lavishly decorated horse with his hound leaping ahead. Stylized trees and a castle can be seen in the background. Inside, the artists – M. M. Crawford for *Sir Gawain* in 1898 and later Caroline M.

Watts – created detailed pictorial representations of key narrative scenes.
The Art Nouveau design was for Nutt and Weston a visual shorthand to
appeal to a particular type of audience; for British readers, it captured a *fin--
de-siècle* Arthurian aesthetic that drew on the work of William Morris, the
Pre-Raphaelites, and Aubrey Beardsley. They also sought to evoke the medieval practices and designs that inspired these artists. The patterned wood-cut
title pages and initials created a sense of manuscript-like authenticity for
the turn-of-the-century reader, while the dramatic, flowing black-and-white
ink illustrations evoked a very contemporary and relevant aspect of modern
culture. Reviewers responded positively to the aesthetic; *Sir Gawain and the
Green Knight* was said to be "quaintly and prettily bound."[23]

The other series designed by Nutt for a popular audience was "Popular
Studies in Mythology," composed of short pamphlets written by leading
folklorists and mythologists of the day: Nutt wrote five. Weston's first contribution was a general introduction to Arthurian literature called simply *King
Arthur and His Knights*.[24] She followed this in 1901 with a similarly broad
work, *The Romance Cycle of Charlemagne and His Peers*.[25]

These three series produced for the David Nutt company – the translations of "Arthurian Romances Unrepresented in Malory's *Morte D'Arthur*,"
the "Grimm Library," and the "Popular Studies in Mythology" – demonstrate not only how prolific Weston was, but how significant the publication history of her translations and other works is to modern understanding
of her scholarly project. Her idiosyncratic theories and styles of translation
were developing within them, but the works were externally organized and
packaged as products in a particular range, and this required her to vary her
tone, style, and level of complexity for a range of audiences. Nutt felt that
these often little-known texts were essential fodder for research into folklore, recognizing "the importance of accurate texts to the creation of sound
theory."[26]

To define Weston's scholarship by modern standards is difficult, as her
work engaged with many newly developing disciplines: folklore, mythology,
anthropology, comparative religion, Arthurian studies, and Middle English
literary studies. Writing for two audiences – popular and scholarly – influenced the way Weston translated and interpreted her texts, but it also
presented her with a unique opportunity to utilize contemporary interest in
the Arthurian world in addressing and propagating her new and developing
ideas.

"Miss Weston's Gawain-Complex"

Weston's theories sprawl across dozens of publications, yet there was one
figure who appeared in her work with notable regularity and who became

vitally important to Weston's scholarly project: Sir Gawain. Contesting Alfred Nutt's favoring of Perceval as the Grail hero, or A. E. Waite's championing of Galahad, Weston wore Gawain's colors proudly in debates that represented nothing so much as scholarly tournaments. One opponent, the American scholar James Douglas Bruce, took particular objection to her favoritism and labeled it "Miss Weston's Gawain-complex," implying, in Janet Grayson's words, "the *idée fixe* of her work and mind."[27] Yet this focus was not a baseless psychological obsession. Gawain acted as the lynchpin in Weston's theories: she rewrote the history and pre-history of the character, and sought to determine its origins in ancient ritual and myth.

As the most malleable and complex hero in the Arthurian tradition, Gawain was immensely useful to Jessie Weston, and came to carry the interpretative load of her entire approach to romance and religion. This involved three linked aims: to rescue Gawain's reputation and popularize the hero; to associate him with the Grail quest and reveal him to be the earliest, most "authentic" Grail hero; and to recast him as a figure of ritual, a pre-Christian deity.

Within the extant literary corpus, Gawain had perhaps the most unstable reputation of all Arthur's knights, running the gamut from courteous and noble to irreverent and lascivious.[28] In the chronicles of medieval Britain – William of Malmesbury's *Gesta regum Anglorum* (c.1125) and Geoffrey of Monmouth's *Historia regum Britanniae* (1136) – Gawain is a warlike figure, "fearless in his courage," who is known for his bravery.[29] His next extant appearance in medieval literature was in the twelfth-century romances of Chrétien de Troyes. In Chrétien's works, Gawain is always courteous but is often overshadowed by other knights. In the Grail quests, Gawain is viewed as too worldly and amorous in comparison with the spiritual Perceval.

When English literature began to turn to romance, it drew heavily from the French tradition. English poets often selected the most positive aspects of his character, particularly his courtesy, so that the English verse tradition developed a "hagiology of Gawain."[30] Gawain appears in poems of the fourteenth century, such as *Ywain and Gawain* and *Libeaus Desconus*. In *Sir Gawain and the Green Knight*, dating from the late fourteenth century, his character is at its chivalric height. This poet was conscious of Gawain's muddled character – using his racy French reputation to add tension and irony to the bedroom temptation scenes – and yet preserves him as a morally and spiritually pure figure. The martial Gawain of the chronicle tradition influenced other English texts – the *Alliterative Morte Arthure* and *Brut* – in which his bravery and valor were emphasized, rather than his courtly qualities.

During the fifteenth century Gawain became the cult hero of a popular English tradition: based, critically for Weston, on traditional, orally-evolved folk-tales. Here Gawain was developed as a popular chivalric hero; these texts include *Gawain and the Carle of Carlisle* and *The Wedding of Sir Gawain and Dame Ragnelle*. In this tradition Gawain is always brave, loyal, and courteous. He is often associated with the "Loathly Lady" motif, during which he always behaves with impeccable manners.

Yet in Sir Thomas Malory's fifteenth-century prose epic *Le Morte Darthur*, Gawain is a more complex and inconsistent figure. Malory's main source was the French prose tradition in which Gawain's reputation had deteriorated; his status as a lover of ladies from the verse tradition became something lewder and he was associated with rape and murder. The Gawain of the Vulgate cycle is spiritually unfit to seek the Grail. In *Le Morte Darthur*, Gawain is "wycked and synfull"; a hermit tells him, "ye have used the moste untrewyst lyff that ever I herd knyght lyve."[31] Although Gawain has been sorely wronged and gains the reader's sympathy, his implacable anger plays a crucial role in Arthur's tragic downfall.

This version was to be the most influential on the modern imagination. Following the eighteenth-century collection of late-medieval popular ballads and romances in Thomas Percy's Folio Manuscript, some authors were inspired to write Gawains who matched the courteous and comical folk creation.[32] In Edward Bulwer-Lytton's *King Arthur* (1848), he declares sympathy for the figure: "poor Gawaine himself, the mirror of chivalry in most of the Fabliaux is, as Southey observes, 'shamefully calumniated' in the *Morte d'Arthur* as the 'false Gawaine'."[33] Frederic Madden's 1839 edition of Gawain romances for the Bannatyne Club, including the first edition of *Sir Gawain and the Green Knight* from the recently discovered manuscript Cotton Nero A.x, was another influence on these interpretations.[34] However, while these retellings prevailed in the early century, the Malorian vision soon became more influential. It was Tennyson's *Idylls of the King* that dominated the Victorian cultural imagination.

Although Tennyson's interest in Arthurian literature pre-dated his reading of Malory, he took much of his material for *The Idylls of the King* directly from the *Morte Darthur*. It is a late-medieval Malorian aesthetic that prevails in the *Idylls*. In adjusting the plot to fit his twelve idylls, Tennyson focuses on episodes in which Gawain fares worst in Malory: "Pelleas and Ettarre" and "Lancelot and Elaine." B. J. Whiting describes the latter tale as "a little masterpiece in malice," where Gawain proves that although he is "surnamed The Courteous, fair and strong," he is not to be trusted, "Nor often loyal to his word."[35] Throughout the *Idylls*, Gawain is "a reckless and irreverent knight."[36] Worse still, he is impious and lustful: a symbol of the depravity and corruption that despoiled the purity of the Round Table. When writers, poets, and artists engaged with Arthurian themes in the nineteenth century, they were usually responding to Malory's depiction of the Arthurian court, and to Tennyson, who published the first four *Idylls* in 1859. The most popular image of Sir Gawain in the public mind at the end of the nineteenth century, therefore, was of a less-than-perfect knight.

It was in this context that Weston and Nutt promoted their "Arthurian Romances Unrepresented in Malory's *Morte D'Arthur*." These works allowed Weston to promote the "good" Gawain: the courteous hero of the British popular tradition. By deliberately positioning her translations as outside Malory's influence, she also sought to avoid the shadow of Tennyson and his well-established Arthurian world, drawing a line between fanciful literature and authentic legend:

> Malory's prose epic, which, fine as it is, is an example rather of excel-lence of style than a faithful representation of the original legend, was till this nineteenth century the sole great monument which English literature had dedicated to the memory of Arthur. Tennyson's collec-tion of Arthurian poems and Idylls has freed us from a well-deserved reproach, though, from a critical point of view, it must be admitted that his work is open to much the same objection as is Malory's – it is admirable considered as *literature*, as *legend* it does even less justice to the original characters of the story.[37]

Sir Gawain and the Green Knight was crucial to that distinction. She trans-lated the text – the "jewel of English medieval literature" – twice in her career.[38] Her first text, "retold in modern prose," was published in 1898 in "Arthurian Romances Unrepresented in Malory's *Morte D'Arthur*." Her second was a translation in the "original metre" as part of her anthology for Houghton Mifflin, *Romance, Vision, and Satire* (1912).

As Whiting has noted,

> If [modern readers] are familiar with *Sir Gawain and the Green Knight*, where Gawain embodies nearly all the chivalric virtues, they think they see a progressive degradation of character from the medieval to the renaissance to the Victorian concept, an almost perfect example of epic degeneration.[39]

Sir Gawain and the Green Knight, Weston felt, represented better than any other text the British, courteous Gawain that she was simultaneously uncov-ering through her scholarly research. She believed that:

> the author of the most important English metrical romance dealing with Arthurian legend faithfully adheres to the original conception of Gawain's character, as drawn before the monkish lovers of edifica-

tion laid their ruthless hands on his legend, and turned the model of knightly virtues and courtesy into a mere vulgar libertine.[40]

Through translating and popularizing this poem, more than any other, Weston sought to represent her scholarly beliefs about the national and religious origins of Arthurian legend.

Weston's aim was to enable a broad range of readers to access the authentic character of Gawain that she believed in, and which she felt was embodied in this text. Her first translation of 1898 was written purposely to exclude the scholar, "This little book is not for them," she states:

> and if to those to whom the tale would otherwise be a sealed treasure these pages bring some new knowledge […] [if] they gain a keener appreciation of our national heroes, a wider knowledge of our national literature, then the spirit of the long-dead poet will doubtless not be the slowest to pardon my handling of his masterpiece.[41]

Weston saw it as her role to unseal the treasure and make her text as accessible as possible, using modern prose to overcome what she called the "real difficulty and obscurity of the language."[42] Stephanie Barczewski describes Weston's text as "catholic in its appeal," and asks, "From what source flowed this new concern to democratize medieval literature? Doubtless the profit motive should not be underestimated; nineteenth-century editors and publishers were certainly eager to capitalize upon the contemporary predilection for all things medieval."[43] While Weston and Nutt no doubt perceived the financial benefits, she in particular had complex motives for reaching a wider readership.

That Weston felt it important to address the popular reader's needs in her translation – and exclude the scholar's – is linked to her status as a woman scholar. Although her combative style and controversial theories might have made Weston an academic outsider in any period, her position was deeply embedded in gender politics at the turn of the century. Recent work on women's scholarship has explored the relation of women to the academy, and the liminal spaces between academic and popular writing – such as translations or children's versions – that women often needed to inhabit in order to forge a career. As Lorna Hardwick has noted, women built their scholarly careers both by "challenge to and complicity with dominant traditions."[44] Jane Chance comments that Weston "circumvented academic structures" and was "pilloried […] for [her] independent, often speculative and unfounded ventures."[45] This narrative is complicated further by the fact that medieval and folklore studies did not exist within a coherent academy for much of the nineteenth century: there were many male scholars who lacked institutional support. Although educational opportunities for women improved in the new century, the formalization of the academy – and therefore of the qualifications and status needed to enter it – at first resulted in greater exclusion of women from scholarship.[46]

There were elements of Weston's career that were hindered or influenced by contemporary gender politics. She studied with Gaston Paris, but never received an official degree, only began to publish at the age of forty-four, and never held an official academic position, let alone a chair. Unmarried and childless, Weston lived and worked peripatetically, without institutional moorings. This marginality has even influenced the way we now understand her career; one of the likely reasons for the paucity of surviving material is that she lacked an institution to preserve it. Although she received an obituary in *The Times*, the journal *Romania*, to which she had been a frequent contributor and which had been founded by her mentor Paris, "barely noticed" her death.[47] She certainly faced prejudice in some of her scholarly exchanges. The Swiss scholar Ernst Brugger dismissed her reconstruction of Borron's verse *Perceval*, calling it "*müssige Spielerei*" ("idle child's play"). Weston wrote in the book's introduction, "has not the writer of these studies been solemnly warned off ground sacred to scholars of another sex, and dare we say of another nation?"[48]

However, despite noting this warning, Weston regularly contributed to journals and entered debates and disagreements with her Germanic counterparts, seemingly without trepidation. It must have been a very different matter for the medieval historian and editor Lucy Toulmin Smith (1838– 1911), contributing as a very rare "Miss" among the male contributors – most of whom were "Dr" or "Professor" – to *Anglia* and *Englische Studien* in the 1880s.[49] By Weston's time, and particularly in Weston's field, women scholars were more numerous. The editor of *Folklore* from 1900 to 1908 and president of the Folklore Society from 1909 to 1910 was Charlotte Burne (1850– 1923), known for her work on Shropshire folklore. When Burne delivered her Presidential Address in 1910, she indicated that the Folklore Society – a relative newcomer in the world of learned societies, having been formed in 1878 – was something of a trailblazer in this respect: "This is, to the best of my belief, the first time, – at all events in the Old World, – that the duty of delivering the Annual Presidential Address to a learned Society has been entrusted to a woman."[50] In the pages of the journal *Folklore* are conversations between women scholars: Weston reviewed the American folklore scholar Lucy A. Paton's *Studies in the Fairy Mythology in Arthurian Romance*, and when *From Ritual to Romance* was reviewed in *Folklore* by Eleanor Hull, Weston responded to her criticisms in the same journal.[51]

Although she did not work within a formal academy of scholarship, she was a member of a figurative community of Arthurianists; *The Times* called them, in her obituary, "that small and early band of workers who, with unflagging enthusiasm, devoted their lives to the elucidation of the hidden truths of Arthurian romance."[52] Janet Grayson writes that her "strong and charming personality and her great sense of humour won her the enduring affection of a host of friends all over the world," including "W. P. Ker, W. W. Greg, Walter Raleigh; [...] Ferdinand Lot, Joseph Bedier; [...] Gaston Paris; Celticists Alfred Nutt, John Rhys, and the young Roger Sherman Loomis; anthropologist Sir James Frazer and classicist Jane Harrison."[53] Although she had not had the accolades or support of an institution during her publishing career, she did receive formal recognition late in her career: the Rose Mary Crawshay Prize for Women Writers in 1920 and a D.Litt. from the University of Wales in 1923, where the Professor of French Literature Mary Williams (herself a pioneering woman scholar) introduced her by saying,

> I venture to believe that no one, be it man or woman, is better known on the Continent as well as in these islands for her studies in the domain of Arthurian romance. Her researches have ever been pros-ecuted with that patience, zeal and love of the truth which are charac-teristic of the great scholar.[54]

Weston was, therefore, not "of the academy" – as far as one existed for her field – but nor was she, evidently, a casual interested reader, nor an "amateur" translator – if amateurs and professionals can be divided so neatly at this period. We cannot suggest a dichotomy between male scholarly works and female popular ones as works that contradict both categories abound. As the range of Weston's publications has demonstrated, she could switch between the competitive scholarly mode of a journal article and the popular style of a translation. Yet, Weston's position made her more than usually aware of the needs of the popular market, and how they might find medieval literature a "sealed treasure." Translation into modern English had long been an auxil-iary element of scholarship, deemed appropriate "woman's work."[55] In the preface to her 1898 translation of *Sir Gawain and the Green Knight*, Weston stated that she sought "to render it more accessible to the general public, by giving it a form that shall be easily intelligible, and at the same time preserve as closely as possible the style of the author."[56] Her ambiguous status gave her the freedom to deviate from scholarly norms – although other women scholars felt compelled to adhere to them all the more strictly in similar circumstances – but also a far-reaching sight beyond the academy's walls, feeding her career-long desire to produce works that were "accessible to the general public" and "easily intelligible." Weston could challenge her male contemporaries with more confidence than women scholars of any previous generation. Yet in these works she sought to write around the scholarly tradition; this "little book" was "not for them." Weston's popular publications did not only seek to benefit the uneducated reader; they gave her the necessary freedom to pursue her own ideological path.

Weston's primary way of marrying the conflicting aims of being accessible and "preserving" the author's style was through the use of archaism: what she sees as preservation is – by the nature of translation – a form of re-creation. This was achieved by her "modern prose," generous use of alliteration, and choice of ancient-sounding terms. Thus we find phrases in her "modern prose" such as "thither came the king," they "made much mirth withal," "the knight rideth," "Gramercy," "Forsooth," "ere they gat them to bed," "'Now, I wis,' quoth the knight."[57] She simplified the narrative, making silent abridgements, and engaged in a "softening of mediæval manners and customs" on grounds of taste, which her critics disliked.[58]

When she retranslated the text in 1912 for her anthology of alliterative verse, *Romance, Vision, and Satire*, she went further in attempting to mimic her medieval source, recognizing that it came from a period when "a sense of form was making itself felt."[59] Although Weston claims these verse translations were done "in the original metres," the form of the work is in fact of her own invention, and the meter is about as original as her prose was modern. Calling herself a "versifier," rather than a poet, she uses alliteration – which is here stylistic rather than truly metrical – on top of an accentual-syllabic meter (as opposed to purely accentual), and rhymes on every line. Weston's antiquated diction is even more prevalent than in her previous translation. Some contemporary critics disapproved of Weston's strange hybrid meter and her use of obsolete and archaistic words.[60] Yet for Weston these effects were crucial to her attempt to make her texts "appeal to the modern reader, not as curious specimens of writing in a dead past, but, what they would indeed be, a living literature."[61] The "wheel" in which the *Gawain*-poet describes the Green Knight for the first time illustrates Weston's emphasis on mimicry of the original, rather than rephrasing for the sake of clarity:

> Men marvelled at his hue,
> So was his semblaunce seen,
> He fared as one on feud,
> And over all was green![62]

She intended it to be the closest a non-reader of Middle English could get to reading *Sir Gawain and the Green Knight*. Although Weston's translations can often seem to alter the original text, this was always intended as a more accurate or authentic way of keeping it the same: "I have held myself free to express the poet's idea in somewhat different words."[63] The ambiguities of the *Gawain*-poet's language and his intricate style have remained problematic for translators; Weston's archaism, rhyme, and mixing of meters are her early twentieth-century method of approaching such difficulties.

If she succeeded in making her *Sir Gawain and the Green Knight* both accessible and authentic, then Weston was sure she could provide a superior Gawain to the one that her readers already knew. We read Malory or Tennyson, she insisted, with "a feeling of dissatisfaction"; she asks, "How did the Gawain of their imagination, this empty-headed, empty-hearted worldling, cruel murderer, and treacherous friend, ever come to be the typical English hero?" and continues, "Then we turn back to these faded pages, and read the quaintly earnest words in which the old writer reveals the hidden meaning."[64] Weston's alternative version of the hero was reflected in several contemporary texts that took the English popular Gawain as their inspiration: one play adaptation of *Sir Gawain and the Green Knight* for children points its readers to Weston's translation.[65]

Weston developed this approach in her other contributions to the series "Arthurian Romances Unrepresented in Malory's *Morte D'Arthur*." Her translation of *Libeaus Desconus*, in which Gawain appears, was published in 1902.[66] In her following two volumes – *Sir Gawain at the Grail Castle* and *Sir Gawain and the Lady of Lys* – Weston selected and translated episodes featuring Gawain from obscure Arthurian texts that Nutt's readers were unlikely to have read in the original languages. In this way, she was able selectively to foreground certain aspects of Gawain's character, and to guide her readers' interpretation of them.

Volume six of the series, *Sir Gawain at the Grail Castle* (1904), featured carefully selected episodes from several medieval sources on the theme of "the adventures of Sir Gawain in search of the Grail."[67] She chose the texts to demonstrate that

> the student who will devote time and research to the subject will before very long discover, probably to his, or her, surprise, that no knight in the whole cycle, save Perceval himself (and scarcely even he) is associated with the Grail under so many and varying conditions as is Sir Gawain.[68]

The stories she included to show "the chief hero of early Arthurian tradition in an unfamiliar light" had the exact same format, style of illustration, and a similarly accessible modern prose style as her *Sir Gawain and the Green Knight* of 1898.[69]

In *Sir Gawain and the Lady of Lys*, volume seven (1907), Weston continued to translate excerpts from the same texts that appeared in her more serious studies. She thus made accessible the materials that underpinned her scholarly arguments, and introduced them to new readerships, seemingly only for "the interest of the story itself, and its connection with our vernacular literature, [which] were sufficient to warrant a full translation being placed at the disposal of English readers."[70] She reveals in her introduction that she is hoping to incite among her readership, characterized as the humble "English folk," a "demand" for Gawain's "real story." She seeks not to convey the medieval text as it exists in manuscript or edited form, but to do justice to an intangible conceptual text. She writes, with heady rhetoric:

> Is it too much to ask of the students of Malory, fascinated by the noble style in which he has clothed and disguised the real poverty of his *réchauffée*, that they should for a short time lay him aside, and turning back to the true Arthurian legend, learn at last to do justice to one of the most gracious and picturesque figures in literature – a figure to which gross injustice has been done – that, rejecting Malory's libel, they do tardy justice to our own insular hero – for not the most fanatical partisan of the Continental school has ever ventured to claim him – to the true Sir Gawain?[71]

Weston's vision stretched across more than one of her texts; her series of hand-picked translations are a coordinated effort to garner enthusiasm for the brave and courteous Gawain.

As some elements of this material have hinted, Weston did not rest with defending Gawain's good name. When we consider the translations alongside Weston's more scholarly works – particularly those appearing in Nutt's "Grimm Library" – we can observe that the popular works reflect the conclusions that Weston was reaching in her scholarship. Weston had begun her career by translating a legend of Sir Perceval, whose reputation was far more cohesive than Gawain's. In Chrétien's *Perceval* and Wolfram's *Parzival*, Perceval is a pure knight who engages in a Grail quest, who heals the Fisher King and who, in Wolfram at least, has his name appear on the Grail as the new Grail King. Weston, influenced by Wagner and Nutt, originally felt convinced of his centrality and importance.[72] Yet even within her translation of *Parzival*, Weston was proud that she – unlike the previous translator – had included the lengthy episodes about Gawain.[73]

Weston's first scholarly study for the "Grimm Library" was *The Legend of Sir Gawain* of 1897, which set out to untangle the many threads of Gawain's history. In this, her earliest interpretation of his reputation, published a year before her first translation of *Sir Gawain and the Green Knight*, she notes that "it is unfortunately the case that later writers have followed in the track of Malory rather than that of Chrétien; and the English nineteenth-century representations of Gawain are even more unjust to the original than are the fifteenth."[74] She declares herself perplexed that Gawain "has hitherto failed to meet with the favour accorded to his companions."[75] She denies that undiscriminating love affairs are truly part of Gawain's character, suggesting that the figure of faery who traditionally resided in the Maidens' Isle and was courteous to all women was misunderstood by later Christian writers.[76]

Gawain was demonstrably part of an older tradition than Chrétien, a position shared only by Arthur. In Weston's arguments, his existence reaffirmed the Insular school's position that Arthurian literature was at root a Celtic practice; she stated, "we make a grave mistake when we pursue our researches as far back as the French poet and no further."[77] Moreover, Weston believed that Gawain was not only pre-Chrétien, but pre-Christian. She links him to the Irish hero Cuchulinn, who is also called up to behead a hideous knight in the tale *Fled Bricend*, and suggests that the figure "was at one time a solar divinity."[78] At this date she claims no relation between Gawain and the Grail, believing that "that famous quest was no part of his own story."[79] She links him with the "world of the departed," the Celtic other-world, and states that rather than having "most numerous and least edifying love affairs," he is "rather the courteous and disinterested champion of *all* maidens than lover of *one*."[80] She posits "the ultimate source of the Gawain story" as a Celtic tale, "one special adventure with strongly marked other-world features" into which other incidents, such as the episode with the Green Knight and the marriage incident, had once fitted.[81] Such a theory did not persuade all her readers; Ker found in Weston's insistence on a primitive Gawain story, "not enough allowance [...] for the possibilities of coincidence, for the familiar machinery of folklore."[82]

Despite such suggestions, Weston continued to accrete further evidence upon the theme in a later work for the "Grimm Library," *The Legend of Sir Perceval*, published in two volumes in 1906 and 1909. Although the subject was nominally Perceval, this text was an opportunity for Weston to continue her discussions about Gawain. She asks:

> [...] is Perceval connected with the Grail by virtue of any peculiarity essentially and originally bound up with his legend? Before I began the close study of the texts, I was decidedly of that opinion, now I can no longer think so. I feel sure now that the original hero was Gawain and that Perceval's connection with the Grail is accidental rather than inevitable. [...] As the Grail story became Christianized, Perceval simply replaced Gawain, his story lending itself more easily to a moral and edifying development.[83]

Weston felt the influence of the Christian religion was largely responsible for the degradation of Gawain's reputation. "[B]ent on spiritual edification," Christian writers found Gawain a "stumbling block": "In those versions which are devoted to the most highly-developed and ecclesiasticised form of the Grail legend, the character of Gawain undergoes a remarkable and striking change: he becomes a mere libertine, cruel and lecherous."[84] This approach can also be discerned in the way she "could barely conceal contempt for the Galahad quest altogether and specifically for the monkish character of the hero"; she felt the Galahad stories were late additions, after the Grail stories had been altered to fit with the newer concepts of Christian mysticism.[85]

The earliest Grail legends featuring Gawain were "a confused remembrance of a most ancient and widespread form of Nature worship, the cult of Adonis, or Tammuz, which underlies many of the ancient mysteries, and was as *The Golden Bough* has taught us, of practically universal observance."[86] Weston had become familiar with James Frazer's work since she had written *The Legend of Sir Gawain* and her early thoughts about Gawain as a solar deity were easily mapped on to Frazer's ideas. That Weston had also made the jump from utterly dissociating Gawain with the Grail to linking him closely and consistently to it is vitally important to her depiction of Gawain as the mythological hero of pre-Christian worship. She here asserts that "the Grail was originally a vessel which played a rôle in these rites of some form of Nature worship. [...] Thus, in its original, of which the Gawain stories are the survival, the Grail was purely Pagan."[87] By defending Gawain's reputation, locating him in the pre-historical past as a figure of ritual, and by linking him to the earliest accounts of the Grail quest, Weston strengthened the implied link between the three concepts, and thus supported her controversial notion of the pagan Grail, which would form a vital element of *From Ritual to Romance*. Stripping away the Christianized layers of Gawain's "later" reputation, Weston reveals a purely mythical hero; her complex and sustained exposition of his character is an integral part of her quest for the origins of Arthurian literature and legend.

Unlike many nineteenth-century textual scholars, who sought when editing a manuscript to find the Ur-text, the authorial version that was authentic and reliable, Weston based her Gawain theories on a theoretical group of texts that descended through popular folk-tale telling from an Ur-myth. Weston's theory pushed back Gawain's first appearance to the "poems" of the Welsh bard Bleheris, the "Geste of Sir Gawain," a difficult task since all her arguments for the existence of non-extant literature had to be based on evidence within the extant literature. Not much more is known about Bleheris other than his name, and certainly no written Arthurian poems by him survive. To Weston, Bleheris was not an author whose creative genius was responsible for Arthurian literature – like Chrétien to the continentalists – but a collector and compiler.[88] She describes a "group of short episodic poems": they are "the earliest stratum of the Arthurian romantic tradition we as yet possess [...] the character of this group was that of popular folk-tale rather than of deliberate and inventive literature."[89] She believed in particular that existing stories of Gawain and the "Chastel Orguellous" were known to Wauchier de Denain and Chrétien's other continuators and therefore that they influenced the same texts that she printed in *Gawain at the Grail Castle* and *Gawain and the Lady of Lys*. She found within the written texts evidence of a "special field [which] was of much earlier date, and of much more extended character than we have hitherto recognised."[90] She links the English popular romances featuring Gawain to the "Chastel Orguellous" group, describing them as "one and the same collection of tales."[91]

Weston then promoted her opinions in her popular works and among the scholarly community. She noted in *Sir Gawain and the Lady of Lys*:

> Since the publication of the last volume of this series we have become aware of certain facts, small in themselves, but weighty in their connection and ensemble, which go to prove that there existed at an early date a collection of poems dealing with the feats of Gawain and his kin, which may be styled "The Geste of Sir Gawain," the authorship of which was ascribed to a certain Bleheris. Of this collection the story in Vol. I, *Sir Gawain and the Green Knight*; the first visit of Gawain to the Grail Castle in Vol. IV; and the stories here given all formed part, while our English Gawain poems are a late and fragmentary survival of the same collection.[92]

In 1906 she read a paper to the Folklore Society entitled "The Grail and the Mysteries of Adonis"; the reading was attended by F. J. Furnivall, G. Laurence Gomme, A. B. Cook, and W. B. Yeats, who participated in the ensuing discussion.[93] She took the opportunity to reinforce her recent "discoveries": "we know that the earliest attainable Grail story is that of which not Perceval but Gawain was the hero, and the authorship of which is ascribed not to Chrétien de Troyes, but to Bleheris the Welshman."[94] She later puffed her claims further, stating that "as Dr Brugger, the leading German critic of Arthurian literature, has frankly admitted, we must henceforth take the Bleheris-*Gawain* form as our starting-point of investigation."[95] It was Weston's description of the Geste of Syr Gawayne and Bleheris the bard – her "unshakable theory of lost hypothetical originals" – that led Bruce to declare that Weston had a "Gawain-complex."[96] Bruce felt the first extant mention of Gawain was as far back as any critic could legitimately go, and that Weston's conjectures were a step too far.

Weston was afforded the ultimate opportunity to have her version of history recorded as the authoritative account when she was commissioned to write all the Arthurian entries for the *Encyclopaedia Britannica* in 1911. The entry for Gawain is the only one that is unsigned, although it could hardly have been written by anyone else.[97] Weston thus presented her perspective on this contested personality as an anonymous authorized version. She gives a potted overview of the various Gawain traditions in chronicle and romance, and makes clear how she believes the current perception to be false:

> Most unfortunately our English version of the romances, Malory's *Morte Arthur*, being derived from these later forms ["the *Merlin* continuations, the *Tristan*, and the final *Lancelot* compilation"] (though his treatment of Gawain is by no means uniformly consistent), this unfavourable aspect is that under which the hero has become known to the modern reader. Tennyson, who only knew the Arthurian story through the medium of Malory, has, by exaggeration, largely contributed to this misunderstanding.[98]

She makes her key points about Gawain preceding Perceval as the Grail hero and refers, without mention of her own name, to "recent discoveries" that have made it "practically certain" that the "Geste of Gawain" poems existed. She places Gawain firmly in pre-Christian tradition, and concludes, "Chaucer, when he spoke of Gawain coming 'again out of faerie,' spoke better than he knew; the home of that very gallant and courteous knight is indeed *Fairy*-land, and the true Gawain-tradition is informed with fairy glamour and grace."[99] In her bibliography, she recommends for interested readers five of her own works in which she laid out her "Gawain-complex" for scholarly and popular readers: *The Legend of Sir Gawain, The Legend of Sir Perceval, Sir Gawain and the Green Knight, Sir Gawain at the Grail Castle, Sir Gawain and the Lady of Lys*. Together, these texts – "weighty in their connection and ensemble" – present a coherent, seemingly objective story, and she recommended them to any reader who was interested enough to look up Gawain in the *Encyclopaedia*.

From Romance to Ritual

Jessie Weston's project to rehabilitate Sir Gawain was a scholarly rebellion, a moral exoneration, and a search for origins. For her, there was always a more authentic version of a legend that was prior to the textual form. Although, as we have seen, Weston's ideas were developed through the reproduction and interpretation of medieval literature, particularly romance, Weston was no literary scholar. Her concern was with the past that preceded a work of literature and survivals of that past to her day, and not the work's own creative present. This attitude is often apparent in her works: she felt that "direct literary invention has played but a secondary part in the growth of this wonderful body of romance" and believed that "much of the subtle glamour and pervasive charm of the themes has vanished in the process of transformation from folk-tale to classical literature."[100]

This favoring of spiritual impulse over authorial intent was another disputed topic. C. S. Lewis, discussing "The Anthropological Approach" of John Spiers in 1962, argued that while "literary texts can sometimes be of great use to the anthropologist," it "does not immediately follow […] that anthropological study can make in return any valuable contribution to literary criticism."[101] This was precisely the approach Weston had inherited from Alfred Nutt, the "daring to use medieval folk-tales in elucidation of medieval romance." Lewis continues:

> When savage beliefs or practices inform a work of art, that work is not a puzzle to which those beliefs and practices are the clue. The savage origins are the puzzle; the surviving work of art is the only clue by which we can hope to penetrate the inwardness of the origins. It is either in art, or nowhere, that the dry bones are made to live again.[102]

Lewis was interested in the work of art, and Weston in the savage beliefs. In similar language Weston described the Grail as: "the symbol and witness to unseen realities, transcending the world of sense; […] the attempt to penetrate from the outer to the inner, to apprehend behind the sign the thing signified […]."[103] This flight from the textual and historical to the pre-textual and pre-historical makes Weston's work remote from the realities of medieval textuality. Her favored text, *Sir Gawain and the Green Knight*, was a fourteenth-century work by a Christian poet with Christian themes, and yet Weston interpreted it to support her version of a figure who, she believed, as "hero of a distinctively Christian legend […] would certainly be out of place."[104]

Weston sought to transcend literature and historical time, to deal only in "essential elements." When she discusses the possible dates of Bleheris, we find evidence of a distinct resistance to historical specificity. She constantly strives to push the dates further back; she states, "it is scarcely possible, in dealing with matter of this character, to err by placing it too early."[105] She recalls that Gerald of Wales

> says he lived "a little before our time," words which may mean anything. Giraldus may be using the editorial "we," and may mean "a little before my time," which, as he was writing in the latter half of the twelfth century, might imply that Bledhericus lived in the earlier half. But he may also have used the pronoun quite indefinitely; as M. Ferdinand Lot, with whom I discussed the question, remarked, "it may mean anything from ten to a hundred years; we might say that Bonaparte

lived 'a little before our time'." [...] it seems most probable that he lived at a period sufficiently remote to allow of the precise details concerning his life and work to become obscured, while the tradition of his close connection with Arthurian romance was retained.[106]

It is typical of Weston to be drawn to the indefinite interpretation; words, which "may mean anything," allow Weston to place her author in any time. She uses an example that stretches her time back to the beginning of the nineteenth century, and thus frees up medieval time for easier manipulation. Weston describes the early periods that precede written romance as

> this *terra incognita* that I hope to penetrate [...] [which] is, let us hope, henceforth no longer a Forbidden Land, but rather a Land of Promise, to be entered very cautiously no doubt, but still to be entered with every hope of bringing thence some fruit to reward our toil.[107]

The more unknown the field of study, the more promising the land, and the more ripe for interpretation. Weston dismisses the historical tradition of Arthurian literature, which in terms of extant written accounts precedes the romance tradition, and argues instead that romance, disguised as folklore, really came first:

> Arthur as "dux bellorum" may very well date from the fifth century; Arthur and his knights as first folk-lore, then romantic heroes, are survivals of the Celtic wonder-world; and that in its essential elements, preceded the birth of history, and will endure till the need for history shall pass away.[108]

Weston's treatment of Gawain in her translations and scholarly works was highly systematic; through Gawain she led her readers on a quest that drew them back from medieval literature into the mythical past, from romance to ritual. When her publications are viewed together, we can see that she was working towards establishing and popularizing a coherent theory of Arthurian legend; she was able to dictate the terms of that theory completely once she had moved the debate back, past Chrétien to the British past, then past Bleheris to the "Forbidden Land" of folklore and myth, discarding the inconveniences of historical and linguistic specificity. Weston sought to show her readers, through authentically archaic translations – by careful construction of language and meter – the "real" story of Gawain. What she presented as transparent translations were in fact deeply invested in her scholarly vision. It was ultimately a philosophical quest, through which she sought to make the occult visible and the bones of the dead live.[109] Her scholarly works

delved ever deeper into time to find the desired origins, while her translations sought to represent the "precious survivals" or "remembrances" of
those origins as accessibly and authentically as she could. Weston criticized
what she saw as the misunderstandings and alterations of earlier writers; this
exploration reveals that some of the most interesting manipulations that the
figure of Gawain has undergone were at her own hands.

NOTES

1. Jessie L. Weston, *The Legend of Sir Perceval: Studies upon its Origin, Development,
and Position in the Arthurian Cycle*, 2 vols. (London: David Nutt, 1906), I:335.
2. This article is based on my doctoral research: "Chapter Four: Jessie L. Weston
(1850–1928)," "From the Margins: Scholarly Women and the Translation and Editing of
Medieval English Literature in the Nineteenth Century," University of Cambridge, 2010.
3. Norris J. Lacy, "Jessie Laidlay Weston (1850–1928)," in *On Arthurian Women: Essays
in Memory of Maureen Fries*, ed. Bonnie Wheeler and Fiona Tolhurst (Dallas: Scriptorium
Press, 2001), 339.
4. T. S. Eliot, *The Waste Land* (New York: Boni and Liveright, 1922), 53; T. S. Eliot,
On Poetry and Poets (London: Faber & Faber, 1957), 109–10; Hugh Kenner, *The Invisible Poet*
(New York: Obolensky, 1959), 152.
5. Gillian Thomas, "Weston, Jessie Laidlay (1850–1928)," in *Oxford Dictionary of
National Biography* (accessed 26 May 2009). Leon Surette chooses to separate Weston from
"respectable, mainstream" scholarship and attributes to her an "occult belief"; Surette, "*The
Waste Land* and Jessie Weston: A Reassessment," *Twentieth-Century Literature* 34 (1988):
223–45 (224). Angela Jane Weisl condemns the "unnecessary zeal with which Eliot scholars
criticize Weston"; Weisl, "By Her Works Shall Ye Know Her: The Quest for Jessie L. Weston,"
in *Women Medievalists and the Academy*, ed. Jane Chance (Madison: University of Wisconsin
Press, 2005), 48.
6. Weisl named her biography "By Her Works Shall Ye Know Her," while Grayson
notes that, with Weston's first book, "like Athena she came fully grown out of the head of
the god"; Janet Grayson, "In Quest of Jessie Weston," *Arthurian Literature*, 11 (1992): 1–80
(3). The little of Weston's biography that is known is discussed in these works and in Thomas,
"Weston, Jessie Laidlay (1850–1928)"; "Miss Jessie Weston. Arthurian Romance," *The Times*,
1 October 1928, 19.
7. Lacy, "Jessie Laidlay Weston (1850–1928)," 336–37.
8. "Miss Jessie Weston. Arthurian Romance."
9. A full bibliography is provided in Grayson, "In Quest of Jessie Weston," 52–61.
10. Thomas, "Weston, Jessie Laidlay (1850–1928)."
11. Jessie L. Weston, *Parzival: A Knightly Epic* (London: David Nutt, 1894).
12. Jessie L. Weston, "Alfred Nutt: An Appreciation", *Folklore* 21 (1910): 512–14 (512).
13. Jessie L. Weston, *Romance, Vision, and Satire: English Alliterative Poems of the Fourteenth Century* (New York: Houghton Mifflin, 1912); Jessie L. Weston, *The Chief Middle
English Poets: Selected Poems* (New York: Houghton Mifflin, 1914).

14. Grayson, "In Quest of Jessie Weston," 43.

15. Jessie L. Weston, "Legendary Cycles of the Middle Ages," in *The Cambridge Medieval History*, ed. J. B. Bury and H. H. Gwatkin (Cambridge: Cambridge University Press, 1928).

16. Weston, "Alfred Nutt," 514.

17. Grayson, "In Quest of Jessie Weston," 27.

18. Juliette Wood, "Folklore Studies at the Celtic Dawn: The Rôle of Alfred Nutt as Publisher and Scholar," *Folklore* 110 (1999): 3–12 (4).

19. Jessie L. Weston, *The Legend of Sir Gawain: Studies upon its Original and Significance* (London David Nutt, 1897), 4.

20. Weston, *The Legend of Sir Gawain*, 4.

21. "The Legend of Sir Gawain," *The Academy* 1334 (November 27, 1897): 447.

22. Jessie L. Weston, *The Story of Tristan and Iseult, Rendered into English from the German of Gottfried von Strassburg*, 2 vols. (London: David Nutt, 1899); Jessie L. Weston, *Guingamor; Lanval; Tyolet; Le Bisclaveret; Four Lais Rendered into English Prose from the French of Marie de France and Others*, trans. Jessie L. Weston (London: David Nutt, 1900); Jessie L. Weston, *Morien: A Metrical Romance Rendered into English Prose from the Mediaeval Dutch* (London: David Nutt, 1901); Jessie L. Weston, *Two Old English Metrical Romances Rendered into Prose Sir Cleges and Sir Libeaus Desconus* (London: David Nutt, 1902); Jessie L. Weston, *Sir Gawain at the Grail Castle* (London: David Nutt, 1904); Jessie L. Weston, *Sir Gawain and the Lady of Lys* (London: David Nutt, 1907).

23. "Sir Gawain and the Green Knight: A Middle English Arthurian Romance Retold in Modern Prose," *The Bookman* 15 (February 1899): 159.

24. Jessie L. Weston, *King Arthur and His Knights: A Survey of Arthurian Romance* (London: David Nutt, 1899).

25. Jessie L. Weston, *The Romance Cycle of Charlemagne and His Peers* (London: David Nutt, 1901).

26. Wood, "Folklore Studies at the Celtic Dawn," 7.

27. James Douglas Bruce, *The Evolution of Arthurian Romance* (Baltimore, MD: Johns Hopkins University Press, 1923), 2, 94. Grayson, "In Quest of Jessie Weston," 13.

28. See "Gawain" in *A Dictionary of Medieval Heroes*, ed. Willem P. Gerritsen and Anthony G. van Melle (Woodbridge: Boydell Press, 1998), 113–20; B. J. Whiting, "Gawain: His Reputation, His Courtesy, and His Appearance in Chaucer's *Squire's Tale*," in *Gawain: A Casebook*, ed. Raymond H. Thompson and Keith Busby (Abingdon: Routledge, 2006), 45–94.

29. Geoffrey of Monmouth, *The History of the Kings of Britain*, trans. Lewis Thorpe (London: Penguin, 1966), 254.

30. W. J. R. Barron, "Golagros and Gawayne," in *The Arthur of the English*, ed. W. J. R. Barron (Cardiff: University of Wales Press, 1999), 120–21.

31. XII.16 in "The Tale of the Sankgreal," in *Malory: Complete Works*, ed. Eugène Vinaver (Oxford: Oxford University Press, 1971), 534–35.

32. *Bishop Percy's Folio Manuscript: Ballads and Romances*, ed. J. W. Hales and F. J. Furnivall (London: Trubner, 1867).

33. Raymond H. Thompson, "Gawain in Post-Medieval English Literature," in *Gawain: A Casebook*, 297–318 (299).

34. *Syr Gawayne: A Collection of Ancient Romance – Poems by Scotish and English Authors, Relating to that Celebrated Knight of the Round Table*, ed. Sir Frederic Madden (London: Bannatyne Club Publications; printed by R. & J. E. Taylor, 1839).

35. Whiting, "Gawain," 60; Alfred Lord Tennyson, *Idylls of the King*, ed. J. M. Gray, 2nd edn. (London: Penguin, 1996), 182.

36. Line 853 in "The Holy Grail," in Tennyson, *Idylls of the King*, 229.

37. Weston, *The Legend of Sir Gawain*, 2–3.

38. Jessie L. Weston, *Sir Gawain and the Green Knight: A Middle-English Arthurian Romance Retold in Modern Prose, with Introduction and Notes*, trans. Jessie L. Weston (London: David Nutt, 1898), xii.

39. Whiting, "Gawain," 48.

40. Weston, *Sir Gawain […] in Modern Prose*, x.

41. Weston, *Sir Gawain […] in Modern Prose*, xii.

42. Weston, *Sir Gawain […] in Modern Prose*, vi.

43. Stephanie L. Barczewski, *Myth and National Identity in Nineteenth-Century Britain: The Legends of King Arthur and Robin Hood* (Oxford: Oxford University Press, 2000), 90.

44. Lorna Hardwick, "Women, Translation, and Empowerment," in *Women, Scholarship and Criticism: Gender and Knowledge, 1790–1900*, ed. Joan Bellamy, Anne Laurence, and Gillian Perry (Manchester: Manchester University Press, 2000), 180–203 (180).

45. Jane Chance, *Women Medievalists and the Academy* (Madison: Wisconsin University Press, 2005), xxxi.

46. I discuss the difficulties involved in constructing a narrative of female scholarship in medieval studies in my doctoral dissertation, "From the Margins."

47. Grayson, "In Quest of Jessie Weston," 2.

48. Jessie L. Weston, *The Legend of Sir Perceval: Studies upon its Origin, Development, and Position in the Arthurian Cycle*, 2 vols. (London: David Nutt, 1909), II:98.

49. I have also examined Smith's biography and career at length in the third chapter of my dissertation: "Lucy Toulmin Smith (1838–1911)."

50. Charlotte Burne, "Presidential Address: The Value of European Folklore in the History of Culture," *Folklore* 21 (1910): 14–41 (14).

51. Jessie L. Weston, "Review of *Studies in the Fairy Mythology in Arthurian Romance*, by Lucy A. Paton," *Folklore* 14 (1903): 437–43; Eleanor Hull, "Review of *From Ritual to Romance*, by Jessie L. Weston," *Folklore* 31 (1920): 163–68; Jessie L. Weston, "From Ritual to Romance," *Folklore* 31 (1920): 334–35.

52. "Miss Jessie Weston. Arthurian Romance."

53. Grayson, "In Quest of Jessie Weston," 3.

54. Grayson, "In Quest of Jessie Weston," 43.

55. Susanne Stark, "Women," in *The Oxford History of Literary Translation, Volume Four: 1790–1900*, ed. Peter France and Kenneth Haynes (Oxford: Oxford University Press, 2006), 125–32.

56. Weston, *Sir Gawain […] in Modern Prose*, vi.

57. Norris J. Lacy singled out "What boots it to make long my tale?" Lacy, "Jessie Laidlay Weston (1850–1928)," 336. See Weston, *Morien*, 107, 139.

58. "The Story of Tristan and Iseult," *The Academy* 1440 (9 December 1899): 680.

59. Weston, *Romance, Vision, and Satire*, vi.

60. John M. Manly, "Romance, Vision, and Satire," *Poetry* 2 (1913): 145–48 (145–46); Arthur C. L. Brown, "Romance, Vision, and Satire," *The Dial* 55 (1913): 17–18 (17).

61. Weston, *Romance, Vision, and Satire*, viii.

62. Weston, *Romance, Vision, and Satire*, 8–9. The original is:

> For wonder of his hwe men hade,
> Set in his semblaunt sene;
> He ferde as freke were fade,
> And overal enker grene. (lines 147–50)

Sir Gawain and the Green Knight, ed. J. R. R. Tolkien and E. V. Gordon, rev. N. Davis (Oxford: Clarendon, 1967), 5.

63. Weston, *Romance, Vision, and Satire*, viii.

64. Weston, *Sir Gawain [...] in Modern Prose*, xi.

65. James Yeames, *Sir Gawain and the Green Knight, a Play* (Detroit: The Knights of King Arthur, 1911).

66. Weston, *Two Old English Metrical Romances*.

67. Weston, *Sir Gawain at the Grail Castle*, vii.

68. Weston, *Sir Gawain at the Grail Castle*, vii–viii.

69. Weston, *Sir Gawain at the Grail Castle*, x.

70. Weston, *Sir Gawain and the Lady of Lys*, xii.

71. Weston, *Sir Gawain and the Lady of Lys*, xiv–xv.

72. Her Arthurian verse, "Knights of King Arthur's Court," written in 1896, very early in her career, in *The Rose-Tree of Hildesheim* reflects this. Is Perceval, she asks, the one "of the heroes, among them all, / [who] shall lift up a fearless head, / And walk the pavement of Heaven's High Hall / With unashamèd tread?"; "Knights of King Arthur's Court," in Jessie L. Weston, *The Rose-Tree of Hildesheim, and Other Poems* (London: David Nutt, 1896), 50.

73. Weston, *Parzival: A Knightly Epic*, xiii.

74. Weston, *The Legend of Sir Gawain*, 11.

75. Weston, *The Legend of Sir Gawain*, 3, 6.

76. Jessie L. Weston, "Gawain," *Encyclopaedia Britannica* (1911); Weston, *The Legend of Sir Gawain*, 45. B. J. Whiting was particularly opposed to this interpretation; Whiting, "Gawain," 60. Weston had supplemented this argument by quoting from her own poetry – declaring that Gawain resides "In the Maidens' Isle for aye" – on the title page of *The Legend of Sir Gawain*. The line between scholarship and re-creation was not a clearly defined one for Weston.

77. Weston, *The Legend of Sir Gawain*, 109–10.

78. Weston, *The Legend of Sir Gawain*, 13.

79. Weston, *The Legend of Sir Gawain*, 42.

80. Weston, *The Legend of Sir Gawain*, 44–45.

81. Weston, *The Legend of Sir Gawain*, 111.

82. W. P. Ker, "The Legend of Sir Gawain," *Folklore* 9 (1898): 265–71 (265–66). Ker also warns that the literature should not be used "for pure folklore without scrutiny of their literary methods" (267).

83. Weston, *The Legend of Sir Perceval*, I:171.

84. Weston, *The Legend of Sir Gawain*, 8.

85. Grayson, "In Quest of Jessie Weston," 36.

86. Weston, *The Legend of Sir Perceval*, I:330.

87. Weston, *The Legend of Sir Perceval*, I:332.

88. For more on these disputes, see Grayson, "In Quest of Jessie Weston," 10–14.

89. Weston, *The Legend of Sir Perceval*, I:178.

90. Weston, *The Legend of Sir Perceval*, I:183.

91. Weston, *The Legend of Sir Perceval*, I:286.

92. Weston, *Sir Gawain and the Lady of Lys*, xii.

93. According to the journal *Folklore*, in which the paper was published, the reading was not attended by Alfred Nutt, as stated in Grayson, "In Quest of Jessie Weston," 62; "Minutes of Meetings," *Folklore* 18 (1907): 1–5 (4). His comments on the paper were read aloud.

94. Jessie L. Weston, "The Grail and the Rites of Adonis," *Folklore* 18 (1907): 283–305 (284).

95. Jessie L. Weston, *The Quest of the Holy Grail* (London: G. Bell, 1913), 52–53.

96. Grayson, "In Quest of Jessie Weston," 11.

97. Jessie L. Weston, "Arthur"; "Arthurian Legend"; "The Holy Grail"; "Guinevere"; "Lancelot"; "Sir Thomas Malory"; "Walter Map"; "Merlin"; "Perceval"; "The Round Table"; "Tristan"; "Wolfram von Eschenbach"; "Gawain"; *Encyclopaedia Britannica* (1911). Hyman states that "the unsigned article on Gawain [...] clearly expressed her views in her characteristic language"; Stanley Edgar Hyman, "Jessie Weston and the Forest of Broceliande," *Centennial Review* 9 (1966): 509–21 (513). As in Weston's signed entries, the author of "Gawain" cites Weston's work first and foremost in the references and does not refer to Weston in the third person in the article.

98. "Gawain," *Encyclopaedia Britannica*, 539–40.

99. Weston, "Gawain." In *The Squire's Tale*, Chaucer refers to "That Gawayn, with his olde curteisye, / Though he were comen ayeyn out of Fairye"; Geoffrey Chaucer, "The Squire's Tale," in *The Riverside Chaucer*, ed. Larry D. Benson (Oxford: Oxford University Press, 1987), 169–77 (170), lines 95–96.

100. Weston, "Alfred Nutt," 512. Weston, *Sir Gawain at the Grail Castle*, xvi.

101. C. S. Lewis, "The Anthropological Approach," in *English and Medieval Studies Presented to J. R. R. Tolkien on the Occasion of His Seventieth Birthday*, ed. Norman Davis and C. L. Wrenn (London: Allen & Unwin, 1962), 219–30 (219).

102. Lewis, "The Anthropological Approach," 223.

103. Weston, *The Legend of Sir Perceval*, I:336.

104. Weston, *The Legend of Sir Perceval*, I:335.

105. Weston, *The Legend of Sir Perceval*, I:328.

106. Weston, "The Grail and the Rites of Adonis," 284–85.

107. Weston, *The Legend of Sir Perceval*, I:vi.

108. Weston, *The Legend of Sir Perceval*, I:336.

109. This desire is also evident in Weston's fictional writings: Jessie L. Weston, "The Ruined Temple," *Quest* 8 (1916): 127–39; Jessie L. Weston, "Debout, Les Morts! A Legend of the Pyrenees," *Quest* 9 (1918): 297–308.

The Cinematic Sign of the Grail

J. Rubén Valdés Miyares

Introduction

One of the greatest challenges in modernizing medieval romances has been to represent the elusive image of the grail in film. From the earliest narratives the grail has been open to multiple significations. Thus, its Christian significance, which eventually turned it into the legendary Holy Grail, is not self-evident in the earliest surviving accounts, such as Chrétien de Troyes' *Le Conte du Graal* or the anonymous *Peredur* from Wales. In those narratives it took different forms, ranging from a severed head or a stone, to a dish or a chalice, so that "the history of both the representation and identification of the Grail was far less iconic than our contemporary perception of it."[1] Modern cinema inherited the grail story heavily marked by the Christian legend of Joseph of Arimathea, which originated in Robert de Boron's thirteenth-century text *Joseph*, was vastly developed in the Arthurian Vulgate cycle, and was consecrated within English culture by Thomas Malory. While a new focus on the iconic nature of the grail appears in nineteenth-century painting,[2] the story itself underwent no essential transformation until it reached the silver screen,[3] which makes the grail a privileged motif for a case study of medievalism in cinema. Ultimately drawing on Peircean semiotics,[4] I propose to trace the ways in which various movies have adapted the medieval symbol to their own iconic purposes, or failed significantly to do so.

The Radiant Grail of the Seventh Art

The medieval story of the quest for the Holy Grail appealed to film-makers from the very inception of cinematic art. But the ventures resulting from this interest often failed to gain the popular or critical acclaim they sought. The oldest known film on the subject, and the first example of Arthurian cinema as a whole, was a version of Wagner's opera *Parsifal* that was commissioned by Thomas Edison from Edwin S. Porter in 1904. The movie fell far short of the opera's popularity at the Metropolitan, but that did not deter later film productions of the work, including H. J. Syberberg's 1982 German *Parsifal*. This extraordinarily innovative version does not present the rise of a glowing Holy Grail at its finale, but rather the wound of a swan, suggesting Parsifal's sense of guilt. The swan-wound image is reached through a Grail Castle with a hall of flags, including banners with a swastika, a white crucifix, a black iron-cross, and a white dove, pointing to the polysemic range acquired by the grail in the course of time. However, this capacity of the grail to present itself from multiple perspectives, which, as Roberta Davidson explains, makes it a perfect example of a metaimage,[5] was not often exploited in earlier films.

In the early days of cinema, representations of the grail tended to draw on images from the pictorial arts. In 1915 D. W. Griffith planned to make a picture called *The Quest of the Holy Grail* based on the series of grail murals by Edward Austin Abbey in the Boston Public Library, a series that had in turn been partly inspired by Porter's *Parsifal*. But Griffith's project was shelved, and an attempt to revive it after the Great War did not come to fruition. Nevertheless, its visual source suggests that, like Porter, Griffith would have lit up the grail to signal its miraculous nature and to fascinate viewers with its power in what amounts to very much of an index for the illusory power of cinema itself.[6] Cinema's dramatic advantage over painting was that the grail could very literally sparkle with light in a darkened theatre, though even as this interpretation of the grail would make it more manifest, it would also make it less meaningful.

There is a trace of this visual notion when a hovering and translucent Holy Grail turns up at the end of Richard Thorpe's *Knights of the Round Table* (1953), the most archetypal classic Hollywood production on the subject. The image of the grail is ultimately just the icing on top of this colorful costume drama and has little narrative significance beyond a token of conventional Christian belief in an afterlife, for, as in Joshua Logan's musical *Camelot* (1967), the movie's focus is almost exclusively on the Arthur-Guinevere-Lancelot love triangle. Indeed, across all pre-1970 American films, which had inherited from modern painting a stress on the iconic power of the grail, the grail legend tends to dwindle in symbolic significance.

The Grail Deconstructed

Some European film-makers were more daring in their representation of the grail. In Robert Bresson's *Lancelot du Lac* (1974), which was originally titled *Le Graal*, the grail is conspicuous in its absence, as the action takes place when the knights are back from their failed quests and begin destroying one another. The plot plays upon the resonance of the grail as signifier, much as the film uses strong sounds as a device to stress the action off-camera. In Peircean terms, it plays upon the iconic value of names and sounds, rather than their symbolism.

Even more influenced by "the politics of reflexivity,"[7] *Monty Python and the Holy Grail* (released in 1975) takes issue with the emphasis that Bresson laid on off-camera sounds, such as the clanking of armor, the clopping of hoof-beats, and the whinnying of horses. By, for example, explicitly substituting the sound of clapping coconut shells for the sound of pounding hooves, it becomes a thorough and parodic deconstruction of Arthurian realism in film, while also restoring some rare details from the medieval stories, such as the contrived theatricality of romance settings. Once again the purely iconic sign replaces symbolic values. Indeed, in this film, the grail itself is but a cartoon image, and so is God, who appears (in a most unmedieval way) personally to set the knights on the quest.

By contrast, Eric Rohmer's *Perceval le Gallois* (1978) has often been regarded as the most accurate rendering of a medieval romance text, though Rohmer makes his Christian belief a great deal more explicit than Chrétien de Troyes did in *The Story of the Grail*. As in the medieval story, the hero sees the grail carried in procession at the Fisher King's castle, but fails to understand it at first. However, Rohmer finally has Perceval turned into a Christ-figure and crucified in a passion play that was not in Chrétien's text. Rohmer's overdetermination of Christian symbolism actually results in stressing the iconicity of the film's medieval iconography, particularly the image of a Perceval who becomes a Christ-image.

John Boorman's *Excalibur* (1981) implies a further reversal of the treatment of the grail, as it tries to strip it of Christian meaning, chiefly by resorting to Frazerian anthropology via Jessie Weston's *From Ritual to Romance*. Yet the icon of the chalice, as well as references to rebirth and to emptiness of the soul, makes Christianity inescapable. The symbolism of Christian iconography, providing "hints we can hardly ignore,"[8] prevails over this attempt to deconstruct its meaning, particularly because, despite the film's claims to be set in "the Dark Ages" (with forests instead of churches, and druids instead of priests), its medieval Christian atmosphere (knights in heavy armor, tournaments, and chalices) is evident. In his characteristic conflation of various figures and images (Perceval and Galahad, Morgan and Morgause, Lancelot/Guinevere/Arthur and Tristan/Isolde/Mark love triangles, the Wasteland and Arthur's kingdom, etc.), Boorman ends up identifying Arthur with the grail, which indeed might involve "expanding the *Arthurian* legend at the expense of the *Grail* legend," as Norris J. Lacy concludes in an influential essay,[9] but, particularly when the grail becomes Arthur himself in his shiny armor, also subsumes the king's significance under the potent icon.

Not all films about the grail, however, have a medieval or Arthurian setting, a fact that involves the controversial questions of genre,[10] on the one hand, and of the boundaries of medievalism, on the other. Grail films might be expected to be an offshoot of Arthurian films, which are themselves a subgenre within medieval films. Yet at least one important grail film does not have an obvious medieval setting. The title of Terry Gilliam's *The Fisher King* (1991) makes it avowedly a grail film, though it also blends Quixotic elements with a touch of Collodi's *Pinocchio* and a New York moral drama in the vein of Oliver Stone's *Wall Street*. The grail actually turns out to be a bowling trophy belonging to a billionaire living in a New York mansion that resembles a castle, and it is in the schizoid mind of a former medievalist, Parry, that it becomes the Holy Grail, after his friend Jack (the former wounded Fisher King, now becoming the Galahad of this quest) gets it for him as a token of friendly love and loyalty that will heal him. Thus, as an indexical object and an icon, the grail is, in itself, quite irrelevant. It is its symbolic value that makes it a sign. Besides, the film contains a more poignant allusion to the grail legend in the recurrent hallucination that Parry has of a Red Knight hunting him through the city. This floating horseman spouting balls of fire and with sprays of red barbs and stalks is a reflection in Parry's deranged mind of his wife's head exploding before his eyes (she was shot by a depressed caller to Jack's radio talk-show who mistakenly took some of Jack's sarcastic advice seriously), a haunting image that invokes an episode from the thirteenth-century Welsh *Mabinogion* in which Peredur sees not a chalice but a man's head surrounded by a profusion of blood and carried on a salver by two maidens. Having deconstructed the medieval/Arthurian film while participating in the Monty Python troupe, Gilliam proves in *The Fisher King*, through Richard LaGravenese's screenplay, that some of the most medieval cinematic grail stories are not set in the Middle Ages (and perhaps *cannot* possibly be) if the grail symbol is to transcend its iconicity. Furthermore, as if to enhance the symbolic complexity of the grail, *The Fisher King* contains a third possible allusion to it: the cup with which Sid, the crippled Vietnam veteran played by Tom Waits, is begging for alms at Grand Central Station. As suggested by the lecture Parry gives his friend Jack while they lie in Central Park's Sheep's Meadow, a simple paper cup, which in this case may be construed as standing for the City's moral conscience, can become the Holy Grail if it is accompanied by an appropriate charitable gesture, such as the healing sip of water that the despairing Fisher King receives on his bedside from a compassionate fool.[11]

The Sword as Grail

While the films discussed in the previous section experiment with the representation of the grail icon and its indexical and symbolic connotations, many other Arthurian films replace the complex sign of the grail with more accessible symbols such as the Sword of Power. This is a decidedly modern trend, for though there are "Books of the Grail" in the medieval sources, there are no works devoted solely to the Sword until comparatively recent Arthurian fiction and film. In the 1949 television production *The Adventures of Sir Galahad*, the medieval knight's exploits revolve around Excalibur. In 1963, Disney's *Sword in the Stone* set an obvious precedent for many other cartoons, such as Warner Brothers' *Quest for Camelot* (1998) and Luc Besson's *Arthur and the Invisibles* (2006), whose only unequivocal Arthurian references are the hero's name and his pulling of the sword.[12] And Boorman's highlighting of the sword *Excalibur* helped fuel a similar trend in live-action movies, though many of these, such as Jerry Bruckheimer's *King Arthur* (2004), Doug Lefler's *The Last Legion* (2007), and Chad Burns' *Pendragon: Sword of His Father* (2008), evade the issue of the grail altogether and focus on the youthful ascent of the epic hero.

Some of these films are undoubtedly influenced by recent literary sources that favor the broad power represented by the sword and give short shrift to the grail quest, such as Hal Foster's comic-strip *Prince Valiant* (Volume VII, 1959–62). As St. Patrick explains to the prince, the grail is a symbol of faith, courage, and hope, but those knights who go on the Quest abandon the Round Table, so it is King Arthur's responsibility to either save the knightly brotherhood or support the symbol.[13] Of course, the prince makes sure that Arthur forgets the grail and saves the Round Table. Thus, the threat to order that the grail involves is not just political but also symbolic, in the sphere of signification. Indeed, it has been argued that in Malory's narrative, the grail "is also the 'anamorphic' blot that remains outside of symbolization ['ther was none myghte see hit'], [...] bringing about the dismemberment of both human bodies and ultimately the body politic."[14] And, not surprisingly, none of *Prince Valiant*'s film versions deals with the grail at all.

The grail also tends to be replaced by the sword in films that, though science fiction with interplanetary settings, are clearly laden with Arthurian motifs of knighthood, questing, magic, and sword-fighting, such as the *Star Wars* saga and the television cartoon series *The Visionaries: Knights of the Magical Sword* (1987). Indeed, with the arguable exception of David Wu's TV mini-series *Merlin's Apprentice: The Search for the Holy Grail* (2006) (where the grail, a glowing chalice, is able to not only execute straightforward justice by pulverizing a villain, but also resurrect the people of Camelot and their enemies after the final battle), the grail as a symbol of redemption has almost entirely disappeared from film, especially movies for juvenile audiences, and has often been replaced by a sword standing for self-righteous power and the knightly brotherhood's unity: a unity of meaning that the grail sign stubbornly refuses to grant.[15]

The Grail as Truth

Meanwhile, the grail has staged a comeback in some action movies and thrillers that have capitalized on the analogy between the Quest for the Holy Grail and detective stories with historical and magical ingredients. Steven Spielberg ventured into it with the first Indiana Jones picture, *Raiders of the Lost Ark* (1981), where the Ark supposedly shares the Holy Grail's ability to grant divine power. Spielberg then replaced the Ark with the grail itself in *Indiana Jones and the Last Crusade* (1989), where Indiana once again faces the Nazis trying to get hold of an object that would decisively aid their struggle for world domination. In both cases Excalibur might have been a more fitting symbol of power.[16]

While the grail's symbolic aspect appears to be replaced by the Sword of Power in some films, in others the sign of the grail remains significant as an icon of mystical utopia, and an index of the alterity of the medieval content that the film mediates. This medieval content is often represented by a written source, which in turn may reveal the true message of the Grail. Richard H. Osberg and Michael E. Crow explain how several films are suggestive of language as an icon: "The representation of words as things, both extradiegetic, in the medium of the film (titles, credits), and diegetic, as props within the film (pages of manuscript, book titles, stone tablets)."[17] That would include the word and the image of the grail-object, as in the cartoons of *Monty Python and the Holy Grail*. It would also include, importantly, "the book of the film" that the Monty Python actors present, the typescript "The Fisher King: A Mythic Journey for Modern Man" by Parry the medievalist in *The Fisher King*, which sounds like the script for the film itself, and acknowledgments of medieval texts by the credits for films like *Knights of the Round Table* and *Excalibur*. *Indiana Jones and the Last Crusade* is very much about the discovery of a true medieval message that the Nazis are trying to appropriate for their propagandistic aims: as Donovan the antiquarian states in the film, "The Nazis want to write themselves into the Grail legend to take on the world." The actual symbolic value of the grail is only just glimpsed in the abyss that opens before Indy as he confuses "j" for "I" in the spelling of God's name, "Iehova," perhaps the abyss of the historical sublime.[18] In Osberg and Crow's structuralist terms, "The loss of the Grail, [is] implicitly the loss of a pre-Babel language in which signifiers and thing signified are one":[19] "a universal language" that D. W. Griffith reportedly hoped film would offer, as "its 'truth' would emerge automatically from the photochemical basis of cinematic representation."[20] In other words, the cinematic sign would be a true index of the real,[21] and the grail would be a direct symbol of truth itself, written univocally in history and in the film's narrative.[22] Indy's final challenge, after learning about humility, knowledge (of God's name), and faith, is to pick out the correct Grail from dozens of candidates, for only one of them is true.[23]

The illusion of an enlightened discovery of the true facts, which is present in *Indiana Jones and the Last Crusade*,[24] is reinforced in perhaps the most recent grail-film of importance, Ron Howard's *The Da Vinci Code* (2006). But while the former is among those films staging the quest for a true spirituality of medieval origins, the latter denounces medieval Christianity for conspiring to obscure the grail's true meaning. Howard's film is an adaptation of Dan Brown's bestselling book of the same name, which defines the Holy Grail in the words of the heroine's grandmother as "simply a grand idea [...], a glorious unattainable treasure that somehow, even in today's world of chaos, inspires us":[25] indeed, as Baelo Allué points out, "In this sentence the whole idea and effect of *The Da Vinci Code* is summarized: the Holy Grail is a grand narrative, a conspiracy that reassures us and that provides an all-encompassing explanation for events."[26] The grail is finally identified with Mary Magdalene's tomb, yet the key iconic visualization of the grail occurs in the film when its V-shape is discovered in the background space between the figures of Christ and "Mary" (the feminine-looking disciple whom tradition assumes to be John) in Leonardo da Vinci's painting *The Last Supper*. Far from being the conventional glowing chalice, it is formed by the space between two bodies,[27] and interpreted as a symbol of the "sacred feminine." The stylization is similar to the sublimated grail image in Denis Llorca's *Les Chevaliers de la table ronde* (1990), "constantly underlined by empty circles as abstract figures of the void," particularly in the "recurrent motif of the cupped hands [of women] holding nothing."[28] Unlike Llorca's subtle geometrical evocations, however, Howard's film is bent on disclosing the ultimate meaning of the grail.

Through a plot blaming the Catholic Church for a millennial conspiracy to hide the truth, the film and Dan Brown's novel interrelate elements from two distinct versions of the grail legend that gained increasing acceptance in the twentieth century: on the one hand, the legend of Mary Magdalene's marriage to Christ and of their descendants bearing the true blood of Christ as symbolized by the grail, and, on the other hand, the matriarchal subtext that gives women the leading role in the Arthurian story. The latter is particularly relevant in the development of the grail story, since an emphasis on the sacred feminine counteracts the general trend of replacing the Holy Grail with the Holy Sword, possibly a reflection of deeply-ingrained phallocentrism in cinema.[29] It is remarkable, for example, how the TV mini-series *The Mists of Avalon*, in adapting Marion Zimmer Bradley's novel about the Arthurian legend from the point of view of the sacred feminine, deletes the very important passages dealing with the grail in the novel, and thereby gives greater prominence to the sword, and confirms the suppression of the feminine grail suggested by Dan Brown's novel and other books.[30] Is the role of women as grail-bearers (confirmed by medieval French romances) the whole truth about it?[31] Again, the nature of that truth is nicely represented by transforming a space into an iconic sign and then investing it with symbolic meaning, which is what Brown's Robert Langdon, a professor of religious symbology turned detective, does with Leonardo's painting. The process has been repeated at different historical moments, with various results,[32] but what prevails in cinema grails, as shall be argued in the next section, is the icon, rather than the symbol or its indexical association with the real.

The Grail as a Cinematic Sign

The cinematic image shares with the grail a fundamental polysemy. While many film versions of the legend of King Arthur and the Knights of the Round Table avoid the key medieval episode of the quest for the Holy Grail altogether, or replace its functional significance with the Sword of Power, many others have attempted to translate it to the medium. In such a translation, as can be expected from an audio-visual art like cinema, the sign of the grail loses much of the symbolic charge of meanings it has in written stories. The grail's sheer iconicity is stressed, which is further strengthened by the lack of sound and movement that characterizes the grail as a material object.[33] The classic Christian image of a glowing chalice remains relatively open to interpretation, depending on various plot readings and different audiences. Monty Python suggested its one-dimensional nature by showing it as a cartoon picture, and Gilliam's *The Fisher King*, while also emphasizing the importance of the visual medium in its plot, goes to the opposite extreme of complexity by splitting its representation between an exploding head in the form of a red knight symbolizing psychic trauma, and a simple sports trophy. Yet this is just one *possible* reading of *The Fisher King*: let us remember the grail as it is also implied by the cup in which the Vietnam veteran is begging for coins, which the character himself calls "a kind of moral traffic light. Like I'm saying, *Red* – go no further" (that red color recalling once again both the red knight and the blood-splattering head). But it is *The Da Vinci Code* movie that, transferring the idea directly from the novel, has finally exposed the most defining feature of the grail in film, by turning it into a bare V-form in the background of a classic painting, and then investing it with meaning from a feminine subtext of the Arthurian legend that also languished on its margins. Thus, *The Da Vinci Code* endows the grail with an "argument" in the Peircean sense (a sign of "necessary truth" from the point of view of its "interpretant," in this case Dan Brown's novel) that is its latest, though certainly not its *last*, plot. It is the visual (and

Peircean) counterpart of Bresson's (Saussurean) play with the grail signifier. The knightly quest for the grail is an endless pursuit of signs.[34]

Whenever modern film has dared to represent the grail, it has done so by focusing on its iconic nature, undermining the certainty of any symbolic meaning. The words in the film – its script, director's comments, or reputed critics' interpretations – may try to "discipline" the grail's polysemy and anchor its meaning in the way accompanying captions do to photographs, according to Barthes,[35] but this explanation will remain a "punctum," that is, a subjective association investing the image with personal desire.[36] The grail in movies is actually characterized by an excess of iconicity that is specific to the cinematic sign, and that auteurs like Bresson or Syberberg tried to mani- fest.[37] We might try to reduce the quest for the Holy Grail to narrative logic, but it will probably "degenerate" to its first mode of being (in the Peircean sense) and revert to an iconic sign, especially when it comes to representing the grail itself on screen. Film criticism after structuralism has indeed gener- ally stressed the iconic, and the indexical or material in signification, at the expense of narrative.[38] As Johannes Ehrat puts it, "A moving picture offers little to express a rule that would suggest how such a picture must be taken or interpreted. It is a curious look at many objects, which could be many things."[39] We may imagine a person with no acquaintance whatsoever with Christianity or the Holy Grail legend watching its image in a film and trying to figure out what to make of it.[40] It is something of a commonplace that cinema is an iconic art, but the result of this is that, in Ehrat's words, "by virtue of its Iconicity," the cinematic sign always signals in excess, that is, more than any individual film-maker or viewer can see at first. As a result it is quite impossible to invest it with stable symbolic significance or fix any final meaning to it.

Only if the iconicity of film is reduced to narrative content can we inter- pret it at any given time. Ehrat is very explicit about what this entails: "These are the films as they end up in books: conclusively interpreted, temporal structure transformed into a teleological goal. Only at this stage do films have messages or morals. Yet this is no longer the specificity of cinema *in se*." Furthermore, Ehrat adds something he calls "the most Peircean element of Peirce's philosophy, as it were":

At this point, some film theorists might be overcome by the *horror vacui*: How is it possible to theorize about such a fluid, intrinsically vanishing object? If cinema is indeed essentially Iconic, there is no meaning in it that can be generalized into theoretical insights of the kind one finds in books.[41]

This might remind us of the monks in *Monty Python and the Holy Grail* banging their heads on blank writing tablets. Thus, one should be wary of final explanations of the grail image in films. It is its iconic nature that may be clearly noticed, while symbolic values will keep shifting, along with their indexical associations with the real.

Conclusion

Film criticism's focus on the iconic, correlating the Peircean emphasis on our experience of material intensities, stands in converse relation to medieval semiotics, where, it has been argued, there was a "marriage of the rational word (verbal medium) and the emotional image (visual medium)."[42] As first devised by Augustine, medieval sign-theory conceived of "natural signs" all around us in the universe as "a sign of something else which God intends an individual to understand," in contrast to the "conventional signs" of human sign-systems.[43] Those natural signs, in such a view, expressed God's Word, a divine truth that human intelligence must strive to understand.[44] The intellect's eye, therefore, had to turn back from the images or symbolic formations, and contemplate the spiritual realities they signified.[45] Perhaps only Rohmer, among the film-makers considered, would adhere to such an aim, for modern film criticism generally reverses the medieval approach by stressing the visual, iconic materiality of the grail, over its narrative meaning. Yet even Rohmer overdetermines the grail sign through an overt emphasis on the original narrative undermined by an excessive stress on Christian meaning.

Today's medievalism, "the continuing process of creating the Middle Ages,"[46] can be understood as part of the post-modern, self-reflective view of the past as nothing but a history of the present, and truth as context-bound and transient; in other words, as a product of our presentation, representation, and performance of the plots of history.[47] One of its aims, from this perspective, is to probe how far we are able to re-present the medieval idea of truth nowadays. Now, to pose the question in a more tentative way, would our "imaginary Middle Ages"[48] – or, rather, our view of what medieval sign theory was – approve of the standard cinematic image of the grail as a glowing chalice? One answer could be sought through Eco's *The Name of the Rose*, when William of Baskerville cites Hugh of St Victor's commentary on Pseudo-Dionysius the Areopagite to the effect that "the more the simile becomes dissimilar, the more the truth is revealed to us under the guise of horrible and indecorous figures, the less the imagination is sated in carnal enjoyment, and is thus obliged to perceive the mysteries hidden under the turpitude of the images."[49] It is an opinion that the villainous blind monk Jorge of Burgos judges to be totally wrong and tries to repress, as he believes that "the man who depicts monsters and portents of nature to reveal the things of God *per speculum et in aenigmate* comes to enjoy the very nature of the monstrosities he creates and to delight in them."[50] When films represent the grail as a beautiful glowing chalice they are true to Jorge's realism; only those very few films that attempt to recover the grotesque aspects of the grail, such as Syberberg's *Parsifal*, Monty Python's cartoon grail, or Gilliam and LaGravenese's exploding head and beggar's cup, do some justice to the view of medieval sign theory we have adopted here, "to turn back once more," in Robert Grosseteste's terms, "from the symbols (*simbola*), as though from images (*ymagines*), by stripping every corporeal formation and figuration from the heavenly substances, and contemplate their simplicity and immateriality."[51] Others, like *The Da Vinci Code*, while remaining valuable experiments in myth-making, reveal more about our own concerns in the twenty-first century – our sense of provisional truth and of the medieval as a source of obscurantist conspiratorial culture – than they do about the medieval grail symbol.

NOTES

1.   Roberta Davidson, "Now You Don't See It, Now You Do: Recognizing the Grail *as* the Grail," *Studies in Medievalism XVIII: Defining Medievalism(s) II*, ed. Karl Fugelso (Cambridge: D. S. Brewer, 2010), 188–202 (188). To mention but two of the many other studies that insist on the various forms the grail adopted in medieval stories, see Dhira B. Mahoney, "Introduction and Comparative Table of Medieval Texts," in *The Grail: A Casebook*, ed. Dhira B. Mahoney (New York: Garland, 2000), 1–99, and María José Álvarez Faedo, "Pompa y ceremonia en el mundo artúrico," *Cuadernos del CEMyR* 17 (December 2009): 11–37.

2.   It is particularly Pre-Raphaelite painters who began to try and suggest the spiritual power of the grail by representing it as a glowing or semi-translucent, hovering chalice. The classic example is James Archer's oil painting *La Mort D'Arthur* (1850). However, as Roberta Davidson reminds us ("Now You Don't," 201, n.1), the most iconic contemporary version of the radiant icon may be M. L. Kirk's 1912 "And Down the Long Beam Stole the Holy Grail."

3.   The most influential literary versions of the Arthuriad before the advent of cinema are Alfred Lord Tennyson's *Idylls of the King* and Mark Twain's *A Connecticut Yankee in King Arthur's Court*. These two works may still be regarded as embodying the two most distinct paradigms of modern interpretation: the romantic and the burlesque. Both approaches, however, also have medieval roots.

4.   It has been argued that Saussure has had more influence than Peirce on film theory: Robert Stam, *Film Theory: An Introduction* (Oxford: Blackwell, 2000), 104. However, several film theories suggest that Peircean semiotics are more capable of accounting for the complexity of the filmic sign. Attempting particularly to overcome Saussurean reductionism and Metz's difficulties with the double articulation of (roughly) expression and sense in film language (Christian Metz, *Film Language: A Semiotics of the Cinema*, trans. Michael Taylor (New York: Oxford University Press, 1974); Stam, *Film Theory*, 112–13), scholars have adopted a Peircean

approach to cinema studies: for instance, Gianfranco Bettetini, *L'indice del realism* (Milan: Bompiani, 1971); Peter Wollen, *Readings and Writings: Semiotic Counter-Strategies* (London: Verso, 1982); Umberto Eco, *Semiotics and the Philosophy of Language* (Bloomington: Indiana University Press, 1984); Gilles Deleuze, *Cinema II: The Time-Image*, trans. Hugh Tomlinson and Robert Galeta (Minneapolis: University of Minnesota Press, 1989); and Johannes Ehrat, *Cinema and Semiotic: Peirce and Film Aesthetics, Narration and Representation* (Toronto: University of Toronto Press, 2005). They take up Peirce's second trichotomy of semiotics, based on the categories of icon, index, and symbol, instead of Saussure's signifier and signified. Peirce's key point is probably a stress on the relational nature of signs: signs do not just replace objects in discourse, what they do is "render inefficient relations efficient": "a sign is something by knowing which we know something more" (Charles S. Peirce, *Collected Papers of Charles Sanders Peirce*, ed. C. Hartshorne, P. Weiss, and A. W. Burks, 8 vols. (Cambridge, MA: Harvard University Press, 1931–58), 8: paragraph 332, from a 1904 letter to Lady Welby). In short, signs establish meaningful relations between things and their linguistic expression.

5.   Davidson uses critical iconology, particularly W. J. T. Mitchell's *Picture Theory* (Chicago: University of Chicago Press, 1994), to conclude that "It is this combination of fascination, mutability, misrecognition, and singularity that places the Grail squarely in the category of a metaimage." "Now You Don't," 192–93.

6.   Nancy Mowll Matthews, *Moving Pictures: American Art and Early Film 1880–1910* (Williamstown, MA: Hudson Hill Press, 2005), 70.

7.   Stam, *Film Theory*, 151–52.

8.   Norris J. Lacy, "Mythopoeia in *Excalibur*," in *Cinema Arthuriana: Twenty Essays*, rev. edn., ed. Kevin J. Harty (Jefferson, NC: McFarland, 2002), 34–43 (39).

9.   Lacy, "Mythopoeia in *Excalibur*," 41.

10.   Stam, *Film Theory*, 14.

11.   Richard LaGravenese, *The Fisher King*, 1990, www.dailyscript.com/scripts/fisher-king_shooting.html (accessed 20 August 2009). Thus, in *The Fisher King*, the play of (mis) recognition that is characteristic of the grail as a metaimage (Davidson, "Now You Don't," 195–96) develops in a remarkable way.

12.   Michael N. Salda, "'What's Up, Duke?' A Brief History of Arthurian Animation," in *King Arthur on Film: New Essays on Arthurian Cinema*, ed. Kevin J. Harty (Jefferson, NC: McFarland & Co., 1999), 203–32.

13.   This modern view might originate in Tennyson's *Idylls of the King 8: The Holy Grail* (1869), lines 319–20 and 308–9, where Arthur implies that "Religion's mysticism distracts from the active quest for social justice." Monica Brzesinski Potkay, *Eternal Chalice: The Grail in Literature and Legend* (Prince Frederick, MD: Recorded Books, LLC, 2006), 29.

14.   Laurie A. Finke and Martin B. Shichtman, *King Arthur and the Myth of History* (Gainesville: University Press of Florida, 2004), 182. See also their "Looking Awry at the Grail: Mourning Becomes Modernity," in Laurie A. Finke and Martin B. Shichtman, *Cinematic Illuminations: The Middle Ages on Film* (Baltimore, MD: Johns Hopkins University Press, 2010), 245–87 (246).

15.   Such modern uses of the sword as an instrument of power and justice in history actually set back the process at work in the medieval *Quest del sant grail*, where Solomon's wife and Perceval's sister re-design the purpose of Galahad's sword to make it spiritual, in "the process of redemption from a fallen state (history) to a sanctified one (eternity)." Michelle

R. Wright, "Designing the End of History in the Arming of Galahad," www.arthuriana.org/access/ASubscribe/wright.html#ftn1 (accessed 19 May 2011).

16. The Danish production *Tempelriddernes skat II* (2007), or *The Lost Treasure of the Knights Templar II*, directed by Giacomo Campeotto, echoes Spielberg's Indiana grail movies: a first part focuses on the Ark, while a second one is on the grail, which is also associated with the Templars. Unlike Spielberg's films, however, Campeotto's do not imply the grail might be used as a weapon, or that it is a symbol of power – the grail is rather a pure index of mystery itself, and the movie mostly consists of detective-like enquiry, as well as chase and combat action, all set in a modern medieval festival.

17. Richard H. Osberg and Michael E. Crow, "Language Then and Language Now in Arthurian Film," in *King Arthur on Film*, 39–66 (47).

18. Provided we interpret that, by spelling the mystery, what Indy is doing is turning myth into narrative history – see Frank R. Ankersmit, *Sublime Historical Experience* (Stanford, CA: Stanford University Press, 2005), especially 364–65.

19. Osberg and Crow, "Language Then and Language Now in Arthurian Film," 59.

20. Miriam Hansen, "Cinema, Language, Film Theory," *Raritan* 4 (1984): 95–108 (100–1).

21. Gianfranco Bettetini, *L'indice del realismo* (Milan: Bompiani, 1971).

22. The quest for a truth that can be definitely discovered was characteristic of the historian's pursuit, approximately from the establishment of academic history in the 1950s to the advent of structuralism and after. Beverley Southgate, *What Is History For?* (London: Routledge, 2005), 14.

23. Semiotics, however, is not about truth, but about signs; in other words, about the material conditions of communication on which truth can be constructed, and the conventions that make meaning possible. Jonathan Culler, *The Pursuit of Signs: Semiotics, Literature, Deconstruction* (London: Routledge & Kegan Paul, 1981), 37.

24. Osberg and Crow, "Language Then and Language Now in Arthurian Film," 48–49.

25. Dan Brown, *The Da Vinci Code* (London: Bantam Press, 2003), 444.

26. Sonia Baelo Allué, "Dan Brown's *The Da Vinci Code*: The Power of a Conspiracy Master Narrative," in *Culture and Power: The Plots of History in Performance*, ed. Rubén Valdés Miyares and Carla Rodríguez González (Newcastle upon Tyne: Cambridge Scholars Publishing, 2008), 246–53 (251).

27. The painting itself is an icon too, and so are the bodies, which form an indexical object, a vessel, to be interpreted within the Christian and Arthurian cultural spaces as a grail symbol. This empty shape formed by the bodies stands for the chalice missing on the table.

28. Sandra Gorgievski, "From Stage to Screen: The Dramatic Compulsion in French Cinema and Denis Llorca's *Les Chevaliers de la table ronde* (1990)," in *Cinema Arthuriana*, 163–76 (172).

29. Laura Mulvey, *Visual and Other Pleasures* (Bloomington: Indiana University Press, 1989).

30. Particularly Michael Baigent, Richard Leigh, and Henry Lincoln, *Holy Blood, Holy Grail* (New York: Dell, 1983).

31. Particularly in *La quest del sant grail* from the thirteenth-century Vulgate Cycle. Cf. the story of Perceval's sister in Malory's *Le Morte Darthur*, Book 17; in Tennyson's *Idylls*,

Book 8; and in Phyllis Ann Karr, "Galahad's Lady," in *Quest for the Holy Grail*, ed. Mike Ashley (London: Raven Books, 1996), 151–77.

32. For example, according to Finke and Shichtman's deconstruction of Bresson's *Lancelot du lac*, "the Grail and Guinevere serve similar structural functions in the film; they are black holes around which the male subject's desire is structured." Finke and Shichtman, "Looking Awry at the Grail," 256.

33. Roger Dawkins, "The Problem of a Material Element in the Cinematic Sign. Deleuze, Metz and Peirce," *Angelaki: Journal of Theoretical Humanities* 8.3 (2003): 155–66.

34. Cf. Culler, *The Pursuit of Signs*, 18–43. I am indebted to Dr Javier García, from the University of Valladolid, who both provided me with the decisive insight into the analogy between the Grail Quest and semiotics (which he had found himself in David Lodge's novel *Small World*), and directed me to Peirce's philosophy. He did so through his lecture "Peirce/Percival/Persee McGarrigle: en busca del Grial. Una aventura por la Semiótica, los libros de caballería y la novela de campus," within the course *Reescrituras literarias y cinematográficas de las leyendas artúricas: caballeros, dragones, magos y hechiceras* (University of Oviedo, Avilés, July 2007). Special thanks are also due to Dr Alvarez Faedo, who directed the course, for creating the right academic setting for that memorable lecture.

35. Roland Barthes, "Rhetoric of the Image," in *Image, Music, Text*, ed. and trans. Stephen Heath (New York: Hill and Wang, 1977), 32–51.

36. Robert Stam, R. Burgoyne, and S. Fitterman-Lewis, *New Vocabularies in Film Semiotics: Structuralism, Post-Structuralism and Beyond* (London: Routledge, 1992), 31.

37. "Bresson, Rohmer, and Syberberg locate modernity's despair in the failure of signification [...]. They leave us with stranded objects, blots that resist symbolization, refuse explanation." Finke and Shichtman, "Looking Awry at the Grail," 286.

38. Precisely "the root of Deleuze's difficulty with Metz lies with the overarching formalism manifest in his emphasis on narrative." Dawkins, "The Problem of a Material Element," 159.

39. Ehrat, *Cinema and Semiotic*, 145.

40. An extreme example could be a silent movie such as Porter's *Parsifal*, but most other films also fail to provide sufficient narrative information to explain the grail, as they generally rely on Western audiences' knowledge of the legend. As a metaimage, the grail actually "destabilizes perspective" (Davidson, "Now You Don't," 192), so that even a privileged, knowledgeable perspective on it will be challenged. Syberberg's *Parsifal* actually deploys Brechtian techniques for alienating his viewers from the beginning of the film, as it "presents the story of Parsifal's youth in dumb show, so that someone unfamiliar with the medieval tale of Parsifal [...] would almost certainly be unable to follow it." Finke and Shichtman, "Looking Awry at the Grail," 279.

41. Ehrat, *Cinema and Semiotic*, 146.

42. Robert J. Blanch, "The Fisher King in Gotham: New Age Spiritualism Meets the Grail Legend," in *King Arthur on Film*, 123–39 (130–31). See also Monica Potkay, "The New Dark Ages of Camille Paglia," *AEstel* 1 (1993): 151–74, http://teachingtolkien.org/McNelis/AEstel/AEstel1/Potkay1.html (accessed 20 August 2009).

43. James J. Murphy, *Rhetoric in the Middle Ages: A History of Rhetorical Theory from St Augustine to the Renaissance* (Berkeley: University of California Press, 1974), 287. Drawing on the work of medieval logicians, Ross G. Arthur sums up medieval sign theory thus: "If we

want to understand any sign or grouping of signs, we must consider not only the meaning in isolation, the meaning in propositional context, and the effect on the mind of an ideal perceiver but also the possibility of various receptions by various actual perceivers." Ross G. Arthur, *Medieval Sign Theory and Sir Gawain and the Green Knight* (Toronto: In Parenthesis Publications, 2002), 16. Hence, medieval sign theory was able to distinguish: *significatio*, or pure signification; *suppositio*, i.e., the uses of a sign, determining which of the alternate meanings is appropriate, so as to avoid *equivocatio*; Truth, i.e., *absolute veritas*, as the object of religious faith; and a fourth dimension, the variance of meanings in a broader social context.

44. Intelligence, as Boethius defined it *(Consolatio Philosophiae*, Book V, Prose 5), is a divine attribute of the human soul; for Peirce, on the other hand, intelligence is a natural tool, a continuation of nature used by human beings in response to the environment, not supernatural. Dawkins, "The Problem of a Material Element," 161. However, Augustine's "natural sign," aside from theology, is not unlike Peirce's sign as "something by knowing which we know something more." This would explain why, from Chrétien de Troyes' Perceval romance to Spielberg's grail films, it does not suffice for the hero to see the grail: it must also be recognized, often by asking the right questions. Davidson, "Now You Don't," 189–90 and 193–200.

45. *Medieval Literary Theory and Criticism c.1100–c.1375*, ed. A. J. Minnis and A. B. Scott with David Wallace (Oxford: Clarendon Press, 1988), 192–93.

46. Cited by Kathleen Verduin, "The Founding and the Founder: Medievalism and the Legacy of Leslie J. Workman," from the Preface of *Studies in Medievalism VIII*, 1996, in *Studies in Medievalism XVII: Defining Medievalism(s)*, ed. Karl Fugelso (Cambridge: D. S. Brewer, 2009), 1 (epigram).

47. Valdés Miyares and Rodríguez González, eds., *Culture and Power*, 20–30.

48. Nickolas Haydock, *Movie Medievalism: The Imaginary Middle Ages* (Jefferson, NC: McFarland, 2008).

49. Umberto Eco, *The Name of the Rose*, trans. W. Weaver (London: Secker and Warburg, 1983), 79.

50. Eco, *The Name of the Rose*, 80. Medieval examples of grotesque representation of the grail (the head in *Peredur* may be one) are comparatively rare too. Umberto Eco, whose *A Theory of Semiotics* (1977) and *Semiotics and the Philosophy of Language* (Bloomington: Indiana University Press, 1984) are still solid starting points into the science of signs, has, in *On Ugliness* (2007), not only sampled the grotesque and related aesthetics at length, but, in *Foucault's Pendulum* (1989), also previously parodied the craze for grail conspiracy theory. Moreover, he has provided a useful list of the meanings and uses of the Middle Ages, in Umberto Eco, "Dreaming of the Middle Ages," in *Travels in Hyperreality*, trans. William Weaver (San Diego, CA: Harcourt, 1983): 61–72, though his typology is very general and cannot possibly account for every variation within each instance of medievalism. Elizabeth Emery, "Medievalism and the Middle Ages," *Studies in Medievalism XVII: Defining Medievalism(s)* (Cambridge: D. S. Brewer, 2009), 77–85 (82).

51. As translated in Minnis and Scott's *Medieval Literary Theory and Criticism*, 192.

Destructive *Dominae*: Women and Vengeance in Medievalist Films

Felice Lifshitz

Introduction: The Vengeful Dominae of Die Nibelungen *(1924) and* Excalibur *(1981)*

The representation of women in twentieth-century medievalist films has largely been ignored in previous scholarship, which has tended "to privilege the masculine experience."[1] I propose here that, in the overall trajectory of medievalist film heroines over the course of the century, the dangerous (even bloodthirsty) *femme fatale* has been a key – albeit rare – character in the cinematic repertoire. She is far less common than various alternative, positively coded, types such as the eager helpmeets and passive beauty queens who assist and inspire heroes such as Robin Hood and El Cid.[2] Nevertheless, violently destructive, vengeful *dominae* (ruling women, or female lords/*domini*) are at the narrative heart of two important medievalist films: *Die Nibelungen* (dir. Fritz Lang, Germany, 1924) and *Excalibur* (dir. John Boorman, UK, 1981).[3] The two films were made many decades apart, in radically different contexts. The appearance of the figure of the destructive *domina* in two such superficially different films indicates that she represents one of the fundamental female types of twentieth-century cinematic medievalism.

The *dominae* of *Die Nibelungen* and *Excalibur* are based on characters in the medieval texts that inspired the films, namely the anonymous Middle High German *Nibelungenlied* (*c.* 1200), witnessed by a number of thirteenth-century manuscripts, each of which contains a slightly different version of the text, and Thomas Malory's Middle English *Morte D'Arthur* (*c.* 1470), one of the first texts ever printed – and consequently, stabilized – in England (by Caxton, in 1485).[4] These popular vernacular narratives represent specific written or literary fixings of stories that had been developing over many centuries, in other written versions as well as in oral tradition. The two late

medieval texts, both of which imagined the political and military compe-
titions of the fifth century, were themselves generated in atmospheres of
intense political controversy: in one case, the years during which the dominance of the Staufer dynasty in the Holy Roman Empire was challenged
by the anti-king Otto of Brunswick (1198–1215), who found widespread
support from Italian cities, German princes, and the papacy; in the other,
the final decades of the Wars of the Roses, which pitted the Lancastrian and
Yorkist dynasties against one another for control of the English crown. The
specific written fixings of the two sets of legends represented the culmination
of centuries of accretion and sedimentation, much of which reflected controversies with gendered dimensions. As noted, both textual fixings included a
number of important negatively charged female characters.

Both the *Nibelungenlied* and *Morte D'Arthur* had been, by 1900, canonized
as classics of (German and English) national literature, and were thus ripe for
anti-feminist exploitation in the cinematic age. That they were selected to
be filmed, when so many other subjects (which could have sent a different
message about women and political power) were not, is significant in and
of itself. However, the histrionically negative characteristics of the medieval
female literary characters were amplified by/for/on the big screen, creating
dominae who would horrify twentieth-century audiences. The re-mediation
(or rendering into the modern cultural format of cinema) of the *Nibelungenlied* and *Morte D'Arthur* as twentieth-century films, in the crucible of
twentieth-century contexts and needs, involved the re-accentuation of both
narratives by filmmakers who inflated female characters from the medieval
texts into monstrous figures of vengeful womanhood.[5]

The key to the power of these virulently misogynist twentieth-century
depictions of medieval literary *dominae* is the fact that the screen villainesses
inhabit a fantasy world. Neither film is set in a particular time. Historical
research had clearly established by the time the films were made that the
depicted events belonged (if anywhere) to the fifth century, and designers
could have recreated a specifically late Roman (or early medieval) world for
the screen; yet both films use sets, costumes, and props that evoke the Middle
Ages in general.[6] As a result of their unmooring from any particular time, the
characters become timeless and therefore eternal. A specific historical figure
who displays stereotypically negative characteristics imputed to women
simply reinforces those stereotypes, but a timeless figure turns a stereotype
into an archetype. Specialists in literature, comparative religion, and cultural
anthropology align such female counter-heroes with the powerful *Magna
Dea*, the Great Mother who is both mother of life and mother of death,
simultaneously nurturer and destroyer.[7] For untrained movie-goers, these
dominae are more likely simply Woman. Audiences hear them roar, and
watch as their rage and ambition destroys civilization.

Yet, this treacherous Woman only made screen appearances at certain times and in certain places, as anti-feminist responses to pro-feminist threats. Medievalist films fed a reactionary twentieth-century fantasy that power in the hands of Woman was power misplaced. This essay explores two examples of that fantasy.

Re-Mediation, Re-Accentuation, and First-Wave Feminism:
The Nibelungenlied *becomes* Die Nibelungen

There are two major female characters in the Middle High German poem, the *Nibelungenlied*: Queen Brunhild of Iceland and Princess Kriemhild of Burgundy. One scholar argues that the two women effectively merge into one (literal) *femme fatale*, "lethal on every level […] the agent of destruction of masculine order in its entirety" ("mortelle à tous les niveaux […] l'agent de destruction de l'ordre masculin dans son ensemble").[8] The duplicitous defeat of the fiercely independent Brunhild by Siegfried (with the help of magical objects), which results in her being forced to marry – and become silently subservient to – King Gunther of Burgundy, is an important aspect of the overall gendered message of the poem. But most of the discussion of women and gender in the poem centers on the figure of Kriemhild, whom many consider to be the most important character of the poem, which begins by introducing her and ends with her death.[9]

Widowed by Hagen's murder of Siegfried (made possible only by her own foolish betrayal of the secret of his vulnerable spot), Kriemhild's thirst for bloody revenge drives the action of most of the narrative, through a cataclysmic denouement that not only destroys the army of Burgundy but also leaves the kingdom of Attila the Hun, her second husband (known as Etzel in the poem), in flaming ruins. So described, the medieval literary Kriemhild is clearly already a less than completely sympathetic figure, and it is true that many anti-female elements were already present in the medieval literary tradition. However, the medieval situation – unlike the modern one – was more complicated than is implied by that skeletal plot summary, or by the pointedly monstrous character of the cinematic Kriemhild, who was described in Anglophone countries on advertising posters and souvenir programs for part II of the duology ("Kriemhilds Rache" or "Kriemhild's Revenge," part I having been focused on "Siegfried") as "She-Devil."[10]

As noted, the manuscripts of *Das Nibelungenlied* contain variant versions of the poem. The two most important copies (manuscripts B and C) diverge from one another primarily over the extent to which Kriemhild is villainized and vilified. The *C text, and all the manuscripts in that tradition, have been read as sympathetic to Kriemhild, indeed as so pro-feminist that one scholar has even attributed the written fixing of this version to a nun.[11]

Furthermore, there are additional medieval literary texts that rework the Nibelungen material, sometimes explicitly in order to defend Kriemhild (as in the various versions of the *Nibelungenklage*, which accompanies the *Nibelugenlied* in all the significant extant manuscripts of the poem), sometimes in order to revisit her seemingly unmanageable, stubborn character and show how (in the classic "taming of the shrew" emplotment) she was able to change for the better.[12] Even the most negative medieval take on Kriemhild, that of the *B version of the *Nibelungenlied* proper, recognizes the internal logic (indeed, almost the necessity) of her quest for vengeance (understood as justice).[13] Finally, careful attention to the scribal interventions in the text by the redactor of the *B version, that is where he breaks into the narrative with epic anticipations, reflections, and outright commentary, has led one scholar to conclude that even this version explicitly renders Hagen responsible for the entire tragedy.[14] It is a measure of the complexity of the medieval Kriemhild that the thirteenth-century author of a model sermon "on the perfidy of female power," whose main argument was that "powerful women are invariably sinful, in that they bring about the downfall of men at all times and in all places," specifically cautioned preachers against using Kriemhild to exemplify this danger, for she did not possess any generally accepted discursive meaning as evil.[15]

Centuries of cultural dynamics turned the multi-vocality of the thirteenth-century Kriemhild into a modern monotone.[16] Only the *Nibelungenlied* proper (not the various other literary works referenced above) drew the spotlight of canonization as *the* German national epic, while the most anti-Kriemhild version of the epic (the *B recension) was pegged – beginning in 1856 – as the genuine expression of the poetic tradition.[17] The poem was almost unimaginably popular during the Romantic era of the nineteenth century; for instance, no other work in all of world literature was more frequently depicted in visual arts of the day, and only the Bible even came close.[18] The published edition of this version became the standard form of the text, running through at least twenty-two re-editions, and serving as the basis of all translations into modern languages.[19] The "She-Devil" of the American film poster translated the Middle High German "*vâlendinne*," found in the *B recension. This was rendered as "Teufelsweibe" in the modern German of Karl Simrock, whose 1827 verse-translation was largely responsible for the popularity of the epic in nineteenth- and early twentieth-century Germany, and remained the standard modern German version of the tale for well over a century.[20] Perhaps the most widely used modern English translation, by Hatto, also renders "*vâlendinne*" as "she-devil."[21]

Karl Simrock's Kriemhild was effectively the only version of the woman that was available to German-language filmmakers during the early decades of the twentieth century. Indeed, through the end of that century scholarship continued to comment on the epic based almost exclusively on the *B manuscript, and that scholarship has recognized that a hostility to political power in the hands of women ("a sinister form of government") was a central feature of the epic in this widely-read form.[22] The scribe-author of this recension endorsed Siegfried's use of unfair (that is magical) aid to physically subdue Brunhild (when her husband Gunther could not), for otherwise women everywhere might have refused to be subjugated by men; all the main male characters at the Burgundian court explicitly agree (with each other and presumably with the male poet) that it is wrong – indeed, diabolically, hellishly so – for women to be independent or uppity.[23] Events prove them right, for when Kriemhild becomes Etzel's queen she perverts the natural order and gradually appropriates all of his enormous political power for herself, so that his followers act upon *her* orders.[24] "The Huns, indeed, are ruled by a Burgundian queen, not a Hunnish king."[25] This results in catastrophe.

It is, in the first instance, significant that this anti-feminist epic was the material that German filmmakers chose to bring to the screen, during the 1920s, as their instrument for an ambitious project to challenge the dominance of Hollywood, create a German-made international blockbuster, and provide the nation with a great epic film.[26] But additional choices were made in the process of filming the *Nibelungenlied*-B* version of the text. The twentieth century did not simply passively inherit anti-feminist imagery, and the 1924 film did not simply render the *B text of the poem; it developed that imagery, and added new dimensions to the plot, to meet new pro-feminist challenges.

There have always been ambitious women among the elites of Europe, women who either in fact exercised or attempted to gain real political power. Memories of a number of those historical *dominae* even form part of the complex sediment of the *Nibelungenlied* (in all its forms). For instance, it may not be pure coincidence that the downfall of Etzel's Hun Empire in the poem results from his ill-fated marriage with a Christian woman from more developed lands to the west, for the downfall of the empire of the historical Attila the Hun resulted from such an endeavor; his intended bride was the imperial Princess Honoria, sister of Emperor Valentinian III, who proposed to, and contracted a marriage alliance with, Attila in 449 in the hopes that the two of them could depose her brother and rule in his stead. Attila's subsequent (451) attack on Roman imperial forces (after many years of fighting in imperial service) ended in a massive defeat (his first) and inaugurated a downward spiral that would soon lead to his death, and the collapse of the Hun polity.[27] And there was a historical Queen Brunhild, a Visigothic princess who came to rule Burgundy and Austrasia for decades during the late sixth and early seventh centuries, dominating husband, children, and grandchildren. According to Joan Ferrante, "She is certainly a model for the figure of Brunhild, a powerful queen in her own right in Germanic and Norse legend, lover of Siegfried, and wife of a Burgundian king. Traces of that tradition are found in the Nibelungenlied."[28] Finally, although it would surely be mistaken to read the *Nibelungenlied* as a *roman à clef* in which Kriemhild symbolized either of the successive Staufer empresses ruling at Worms (namely Beatrice of Burgundy and Constance of Sicily), both played significant roles in the imperial policies that alienated ever-increasing numbers of German princes in the closing decades of the twelfth century and led to the 1198 election of Otto of Brunswick as anti-king, in opposition to Constance's son and Beatrice's grandson Philip of Swabia; these women must have been in the poet's mind *circa* 1200 as he explored the trials and tribulations of a Burgundian dynasty undergoing collapse in the literary realm, knowing full well that his own ruling dynasty was fighting to avert a similar fate.[29] But the European 1920s were qualitatively as well as quantitatively different from the lifetimes of Honoria and Brunhild and Beatrice and Constance, for in those years the claims to political power by women were not confined to restricted elites at the aristocratic and royal and imperial levels. It was the period of (so-called) First-Wave Feminism in Europe and North America, focused primarily on gaining the right to vote for women as a class.

In the German Weimar Republic, founded in 1918, large numbers of women of all social levels demanded access to political power, as well as other forms of social and economic autonomy. The angry forces of anti-feminist conservatism responded with heavy ammunition in an attempt "to reassert male control, most prominently in the retrenchment of the ideology of motherhood and in new forms of misogyny."[30] *Die Nibelungen* was part of this anti-feminist reaction, featuring a crazed "She-Devil" who, in accordance with the B* version of the medieval poem, deliberately sacrificed her son by Etzel, Ortliep, in order to provoke the Huns to attack the Burgundians.[31] The character of Kriemhild in 1924's *Die Nibelungen* is one of the many "weibliche Stahlgestalten" (female steel-figures) created by screenwriter Thea von Harbou under the impetus of the Great War: "hardened, cold-blooded, ready to kill and to die" ("gestählt, kaltblütig, bereit zu töten und zu sterben").[32]

The paradoxical subjectivity of Thea Gabriele von Harbou (27 December 1888–1 July 1954), who wrote the screenplay for not only *Die Nibelungen* but also dozens of other German films of the first half of the twentieth century, has not gone unnoticed: she was an active and prolific author and filmmaker, who imagined herself above all as a servant of State and Fatherland, while simultaneously opposing attempts by (other) women to involve themselves in spheres (such as politics) in which they did not (in her view) belong.[33]

A Prussian aristocrat who "subscribed to the Kaiser's dictum that German women should serve 'children, church and kitchen' [Kinder, Kirche, und Küche]," her conservative nationalist idealism led her to join the National Socialist party even before Hitler came to power in 1933, attracted as she was by "their call for a return to traditional values."[34] Thus, the person who created the cinematic Kriemhild, and the cinematic Brunhild, did so in the midst of a lively national conversation on the political role of women, a conversation precipitated in large part by the introduction of female suffrage at the creation of the Republic in 1918. In this conversation, many women (above all perhaps the ones likely to flock to the cinema to view a melodramatic screen version of the German national epic) stood firmly with von Harbou on the side of conservatism and nationalism, and in opposition to the participation of women in politics.[35]

Fritz Lang, director of *Die Nibelungen* and husband of von Harbou, is widely considered to be one of the greatest filmmakers of all time. Under the weight of the great-man approach to film history, there is a tendency for von Harbou's leading role in their multiple collaborations (indeed, sometimes for her very presence) to be forgotten.[36] In contrast, scholarship on von Harbou has exploited her surviving screenplays and other documentation connected with her massive filmography to reveal how precisely and richly detailed her instructions for the cinematographic realization of her visions already were – down to camera angles, close-ups, and set designs.[37] In so far as there were social or political agendas embedded in and propagated by films such as *Die Nibelungen*, they were largely von Harbou's. The film must be analyzed with her political orientation (and not just Lang's expressionist artistry) firmly in mind. Just as some women in Germany were assertively claiming political rights, and potentially political power, this conservative woman gave her audiences a powerfully anti-feminist film, utilizing medieval material to warn against the dangers of women in power. For the history and gender of medievalism, it is significant that she chose medieval material for conveying her message, for she set in motion a trend that would dominate in German culture through the 1960s and 1970s, which witnessed repeated depictions of Siegfried as an "uncanny glorification of manliness. This is clearly a reaction to the feminist movement [...] [and] a return to familiar means of oppression."[38]

The film *Die Nibelungen* is one of the most important cultural monuments of twentieth-century Germany. A favorite of both Hitler and Goebbels, it played a key role in shaping a Nazi/fascist citizenry, to some extent from its very release but above all from its re-release – with a score from Wagner – in 1933.[39] This reception was completely in keeping with von Harbou's ambitions for the film, as is clear from her numerous publications connected with the movie; these included *Das Nibelungenbuch*, released six

months before the film to create buzz as well as to direct how the film would
be understood.[40] Von Harbou revered the *Nibelungenlied* as the German
national epic, and believed that the German *Volk* (to whom she dedicated
the film in the opening inter-title card) needed exposure to the epic in order
to be whole with and in themselves; unfortunately, given the stresses of
modern life and work, the *Volk* were too exhausted to read the text. Happily,
this Prussian aristocrat came to the rescue, and conveyed the epic to the *Volk*
in a form that required no exertion on their part:

> The Nibelungen-film is intended to serve this very German *Volk* as its
> singer, its story-telling poet of the self. Viewing calmly, the *Volk* should
> accept the gift, and in receiving it, should experience and thus regain
> what is for it – the *Volk* in its entirety – but a dim memory: a hymn
> in celebration of unconditional loyalty.[41]

The figure who embodied "unconditional loyalty," along with many other
precious qualities, was Hagen.[42] The heroic Hagen, on whose superiority all
scholarly specialists working between the mid-nineteenth and mid-twentieth
century agreed, was already being celebrated in the public spaces of modern
Germany, for instance through a 1905 monument erected in his honor in
the Stadtpark Bürgerweide in Worms.[43] When this unassailably upright cinematic hero calls his nemesis, Kriemhild, a "she-devil," there is meant to be no
room for doubt or dispute (as there might have been in the medieval epic,
due to certain comments by the redactor) over who is behaving properly
and who is not:

> Baldly, unabashedly, Kriemhild is transformed from a textbook example
> of a desirable, good object (that is, one who has assumed the proper
> – because properly disempowered – feminine relationship to viewing)
> into a textbook example of a bad object (one whose aspirations to
> authority and control take her far beyond her assigned place).[44]

When the literary Kriemhild was addressed as *vâlandinne* in the medieval
epic, the degree to which the epithet would have been considered apt by
a reader or listener would have been conditioned by their familiarity with
other versions of the character and by the *B scribe's own commentary,
which raised doubts about Hagen's (the speaker's) own moral compass.[45]
When the cinematic Kriemhild was labeled "She-Devil" on a poster, it was
simply a statement of fact, to be passively accepted by an exhausted audience
too busy for independent critique.

The *Volk* accepted von Harbou's gift: high-level government officials
attended the Berlin première, praising the film mightily, and the general

public overwhelmingly chose it in a contemporary survey as the best film of the year.[46] It is likely that the popularity of the film was in part due to the liberties that von Harbou took with the scenario, liberties that rendered the motivations of the characters more accessible to twentieth-century audiences, and thereby increased the relevance of the filmed events to contemporary debates. Von Harbou's most marked re-accentuation as she adapted the *Nibelungenlied* for the screen involved transforming a socio-political struggle between the queens of Burgundy (Brunhild) and the Netherlands (Kriemhild) over wealth, status, and authority into a rivalry between two psycho-pathological types of Woman (Kriemhild the *Bessessene* or one obsessed/possessed by an evil demon, and Brunhild the *Irre* or lunatic) [47] over a man (Siegfried) whom they both loved.[48] Von Harbou's new emplotment was presumably inspired at some level either by the quite different love triangle of Siegfried, Brunhild, and Gutrune (the Kriemhild-equivalent in the Old Norse versions of the material) in Wagner's *Der Ring des Nibelungen* (1876), or by the various Old Norse poems (some of which were used by Wagner) in which Brunhild loves Siegfried.[49] But it must be underlined that the film does not follow Wagner, or any of those Old Norse poems; it is quite simply the (*B version of the) *Nibelungenlied*, with a series of subtle changes designed to turn the dynastic motivations of the leading female characters into emotional and romantic ones. Hatto's introduction to his English translation warns soberly that "it is not permissible to resort to Northern versions of the story in order to show that Brunhild loved Siegfried," but von Harbou had no such scruples when she reduced the complex courtly wrangling of thirteenth-century aristocratic women (which might have been difficult for a 1924 audience to grasp) to a cat fight over a hunk.[50]

The series of changes made by von Harbou to the *Nibelungenlied* poem, necessary to turn the film into a love triangle, may seem small (and to my knowledge they have not been noticed before), but they transform the entire film, particularly as regards the main female characters. Von Harbou's Brunhild is clearly sexually attracted to Siegfried from the moment she lays eyes on him in Iceland, although there is no justification for this in the text of the poem. The autonomy-craving Brunhild of the *Nibelungenlied* is determined to have no husband, yet is forced to marry Gunther. In contrast, the Brunhild of *Die Nibelungen* (for whom eternal autonomy is not an option) desires Siegfried, and is driven insane by jealousy when he marries Kriemhild instead, and she is left with Gunther. In Canto 5, Brunhild watches jealously from a window as Kriemhild and Siegfried discuss (unbeknownst to Brunhild) the armlet that Siegfried stole from Brunhild when he (magically disguised as Gunther) subdued her. This scene is followed by a confrontation between the two queens on the steps of Worms cathedral. The strife between Kriemhild and Brunhild in the poem revolves entirely around the

issue of status; Brunhild is disturbed that Siegfried pays no tribute and does
no service, although – as Brunhild notes – "I heard them both declare – and
Siegfried himself said so – that he was Gunther's vassal, and so I consider
him to be my liegeman."[51] To this the Kriemhild of the poem responds that
Siegfried cannot be a vassal, for "how could my noble brothers have had a
hand in my marrying a liegeman?"[52] In order to put a stop to the endless
back and forth on the same point, Kriemhild eventually (and quite nastily)
tells Brunhild that Siegfried cannot possibly be a vassal because "how could a
vassal's paramour ever wed a king?" She goes on to explain to Brunhild that
"My dear husband Siegfried was the first to enjoy your lovely body, since it
was not my brother who took your maidenhood [...]. Seeing that he is your
vassal, why did you let him love you?"[53]

In the medieval poem, the confrontation between the two queens never
strays from the subject of status. However, in the film, as soon as Kriemhild
reveals the terrible secret to Brunhild, she shifts the discussion onto another
terrain. Instead of it being politically and socially shameful to Brunhild's
honor that she has lain with a man other than her husband (and one she
thinks is of lower rank), it is emotionally and personally painful to Brunhild's
sense of her own attractiveness as a woman that her rapist, Siegfried, did
not really enjoy his sexual interlude with her. Kriemhild, here a bitch who is
clearly defending her man against a sexual rival, tells Brunhild that Siegfried
"disclaimed" her and "threw [her] away" after having his way with her.[54] This
information drives von Harbou's Brunhild insane with rage over the rejection of her charms and beauty (for she has evidently fallen in love with her
rapist), leading her to command Hagen and Gunther explicitly and repeatedly to "kill Siegfried!" Von Harbou's bloodthirsty Brunhild drives Gunther
to repudiate his sworn blood brotherhood with Siegfried, and laughs mania-
cally when she hears that Siegfried is dead, exclaiming "Hail to you, King
Gunther, for the sake of a woman's lie you have slain your most loyal friend."[55]
A cackling and totally crazed Brunhild then haunts the palace in a long black
cape, looking every bit the bat and/or the vampire, until she commits suicide
in the church next to Siegfried's corpse; she could not permit Kriemhild to
possess the man she loved, nor could she herself live without him.[56] Von
Harbou's pathologically evil Brunhild is thus both an accessory to murder
and a suicide, whereas the Brunhild of the medieval poem has nothing to
do with Siegfried's murder (which is entirely Hagen's idea, to avenge the
impugned honor of his liege lady), and simply retreats into the background
of the Worms court, insignificant and silent, once she discovers the truth
about her marriage.[57] In von Harbou's re-accentuation, we see how Hell truly
hath no fury like a woman scorned. The Nibelungen-*B poet *suggests* that the
women are to blame for the ultimate catastrophe ("thanks to the wrangling
of two women, countless warriors met their doom"),[58] but many readers and

listeners apparently thought otherwise.[59] Von Harbou's screenplay makes the guilt of the women undeniable.

In the 1920s Weimer Republic, as many women of all social classes claimed political rights in the modern German public sphere, opponents of this movement – both male and female – used various means to delegitimize their demands. The 1924 film *Die Nibelungen* contributed (intentionally I would argue) to this public debate, by showcasing two emotionally-imbalanced women whose ability to exercise any level of political power ends in cataclysmic disaster. Thea von Harbou's Brunhild and Kriemhild make no true political decisions, but are instead slaves to the affairs of their hearts. The 1924 film goes beyond the thirteenth-century poem in coding females as unsuited for public political life. Their concerns are trivialized, their characters reduced. They deserve no power in the political sphere, but rather treatment in the medical one. They have nothing in common with the ideal woman of Weimar conservatism, for they are indifferent to her core values: Kinder, Kirche, and Küche. Kriemhild sacrifices her child while Brunhild has no children. Kriemhild happily, and with no comment on the matter, marries a heathen,[60] while Brunhild commits suicide. And neither of these irredeemably emotional, pathological leading women ever gets anywhere near a kitchen.

Re-Mediation, Re-Accentuation, and Second-Wave Feminism:
The Morte D'Arthur *becomes* Excalibur

John Boorman never really wanted to make the film *Excalibur* (1981). His thwarted dream was to bring J. R. R. Tolkien's *Lord of the Rings* to the screen, largely because he relished the technical and technological challenges of rendering Tolkien's magical fantastical world visible for all to see through the use of special effects. When he abandoned the Tolkien project, and settled for an Arthurian tale instead, he was able to apply all the solutions to technical problems over which he had been puzzling for years to *Excalibur*.[61] While fantasy effects preoccupied the director, there is absolutely no evidence that he had any conscious social or political agenda in mind when he, along with co-screenwriter Rospo Pallenberg, began work on *Excalibur*. It is, therefore, all the more significant that the film is so ideologically charged, marked – like *Die Nibelungen* – by the trope of the malevolent *domina*. And *Excalibur* departs even farther from its medieval literary source, in this case Malory's *Morte D'Arthur*, than did von Harbou's screen adaptation of the *Nibelungenlied*; correspondingly more of the anti-feminist imagery of *Excalibur* is therefore owed to its twentieth-century creators. The (unconscious?) misogyny of *Excalibur* is barely mitigated by the fact that (in contrast to *Die Nibelungen*) the evil villainess is defeated in the end, for there is a sense in which hope can always be found in the conclusion of the Arthurian legends. Indeed, one commentator has called the *Nibelungenlied* a warning counterpoint to the "cheerfully-played, optimistically dressed-up, idyllically embellished world of Arthurian epic" ("heiter-verspielte, optimistisch schönende, idyllisch verbrämende Welt arthurischer Epik").[62]

Innumerable medieval literary works in various European languages extol the exploits of King Arthur and/or the knights and ladies associated with his court. The first of many retellings of Arthur's story appears in Geoffrey of Monmouth's (Latin) *History of the Kings of Britain*, written in approximately 1136 in the midst of the civil war/succession crisis unleashed by the competing claims of Stephen of Blois and the Empress Matilda to the Anglo-Norman territorial agglomeration created by William the Conqueror in 1066.[63] As such, "its most overt political agenda is a warning against disunity," and the work in fact seems to have been received by contemporaries as "a unifying contribution to a common insular historical heritage."[64] Geoffrey's description of an ideal court of an ideal king on whose right to the throne all could agree was embroidered and developed in manifold directions over the next three centuries, often by writers who suffered (as he did) from the military disputes endemic to aristocratic dynastic politics. For instance, Sir Thomas Malory's *Le Morte D'Arthur*, which "many consider to be the greatest and most powerful expression of the medieval Arthur legend," emerged from the decades-long political chaos of the Wars of the Roses.[65] It was published in 1485, coinciding with the accession of Henry Tudor to the English throne, the king who united the Red Rose of Lancaster with the White Rose of York, and thus brought harmony to the realm. Filled with hope for an even more harmonious future, Henry named his oldest son, born in September of 1486, Arthur, but the latter died in a 1502 epidemic, and was never to rule.[66]

This theme of a recognized ruler who could bring peace to warring factions was not the only leitmotif that ran through the ever-expanding corpus of medieval Arthurian materials (which, by the late fifteenth century was not a single story but a whole series of tales concerning dozens of characters, all loosely connected through some association with Arthur's court), but it was a very important one from the perspective of gender, for through it all the epitome of the charismatic ruler, whose authority should never be challenged and whose loyalty should never be betrayed, was a male king. Yet, betrayed and challenged he was, above all by women, namely his half-sister Morgan and his wife Guinevere.

Like Kriemhild, the character of Morgan was more complex in her medieval literary environment than one might guess from her screen portrait (as Morgana) in *Excalibur*. Morgan (or Morgan le Fay) figures in multiple tellings of the Matter of Britain dating from the twelfth through the fifteenth century. She began (in another work by Geoffrey of Monmouth, the *Vita*

Merlini) as an entirely positive figure, but declined over the centuries into a mainly treacherous presence, "the most extreme villain of Arthurian romance [...]. Her gradual change [...] indicates the inability of male Arthurian authors to cope with the image of a woman of power in positive terms."[67] But the misogynistic leanings of late-medieval vernacular literature such as *Morte D'Arthur* cannot be blamed for the Morgana of a 1981 film. Boorman, and his co-screenwriter Rospo Pallenberg, could have selected a different medieval version of the Arthurian legend, or they could have let themselves be influenced by any number of sympathetic twentieth-century portraits of Morgan, including in two novels also entitled *Excalibur*.[68] They could even have contented themselves simply with filming Malory, for he at least over-came his anxieties concerning women of power sufficiently to code a number of feminine characteristics and actions (such as reading and enchantment), all crucial to creating meaning in the text, as positive.[69]

In the final analysis, Malory's Morgan was only superficially maleficent; her constant challenging of Arthur and his court proves not entirely mali-cious, when we consider how "the trials she provides Arthur's knights serve to increase their abilities and reputations with successful endurance," and how (at the end of the tale) she is one of the women who takes Arthur away on the barge to Avalon, addressing him in affectionate tones as a cherished brother for whom she will serve as "protectrice and healer," "a curiously suggestive image for a retrospective revision of her acts. Here she addresses Arthur not agonistically, but as a fellow player in a drama that has now concluded."[70] The contrast is stark, and the direction of Boorman's re-accentuation is unambiguous; whereas Malory's "feminine is both life-giving, indeed salvation-giving, and demonic [...], in the film, [Morgana] is the sole cause of the destruction of the civilization of the Round Table."[71]

That there are major plot differences between Malory's *Morte D'Arthur* and Boorman's *Excalibur* has been noticed before.[72] Boorman's changes have the effect of turning the entire film into a duology along the lines of *Die Nibelungen*, the two parts of which could have been entitled "Arthur" and "Morgana's Revenge." But just as Siegfried was not the real hero of *Die Nibelungen*, neither is Arthur the real hero of *Excalibur*. Playing Hagen to Morgana's Kriemhild is Merlin, whose status as the real hero of the film would have been clearer had Boorman been able to use his original and intended title, namely "Merlin Lives!"[73] In the first part of the film, Merlin's magic creates Arthur, by enabling Uther Pendragon to impregnate a rival's wife while disguised as her rightful husband. The film adds to this scenario, taken from Malory, the knowing presence of the girl-child Morgana, who has psychically seen the death of her father in a trap set by Merlin and witnesses the rape of her mother by an evident (to her) imposter. Merlin eventually makes the child born of this union, namely Arthur, into the undisputed (except by Morgana) king, while Morgana devotes her entire life to taking revenge on the two men. She does so, like Kriemhild, in an unlimited primal way; rather than targeting solely those who did her wrong, Morgana plots to destroy civilization itself, and turn the world into a wasteland. As noted, she is defeated in the end by Merlin, after she had temporarily neutralized him through magic.

Boorman's vengeful adult Morgana conflates three female characters from Malory's sprawling plot (that is, Morgause, Nyneve, and Morgan le Fay), and transforms all of their motivations to a single-minded quest for vengeance. Not Nyneve (the principal Lady of the Lake) but Morgana becomes Merlin's sorcerer's apprentice. And the outcome of their lessons is completely transformed. Malory's Merlin becomes, at a certain point, not only "superannuated" but an old fool, lusting (unrequitedly) after Nyneve; using the magic he has taught her, she wards off his advances, and indeed disposes of him permanently, ushering in a "timely and appropriate" "shift of authority to feminine disseminators of enchantment" and herself becoming the "advisor and rescuer of Arthur."[74] Malory's impressive and sympathetic Lady of the Lake is suppressed entirely in *Excalibur*. Instead, Morgana temporarily freezes Merlin as part of her deliberate and evil plot to destroy civilization with her murderous rage. Significantly, she only achieves this temporary victory over Merlin because he is weakened at the key moment by Arthur's renunciation of his sword (Excalibur), which he has left as a sign of his presence between the sleeping post-coital bodies of Guinevere and Lancelot; the sword simultaneously pierced the ground between the lovers and Merlin's back, allowing Morgana to overcome him. Without that stroke of luck, presumably Boorman's enchantress (unlike Malory's) could never have bested a male adversary. And when Boorman's Merlin returns ("Merlin Lives!"), the audience must cheer his defeat of this female would-be usurper, and his transformation of her into a shriveled hag, for she has spent her period of supremacy systematically seducing (with her magically-youthful beauty and the false promise of the Holy Grail) and killing Arthur's knights. Boorman apparently found the influence of a wise woman in the political realm even less attractive than did Malory, who kept Merlin permanently out of the picture and reunited Morgan (and Nyneve) with Arthur in the barge to Avalon.

In *Excalibur*, while Merlin is temporarily neutralized, the evil Morgana moves to the next stage of her plan: to conceive a son (who will be named Mordred) by her half-brother Arthur. She uses her magic powers to deceive Arthur, disguising herself as Guinevere, and rendering Arthur a complete innocent in an adulterous act that, in Malory's original, he committed willingly with a different half-sister, Morgause.[75] Mordred will be raised by his mother eventually to challenge his father on the battlefield, an anti-Christ to Arthur's Christ-figure.[76] She even gives birth to Mordred "amid all the trappings of a Satanic rite."[77] But Morgana also wishes to wield power herself, which she does for many years as Arthur lies withering away, felled by the double trauma of his betrayal by Guinevere (who has had sex with Lancelot), and his own (albeit involuntary) incestuous act. As Arthur withers, so does the land, causing universal suffering. As one scholar noted laconically: "Perhaps not surprisingly, this interval is gendered feminine."[78] "Morgan has become unredeemable evil," and female rulership is shown to be an unmitigated disaster.[79]

It is impossible to miss how significantly Boorman and Pallenberg departed from Malory (their explicit source) when making *Excalibur*. These changes can be explained simply as the necessary result of any attempt to adapt Malory's massive compendium of over one thousand printed pages as a manageable screenplay.[80] Furthermore, Morgana's dramatic maleficence is particularly suited to the exigencies of the cinematic medium, "with its need for contrasting characters to represent good and evil."[81] Nickolas Haydock indicted the "poisonous" influence of Boorman's film, which unleashed "a deluge of sword and sorcery films" in which the "medieval" was pure pretext,[82] but Boorman insisted that the many changes never truly affected the essence of the tale. Instead, he emphasized the fact that he made changes in a "respectful" way, "conscious that we were part of a long line of story-tellers of the legend."[83] He also asserted:

> The thing about myths [...] is that they're a body of stories completely homogenous and interrelated, yet also completely flexible. You can rearrange or extend or elide the order of events quite liberally without destroying the meaning. The essentials that make them popular, the *resonances*, remain the same.[84]

To my knowledge, only one commentator has explicitly called Boorman's bluff here, by insisting that the changes (in particular, the misogynistic spin on Morgana) are in fact truly significant. Marian MacCurdy turned a psychoanalytic eye on the director and his contemporaries, attributing "a search for definitive culprits, even scapegoats, who can be blamed for life's pain" to the shared experience of the "repeated and deep traumas" and "elemental terrors" of the two World Wars.[85] In this view, women were effectively the scapegoats responsible for Boorman's having spent his youth in London during the *Blitzkrieg*, an experience he dramatized in his 1987 film *Hope and Glory*. This cannot be the complete explanation, for it fails to account for the specific timing and precise contours of the anti-feminist imagery in *Excalibur*, points to which I shall return. Nevertheless, MacCurdy is clearly onto something when she invokes psychological and even unconscious levels of motivation behind Boorman's cinematic harridan, a pure distillate of castration anxiety if ever there was one. Nothing in the director's published comments on the film indicates that he intended to create such imagery; indeed, he seems blissfully unaware of what he actually put on the screen, although he remains fascinated by it. *Excalibur* is the only one of Boorman's movies that he himself still watches, because (he says) "the power of the story, the myth, outweighs my reservations about the film that I made. [...] it's such a powerful story, it grips me in spite of myself."[86]

Boorman claims that he "felt a sense of destiny" that he "had to make the movie"; once he did, "the burden was lifted."[87] Yet, despite the director's very inflated sense of the deep significance of the film, it is (as Vincent Canby noted in his 1981 *New York Times* review) impossible to tell what the point of the movie even is, "despite the fact that Merlin periodically seems to be telling us"; Canby went on to snipe that Boorman's "big, solemn, grandiose" movie was virtually a one-film ring cycle that seemed ten times as long as the Wagner version.[88] It is hard enough simply to understand Boorman's assertions concerning the message of the film, such as "And that's what my story is about: the coming of Christian man and the disappearance of the old religions which are represented by Merlin. The forces of superstition and magic are swallowed up into the unconscious," and "Merlin is passing out of the world because of Camelot, because science and rationality have taken the place of magic," and that the story falls "on the cusp of the coming of Christianity, of the individual Christian, the individual man, rationality."[89] What is worse is that these pronouncements have no discernible connection with the action on the screen.[90] It is this fundamental incoherence of the film on the level of the surface plot that leads me to follow MacCurdy in proposing that Boorman was, to an unusual degree, under the influence of unconscious psychological motivations and forces.

I would like to illustrate the extent of the unconscious, even self-delusional, aspect of *Excalibur* (particularly as it relates to the theme of gender) through the example of Merlin's silver helmet.[91] Boorman tells us that Merlin is a "man-woman." He intended to signal Merlin's ambiguous gender identity through having the character hairless, but Nicol Williamson, the actor who played the role, refused. (That a director would accede to something so contrary to his own vision already strains credulity.) Therefore, instead of hairlessness as a way to make Merlin a "man-woman," Boorman let Merlin be very hairy, beard and all, but put a silver helmet on his head. Somehow, Boorman apparently believes that he did not stage a gendered conflict, that his Merlin – because of the silver helmet – would be received as sexless. Boorman seems oblivious to the fact that Williamson played Merlin as a male, and to the fact that he himself staged the character that way. Witness, for instance, the rousing night speech that a torch-bearing Merlin makes to Arthur's army in Scene 17, "Fellowship of the Round Table," a scene modeled (according to Boorman himself, in the DVD commentary) on Henry V's speech at Agincourt in the Shakespeare play of that name. In the final shot of the scene, in which no women appear, all the knights hold aloft their swords, in a solidly masculinist display of martial valor.

John Boorman was probably himself only dimly aware, if at all, of all the influences that conditioned his creation of *Excalibur*. I would like now to suggest some forces that I think might have been at work. First of all, it is possible that the 1924 classic film *Die Nibelungen* in fact played a role in the making of *Excalibur*. Specifically, *Die Nibelungen* may well have affected the overall structure of *Excalibur* as a duology built around the vengeance of a *domina*. As a classic film from the golden age of silent cinema, by one of the greatest directors of the twentieth century, it must have been known to all serious filmmakers, particularly those interested in fantasy material and medievalism. Boorman never invoked Lang (or von Harbou), but he never actually invoked *any* previous filmmaker as an influence on his own oeuvre, at least not in connection with *Excalibur*, despite the fact that he must have been familiar with hundreds of films. Boorman did, however, style himself as following in the footsteps of Wagner when he made *Excalibur*. In fact, he went to Bayreuth for inspiration before he began filming, because he saw the parallels between his own interest in the deep myths of western culture (the Arthurian legends) and Wagner's interest in those materials (in his case, the Nibelungen stories).[92] The fact that Boorman prepared to make *Excalibur* by immersing himself in materials related to the Nibelungen stories indicates that the thirteenth-century poem at least, if not the 1924 film, was part of what shaped the final product.

That final product, the film *Excalibur*, had a message not unlike the message of *Die Nibelungen*, namely: power in the hands of women is misplaced and dangerous. One commentator has detected an unintended "feminist sub-text" to the 1981 film, that "men cannot deny women their rightful inheritances and expect the world to live happily ever after."[93] Certainly Morgana's attempt to seize what she felt was coming to her led to utter chaos (indeed, it created a wasteland), but the problem with this feminist interpretation (even if unintended) is that – within the diegesis of the film – Morgana is never recognized as a rightful claimant, nor does she ever put herself forward as a rational political actor staking a claim to an inheritance. Like the pathological women of *Die Nibelungen*, Morgana is motivated entirely by emotional desires. She has been nursing a grudge for decades and is out for revenge. She prosecutes a personal vendetta against Merlin and Arthur to avenge the murder of her father and the rape of her mother, but – like Kriemhild – she cares not a whit if she must destroy the entire world as well in order to truly crush her enemies. This is the same pattern of emotionality and instability that marked von Harbou's women as unsuited for political responsibilities in Weimar Germany, despite the claims of progressives to the contrary.

This negative view of the consequences of female political power could have been counter-balanced in *Excalibur* had Boorman and Pallenberg kept their cinematic Guinevere relatively close to Malory's literary queen; the latter was both a good ruler and a good woman who "balance[d] her personal concerns with political responsibilities and […] [was] heavily involved with not just her affinity but with most of the major affinities of the kingdom."[94] In some ways Malory's Guinevere positively echoed certain aspects of the political role played in the Lancastrian party during the War of the Roses by Queen Margaret of Anjou, and was in general a model of "good lady-ship."[95] It might be that Malory included positive images of royal women in a relatively unthinking manner, simply reflecting some of the political realities around him; however, it has been argued that he went farther than that, explicitly defending Queen Guinevere in outright "anti-misogynist" modes, and blaming the destruction of the Round Table on the grail quest rather than on her adultery.[96] In contrast, the team that produced the 1981 *Excalibur* felt no obligation to reflect positively on the experience of being ruled by a woman. Malory's British queen was a good leader and even a "holy woman"; Boorman's British queen was a non-entity.[97]

The *dominae* of Lang and von Harbou were generated by the specific context of pro-feminist activism and conservative reaction in Weimar Germany, an important moment in First-Wave Feminism. The United Kingdom during the run-up to the making of *Excalibur* held its own terrors for those disturbed by female claims to political power (who perhaps already chafed under the largely symbolic monarchical authority of Queen Elizabeth II), for the country was in the grips of the feminist Second Wave. The first meeting of the women's liberation movement in Britain took place at Ruskin College in 1970, the first women's liberation march took place in London in 1971, the first feminist magazine in Britain (*Spare Rib*) was launched in 1972, the first women were allowed on the floor of the London Stock Exchange in 1973, and the first feminist publishing house in Britain (Virago) was founded in 1974.[98] The activism of the opening years of this key decade began showing major returns by mid-decade, for in 1975 three landmark pieces of legislation (the Sex Discrimination Act, the Employment Protection Act, and the Equal Pay Act) came into force.[99] And in that same year, Margaret Thatcher (born 1925) was elected the leader of the Conservative Party; four years later she would become Britain's first woman Prime Minister, a post she would hold until 1990.[100] This decade of rapid and dramatic change could not fail to elicit a reaction from those unaccustomed to, and uncertain about, women's suitability as political leaders.

In the view of some critics, the government of Margaret Thatcher, latter-day *domina*, was as destructive to British society as the ascendancy of Morgana was to Arthur's realm. Indeed, the Iron Lady (as she was known) famously asserted that "There is no such thing as society."[101] Her recipe for harsh government strayed as far as possible from the sorts of maternal policies that one type of gender stereotyping might associate with a female ruler. Even before becoming Prime Minister she had earned the moniker (as Secretary of State for Education and Science) "Margaret Thatcher, Milk Snatcher" for eliminating free milk distribution to poor school children.[102] "Thatcherism" was so harmful to some segments of society that some critics charged that she deliberately set out to increase unemployment, which (whatever her true intentions were) did soar in the wake of a combination of union busting and de-industrialization, cutting one million manufacturing jobs during the first three years of her government (perhaps not coincidentally the years of production of *Excalibur*).[103] While acquiring unprecedented powers for the country's political police, Thatcher urged people to "glory in inequality" and presided over a process of wealth "trickle-up" that rendered the United Kingdom the western world's most unequal society by the 1990s.[104] Thatcher's Britain led the way in the creation of a class of the "new poor" and in posting newly draconian incarceration rates.[105] But the similarities in their characters and policies aside, the salient point in terms of provoking opposition both to Morgana and to Margaret may simply have been their gender.

Although *Excalibur* is fairly incoherent, there are still sparks of clarity, one being the secret that Percival learns from the grail: "the king and the land are one." Boorman himself called attention to this notion as "central to the whole myth."[106] And it certainly seems to be, given the plot of the film, which identified virile male rulership with prosperity and female rulership with disaster. When King Arthur has a sword/penis and is virile, all is well. When he does not, and a woman usurps, there is catastrophe. It cannot be a complete coincidence that Boorman made a film that sends this message when faced with the reality of a ruling queen, a female Prime Minister, and a very unhappy populace. In 1981, when *Excalibur* was made, the nation witnessed a wave of riots in London, Bristol, Liverpool, and Manchester.[107] Thatcher's job approval rating was at 23 percent, lower than recorded for any previous Prime Minister.[108] And in that year, a young man shot a gun at Elizabeth II as she was riding during the Trooping of the Colour, the only such confirmed incident in her long reign.[109] The horrors of the summer of 1981 were relieved only by the July wedding of Prince Charles and Diana Spencer, at the time a source of unadulterated jubilation (despite its eventual tragic outcome). At the end of *Excalibur*, Arthur says, "One day a king will come and the sword will rise again." Perhaps Boorman hoped that Elizabeth would abdicate and give the throne to a king, thus setting the cosmos aright.

That there is something to this confluence of factors is confirmed by their extraordinary recurrence in early August of 2011, when a series of violent riots once again shocked Britain. It is perhaps significant that the person primarily responsible for internal security was Home Secretary Theresa May, only the fourth woman ever to occupy one of the great offices of state in the United Kingdom.[110] Rioters, however, never mentioned her explicitly. Instead, and quite strikingly, public discourse in the United Kingdom, the United States and Canada presented the crisis as the consequence of continued Thatcherism and painted the sitting Prime Minister, David Cameron, as Thatcher reborn.[111] Sometimes the ghost of the Iron Lady was so strong in the commentary that her responsibility for the troubles was explicitly invoked whereas the actual leaders of the current government were sometimes not mentioned by name at all.[112] Some commentators were extremely pointed, such as the author who – on August 18, 2011 – informed readers, in an article entitled "Riots: Were They Mrs. Thatcher's Fault or Not?" that "IDS blames Mrs. T's 'unfinished business' – others just blame Mrs. T."[113] The people who rioted in August 2011, like their predecessors thirty years earlier, had to look to the extraordinarily long-lived Queen Elizabeth II as the symbol of their nation, but were constantly reminded – again, like the rioters of 1981 – that a king was waiting in the wings. The wedding of Prince William and Catherine Middleton on April 29, 2011 kicked off a summer of day-dreaming and speculation about the future of the English throne. And right on cue, medievalist popular culture fanned the flames of discontent with female rule, as the BBC television series *Merlin* wrapped up its third season and went into summer production mode for season four, set to air in September 2011. Morgana had already turned evil over the course of season two (2009–10), but the 2010–11 season witnessed a Morgana who was "darker and more powerful than ever before." Fans learned in the summer of 2011 what the future held for the inhabitants of Camelot: season four would open with "Merlin powerless against the spirits of the dead that Morgana summons" and "the corrupted Morgana and her sister Morgause" joining forces to attack the rightful (male) rulers.[114] Only detailed, extensive sociological research could establish a firm connection among these various events, but the conjuncture – with its repetition of the factors of 1981 – is certainly food for thought.

Conclusion: Anti-Feminism and Cinematic Medievalism

When Mary Tudor became queen of England, the horrified Protestant reformer John Knox published a blistering condemnation of female rule, *The First Blast of the Trumpet Against the Monstrous Regiment of Women*, in which he characterized political power in the hands of women as unnatural, unlawful, and contrary to scripture.[115] Anti-feminists continue to argue that the movement of large numbers of women into politics constitutes "a social disaster."[116] *Die Nibelungen* and *Excalibur* graphically stage versions of that fearsome disaster, the former deliberately and ideologically, the latter apparently unconsciously. Both are examples of anti-feminist work that emerged in reaction to specific feminist moments in twentieth-century Europe, when conservatives seized upon medieval material as part of their arsenal. National legends, dating from time immemorial, can seem particularly suited for the defense of values and practices deemed to be traditional. Nothing could have fit that bill better in Germany and England than (respectively) the Nibelungen and Arthurian tales, whose histories had already run on parallel tracks during the heyday of political romanticism in the nineteenth century. When nineteenth-century rulers sought subject matter for the décor of key political buildings in both countries, artists knew exactly where to look; thus, the king of Prussia commissioned a series of frescoes illustrating the *Nibelungenlied* for the Marmorpalais at Potsdam, and Prince Albert commissioned a scene depicting "The Return of King Arthur" for the Queen's Robing Room in the new Houses of Parliament.[117] Twentieth-century filmmakers continued along these lines, embracing the fantasy literature of the Middle Ages, which already was tinged with a strong anti-feminist cast. No ruling women were coded as both fully sufficient (without a male consort or savior) and good in medieval courtly literature.[118] The choice to film this material was already a potentially anti-feminist one; the decision to develop the anti-feminist potential of the *Nibelungenlied* and *Morte D'Arthur* to melodramatically misogynistic heights shows how the medieval past could be put to use in modern European culture.

It must be emphasized that the particular characterization of politically powerful women as emotionally-overwrought seekers of vengeance constitutes a novel – and modern – twist on gendered stereotypes, one that does not correspond at all to medieval stereotypes of ruling *dominae*. The stereotypical female role in the medieval political realm was as a peace-weaver, or as a merciful intercessor seeking to temper the stern decrees of male dispensers of justice.[119] Isolated examples of historical *dominae* who did carry out plots to avenge wrongs done to them and/or their families are generally understood in pragmatic political terms, rather than emotional ones; this is true for most historical cases of vengeance carried out by men as well, at least as far as the sources describing the events are concerned.[120] Among Merovingian-era elites, for instance, both women and men shared a notion of honor as an (often ritualized) exchange of violence that required the vindication of wrongs, with no sense of an ideological difference between the sexes.[121] Medieval people could certainly be overcome with emotion and insist upon taking vengeance upon enemies both real and imagined; however, the type of person who engaged in this sort of behavior was typically male.[122] That history is barely reflected in twentieth-century cinema, which has built few plots around the character of the vengeful *dominus*, or the horrific consequences of male political power.

NOTES

1.   Martha W. Driver and Sid Ray, "Preface: Hollywood Knights," in *The Medieval Hero on Screen: Representations from Beowulf to Buffy*, ed. Martha W. Driver and Sid Ray (Jefferson, NC: McFarland, 2004), 5–18 (8).
2.   Consider Maid Marion in *The Adventures of Robin Hood* (dir. Michael Curtiz and William Keighley, 1938) and Ximena in *El Cid* (dir. Anthony Mann, 1961).
3.   My discussion is based on the DVD versions of the films *Excalibur* (Warner Home Video, 1999) and *Die Nibelungen* (Kino Video, 2002, with English inter-titles), and on repeated viewings of *Excalibur* in theatrical release. I have not been able to see the film copy of *Die Nibelungen* with German inter-titles in the Bundesarchiv/Filmarchiv, Koblenz, or to read the German screenplay for *Die Nibelungen* in the Stiftung Deutsche Kinemathek in Berlin. For the term *domina*, see Sean Gilsdorf, *Queenship and Sanctity: The Lives of Mathilda and the Epitaph of Adelheid* (Washington, DC: Catholic University of America Press, 2004), 66.
4.   Michael S. Batts, ed., *Das Nibelungenlied. Paralleldruck der Handschriften A, B, und C nebst Lesarten der übrigen Handschriften* (Tübingen: Max Niemeyer Verlag, 1971); Eugène Vinaver and P. J. C. Field, eds., *The Works of Sir Thomas Malory*, 3 vols. (Oxford: Oxford University Press, 1990).
5.   For re-accentuation, see Theresa Tinkle, *Gender and Power in Medieval Exegesis* (New York: Palgrave, 2010), 19; for re-mediation, see Laurie A. Finke and Martin B. Shichtman, *Cinematic Illuminations: The Middle Ages on Film* (Baltimore, MD: Johns Hopkins University Press, 2010), 24.
6.   John Boorman, who directed and co-wrote the screenplay for *Excalibur*, said of the project: "But the date is the least important thing really. I think of the story, the history, as a myth. The film has to do with *mythical* truth, not historical truth; it has to do with man taking over the world on his own terms for the first time [...]. What I'm doing is setting it in a world, a period, of the imagination [...] I'm trying to suggest a kind of Middle Earth, in Tolkien terms. It's a contiguous world; it's *like* ours but different. I want it to have a primal clarity, a sense that things are happening for the first time" (quoted by Harlan Kennedy, "The World of King Arthur According to John Boorman," *American Film* 6 (1981): 30–37; www.americancinemapapers.com/files/EXCALIBUR.htm (accessed 16 May 2011). Similarly, the scenarist of *Die Nibelungen*, Thea von Harbou, reduced the story to the fundamental elements of all feeling, namely love and hate, which she considered to be timeless and eternal (Reinhold Keiner, *Thea von Harbou und der deutsche Film bis 1933* (Hildesheim: Georg Olms Verlag, 1991), 86–87.
7.   Maureen Fries, "Female Heroes, Heroines and Counter-Heroes: Images of Women in Arthurian Tradition," in *Arthurian Women: A Casebook*, ed. Thelma S. Fenster (New York: Garland, 1996), 59–73 (68); article reprinted from Sally K. Slocum, ed., *Popular Arthurian Traditions* (Bowling Green, OH: Bowling Green State University Popular Press, 1992), 5–17.
8.   Anne Berthelot, "Kriemhild/Brünhild, Yseut la Blonde/Yseut aux Blanches Mains:

Le Malefice de la Feminité Dedoublée," in *La chanson des Nibelungen hier et aujourd'hui. Actes du Colloque Amiens 12 et 13 janvier 1991*, ed. Danielle Buschinger and Wolfgang Spiewok (Amiens: Université de Picardie, 1991), 21–31 (28–29).

9. Wolfgang Spiewok, "Das Nibelungenlied – eine Krimehilden-Tragödie," in *La chanson des Nibelungen*, 159–75; Philip N. Anderson, "Kriemhild's Quest," *Euphorion: Zeitschrift für Literaturgeschichte* 79 (1985): 3–12; Stanley R. Hauer, "The Sources of Fritz Lang's Die Nibelungen," *Literature/Film Quarterly* 18 (1990): 103–10.

10. Karin Bruns, *Kinomythen, 1920–1945: Die Filmentwürfe der Thea von Harbou* (Stuttgart: Verlag J. B. Metzler, 1995), 190; Kevin J. Harty, *The Reel Middle Ages: American, Western and Eastern European, Middle Eastern and Asian Films about Medieval Europe* (Jefferson, NC: McFarland, 1999), 194.

11. Berta Lösel-Wieland-Engelmann, "Verdanken wir das Nibelungenlied einer Niedernburger Nonne?" *Monatshefte für deutschen Unterricht, deutsche Sprache und Literatur* 72 (1980): 3–25; Ursula Hennig, ed., *Das Nibelungenlied nach der Handschrift C* (Tübingen: Maz Niemeyer Verlag, 1977); Otfrid Ehrismann, "Kriemhild-*C," in *Ze Lorse bi dem münster. Das Nibelungenlied (Handschrift C). Literarische Innovation und politische Zeitgeschichte*, ed. Jürgen Breuer (Munich: Wilhelm Fink Verlag, 2006), 225–48 (244); Jean Fourquet, "Un *Nibelungenlied* Feministe: La *Liedfassung*," in *La chanson des Nibelungen*, 71–79. Note that Fourquet ridicules the notion of a feminist *Nibelungenlied*.

12. Joachim Bumke, *Die Vier Fassungen der "Nibelungenklage": Untersuchungen Zur Überlieferungsgeschichte und Textkritik der Hafischen Epik im 13. Jahrhundert* (Berlin: Walter de Gruyter, 1996); Spiewok, "Das Nibelungenlied – eine Kriemhilden-Tragödie," 173–74; Michael Curschmann, "Zur Wechselwirkung von Literatur und Sage. Das Buch von Kriemhild und Dietrich von Bern," *Beiträge zur Geschichte der deutschen Sprache und Literatur* 111 (1989): 380–410 (380–82); Noriaki Watanabe, "Kriemhild als Widerspenstige. 'Rosengarten zu Worms A' und 'Frauenzucht,'" in *Zwischenzeiten – Zwischenwelten. Festschrift für Kozo Hirao*, ed. Josef Fürnkäs with Masato Izumi and Ralf Schnell (Frankfurt am Main: Peter Lang, 2001), 105–19 (106–7, 110–12, 115).

13. Ehrismann, "Kriemhild-*C," 242.

14. Danielle Buschinger, "Les interventions du rédacteur de la version B de la Chanson des Nibelungen," in *L'"Effet auteur" au Moyen Age*, ed. Danielle Buschinger (Amiens: Centre d'Etudes Médiévales, Université de Picardie – Jules Verne, 2003), 18–23.

15. William Layher, "'She Was Completely Wicked': Kriemhild as Exemplum in a 13th-Century Sermon. Image – Topos – Problem," *Zeitschrift für deutsches Altertum und deutsche Literatur* 138 (2009): 344–60 (353, 355, 359).

16. For the modern reception of the *Nibelungenlied* separate from its constant medieval companion of the *Klage*, see Norbert H. Ott, "Ikonen deutscher Ideologie: Der Nibelungenstoff in der Bildkunst vom Mittelalter bis zur Gegenwart," *Zeitschrift für bayerische Landesgeschichte* 63 (2000): 325–56 (327, 336, 340).

17. Bernhard Martin, "Der deutsche Nationalstaat und das Nibelungenlied. Über die gesellschaftspolitische Funktion des Mythos," in *"Waz sider da geschach": American-German Studies on the Nibelungenlied. Text and Reception*, ed. Werner Wunderlich and Ulrich Müller with Detlef Scholz (Göppingen: Kümmerle Verlag, 1992), 179–88; Fourquet, "Un *Nibelungenlied* Feministe," 71; Layher, "'She Was Completely Wicked,'" 354; Edward R. Haymes,

"A Rhetorical Reading of the 'Hortforderungszene' in the *Nibelungenlied*," in *"Waz sider da geschach"*, 81–88 (87).

18. Ott, "Ikonen deutscher Ideologie," 341.

19. Helmut de Boor, ed., *Das Nibelungenlied* (Wiesbaden: Brockhaus, 1996); A. T. Hatto, trans., *The Nibelungenlied* (London: Penguin, 1965), 351; Karl Simrock, trans., *Das Nibelungenlied. Alt- und Neudeutsch*, 2 vols. (Leipzig: Tempel Verlag, 1900), 2:376–77.

20. Bruns, *Kinomythen*, 37.

21. Hatto, trans., *The Nibelungenlied*, 290.

22. Albrecht Classen, "The Defeat of the Matriarch Brünhild in the *Nibelungenlied*, with Some Thoughts on Matriarchy as Evinced in Literary Texts," in *"Waz sider da geschach"*, 89–110 (108).

23. Hatto, trans., *The Nibelungenlied*, 92; Classen, "The Defeat of the Matriarch," 107; Charles D. Nelson, "Virginity (De)Valued: Kriemhild, Brünhild, and All That," in *"Waz sider da geschach"*, 111–30 (122–25).

24. Michael Boehringer, "Sex and Politics? Etzel's Role in the *Nibelungenlied* – A Narratological Approach," in *"Waz sider da geschach"*, 149–65 (161–63).

25. Franz H. Bäuml, "Attila in Medieval German Literature," in *Attila: The Man and his Image*, ed. Franz H. Bäuml and Marianna D. Birnbaum (Budapest: Corvina, 1993), 57–64 (62).

26. Bruns, *Kinomythen*, 37; David J. Levin, *Richard Wagner, Fritz Lang and the Nibelungen: The Dramaturgy of Disavowal* (Princeton, NJ: Princeton University Press, 1998), 116–17 and 124–25.

27. E. A. Thompson, *The Huns* (Oxford: Blackwell, 1996; originally published as *A History of Attila and the Huns* by Oxford University Press in 1946), 145–56. At least one scholar has suggested that Attila's ill-fated liaison, while on campaign, with a maiden who might have been Germanic ("Ildico") is the historical germ of the relationship with Kriemhild (Hauer, "The Sources," 106). For this event, see Thompson, *The Huns*, 164–66. It is notoriously difficult to try to trace such characters through centuries of history and legend; for instance, the late Carolingian Latin poem *Waltharius* has both a Burgundian princess and a Frankish warrior named Hagen as hostages at Attila the Hun's court (Bäuml, "Attila in Medieval German Literature," 58).

28. Joan Ferrante, "Epistolae: Medieval Women's Letters," http://epistolae.ccnmtl.columbia.edu/woman/36.html (accessed 8 May 2011).

29. Heinz Thomas, "Li conte de Bourgogne – li conte de Rome. Die Staufer im *Nibelungenlied*," in *Ze Lorse bi dem münster*, 85–102.

30. John Alexander Williams, "Foreword," in *Weimar Culture Revisited*, ed. John Alexander Williams (New York: Palgrave Macmillan, 2011), ix–xxiv (xv).

31. Fourquet, "Un *Nibelungenlied* Feministe," 72–74.

32. Bruns, *Kinomythen*, 8.

33. Bruns, *Kinomythen*, 7; Karin Bruns, "Talking Film: Writing Skills and Film Aesthetics in the Work of Thea von Harbou," in *Practicing Modernity: Female Creativity in the Weimar Republic*, ed. Christiane Schönfeld and Carmel Finnan (Würzburg: Königshausen & Neumann, 2006), 139–52.

34. The citations are from the description of a planned 2006 TV documentary by Richard Gilzean. I have not been able to determine whether the program was ever made. The

announcement can be found at http://thea-von-harbou.blogspot.com/2006/08/tv-dokumen-tation-ber-thea-von-harbou.html (accessed 24 April 2011), on the "Thea von Harbou Weblog" (http://thea-von-harbou.blogspot.com/). See also Bruns, "Talking Film."

35. Raffael Scheck, "German Conservatism and Female Political Activism in the Early Weimar Republic," *German History* 15 (1997): 34–55.

36. For instance, Douglas Gomery and Clara Pafort-Overduin, *Movie History: A Survey* (New York: Routledge, 2011), 103–4.

37. Bruns, "Talking Film," 145–46; Keiner, *Thea von Harbou*, 84–90.

38. Peter Morris-Keitel, "Siegfried as Idol? The Function of the Hero in Recent West German Adaptations of the *Nibelungenlied*," in *"Waz sider da geschach"*, 189–95 (194); see also Otfrid Ehrismann, "Disapproval, Kitsch, and the Process of Justification: Brünhild's Wedding Nights," in *"Waz sider da geschach"*, 167–77.

39. Jan-Christopher Horak, Introductory Essay (on the DVD itself and printed as an insert), on *Die Nibelungen* DVD. For the appropriation of the entire *Nibelungenstoff* (Nibelungen-material) by the Nazis, see Ingo R. Stoehr, "(Post)Modern Rewritings of the *Nibelungenlied – Der Nibelungen Roman* and Armin Ayren as Meister Konrad," in *Medieval German Voices in the 21st Century: The Paradigmatic Function of Medieval German Studies for German Studies. A Collection of Essays*, ed. Albrecht Classen (Amsterdam: Rodopi, 2000), 165–78 (167–68). I fail to see the evidentiary basis for the statements that "the film was regarded as too dangerous for the people," that it failed with audiences, and was cold-shouldered by the Nazi authorities (Veronica Ortenberg, *In Search of the Holy Grail: The Quest for the Middle Ages* (London: Hambledon Continuum, 2006), 113, 212).

40. Thea von Harbou, "Aus dem Manuskript des Films *Die Nibelungen*," in *Das Kulturfilmbuch*, ed. E. Beyfuss and A. Kossowky (Berlin: Carl Chryselius, 1924), 246–60; Thea von Harbous, *Das Nibelungenbuch* (Munich: Drei Masken Verlag, 1923); Thea von Harbou, "Vom Epos zum Film," *Die Woche* 26.6 (9 February 1924): 138–40.

41. Von Harbou, "Vom Epos zum Film," 39, quoted in the translation by Levin, *Richard Wagner, Fritz Lang and the Nibelungen*, 131.

42. Levin, *Richard Wagner, Fritz Lang and the Nibelungen*, 101, 103, 111–24, 137–40.

43. Fourquet, "Un *Nibelungenlied* Feministe," 75–79.

44. Levin, *Richard Wagner, Fritz Lang and the Nibelungen*, 107.

45. Buschinger, "Les interventions du rédacteur." Other scholars have argued that *vâlandinne* was an apt description of Kriemhild in the *B text, not only when Hagen uses it but also earlier when Dietrich uses it to express his recognition that Kriemhild is pursuing a disastrous course of action (Winder McConnell, "Kriemhild and Gerlind: Some Observations on the *Vâlandinne*-Concept in the *Nibelungenlied* and *Kudrun*," in *The Dark Figure in Medieval German and Germanic Literature*, ed. Edward R. Haymes and Stephanie Cain Van D'Elden (Göppingen: Kümmerle Verlag, 1986), 42–53 (46–47). Yet, it should not be forgotten that Dietrich of Bern becomes one of the speakers who excuses and defends Kriemhild in the *Klage*; for the relationship between the sagas featuring Dietrich and the Nibelungen traditions, see Curschmann, "Zur Wechselwirkung von Literatur und Sage," 396.

46. Alain Kerdelhue, "Die Nibelungen. Matériaux pour une lecture du film de Fritz Lang (1924)," in *La chanson des Nibelungen*, 81–98 (88).

47. Bruns, *Kinomythen*, 39.

48. Horak's introductory essay on the DVD sets out the plot thus: there is jealousy

between the two queens over Siegfried; both love him, but, because they do not realize that consciously, they fight over social status instead, setting the entire tragedy in motion.

49. Rudolph Sabor, *Richard Wagner, Der Ring des Nibelungen: A Companion Volume* (London: Phaidon, 1997), 153–63 ("Synopsis of the *Ring*"); John McKinnell, "Female Reactions to the Death of Sigurth/Sifrit," in *La chanson des Nibelungen*, 99–112; Hauer, "The Sources."

50. Hatto, trans., *The Nibelungenlied*, 332; Nelson, "Virginity (De)Valued," 125.

51. Hatto, trans., *The Nibelungenlied*, 111–18 (112), Chapter 14, "How the Queens Railed at Each Other."

52. Hatto, trans., *The Nibelungenlied*, 112.

53. Hatto, trans., *The Nibelungenlied*, 114.

54. English inter-titles, *Die Nibelungen* (DVD). Hauer, "The Sources," claims that the film retains the social status issue as the true motivator, although "this dispute is simply inadequate to set in motion the murder of Siegfried that follows" and "imposes on the reader and viewer a gap in credibility which most find difficult to overcome." For those unfamiliar with medieval social history and with the thirteenth-century poem, that is certainly true, which is one of the reasons von Harbou did adjust the motivations of the women and did not, *pace* Hauer, "overlook this difficulty." At the same time, von Harbou made a deliberate decision, and the credibility gap may not have been as large as Hauer believed it was. For instance, the German chancellor von Bülow made a speech in 1909 in the Reichstag concerning the relations between Germany and the Austro-Hungarian empire that analogized the situation to the struggle over precedence between the two queens in the *Nibelungenlied* (Ott, "Ikonen deutscher Ideologie," 350); clearly, some (educated) twentieth-century audiences would have been able to understand what was at stake in the medieval poem.

55. English inter-titles, *Die Nibelungen* (DVD).

56. Von Harbou may have borrowed the suicide from the Icelandic prose *Volsungasaga* (Hauer, "The Sources").

57. Nelson, "Virginity (De)Valued," 126.

58. Hatto, trans., *The Nibelungenlied*, 118.

59. See above pp. 163–64 on the *Klage* tradition, etc.

60. In the *C version of the story, Etzel is not a heathen but an apostate whom Kriemhild hopes to reconvert to Christianity (Bäuml, "Attila in Medieval German Literature," 58).

61. "Everything I learned, the technical problems I had to resolve in planning for 'The Lord of the Rings,' I applied to 'Excalibur.' That was my recompense" (John Boorman, Director's Commentary, *Excalibur* DVD); Nickolas Haydock, *Movie Medievalism: The Imaginary Middle Ages* (Jefferson, NC: McFarland, 2008), 68. The problem Boorman had faced for years was the inability to get funding to film Tolkien, and it was also a struggle to finance *Excalibur*. The financial backing for the film ultimately came (after twenty years of trying) from an American production company, namely Orion (Boorman, "Director's Commentary"). For this reason, Harty (*The Reel Middle Ages*, 86) treats *Excalibur* as an American film. However, Hollywood made no medieval films between the mid-1960s and the mid-1990s; *Excalibur* was an exceptional co-production in which Hollywood executives had no real interest, and on which they had no real influence (Ortenberg, *In Search of the Holy Grail*, 194–97). Therefore, I treat *Excalibur* as a European auteur film, as does Ortenberg. Not only Boorman (who was born in London in 1933) but indeed the entire cast and crew of *Excalibur*

were British or Irish, and the film was made in Ireland (where Boorman had lived since 1969, including as President of the Young Irish Film Makers). For information on Boorman, and for the production notes on the film, see the relevant Wikipedia articles (http://en.wikipedia. org/wiki/John_Boorman and http://en.wikipedia.org/wiki/Excalibur_(film) (both accessed 15 May 2011).

62. Spiewok, "Das Nibelungenlied – eine Kriemhilden-Tragödie," 173.

63. Geoffrey of Monmouth, *The History of the Kings of Britain*, trans. Lewis Thorpe (Harmondsworth: Penguin, 1966).

64. Monika Otter, *Inventiones: Fiction and Referentiality in Twelfth-Century English Historical Writing* (Chapel Hill: University of North Carolina Press, 1996), 76, 78.

65. John Aberth, *A Knight at the Movies: Medieval History on Film* (New York: Routledge, 2003), 5.

66. Aberth, *A Knight at the Movies*, 6–9.

67. Fries, "Female Heroes," 70. See also Thelma S. Fenster, "Introduction," in *Arthurian Women*, xvii–lxiv (xxxi–xxxiii), and Santiago Gutiérrez García, "El hada Morgana y la reina de Avalón," *Cultura neolatina* 61 (2001): 301–18 (301–4).

68. Raymond H. Thompson, "The First and Last Love: Morgan Le Fay and Arthur," in *Arthurian Women*, 331–44 (332), essay reprinted from Debra Mancoff, ed., *The Arthurian Revival: Essays on Form, Tradition and Transformation* (New York: Garland, 1992), 130–47.

69. Roberta Davidson, "Reading Like a Woman in Malory's Morte Darthur," *Arthuriana* 16 (2006): 21–33; Geraldine Heng, "Enchanted Ground: The Feminine Subtext in Malory," in *Arthurian Women*, 97–113, reprinted from Keith Busby and Erik Kooper, eds., *Courtly Literature: Culture and Context* (Amsterdam: John Benjamins, 1990), 282–300.

70. Heng, "Enchanted Ground," 107–8. See also Marian MacCurdy, "Bitch or Goddess: Polarized Images of Women in Arthurian Literature and Films," *Platte Valley Review* 18 (1990): 3–24 (14).

71. MacCurdy, "Bitch or Goddess," 12, 14.

72. MacCurdy, "Bitch or Goddess," 20–21. Martin B. Shichtman ("Hollywood's New Weston: The Grail Myth in Francis Ford Coppola's *Apocalypse Now* and John Boorman's *Excalibur*," *Post Script* 4 (1984): 35–49) pegged Jessie Laidlay Weston's 1920 study *From Ritual to Romance* as Boorman's main source of inspiration for the film. Certainly Boorman did take much from Weston, but she was not the source for his portrait of Morgana as a violently destructive, vengeful *domina* or for the causal link between Morgana's ascendancy and the wasteland. For Weston, see Norris J. Lacy, "Jessie Laidlay Weston (1850–1928)," in *On Arthurian Women: Essays in Memory of Maureen Fries*, ed. Bonnie Wheeler and Fiona Tolhurst (Dallas: Scriptorium Press, 2001), 335–42.

73. Aberth, *A Knight at the Movies*, 23.

74. Heng, "Enchanted Ground," 104–5. See also Sue Ellen Holbrook, "Nymue, the Chief Lady of the Lake, in Malory's *Le Morte Darthur*," in *Arthurian Women*, 171–90, reprinted from *Speculum* 53 (1978): 761–77.

75. Jacqueline de Weever, "Morgan and the Problem of Incest," in *Cinema Arthuriana: Twenty Essays*, ed. Kevin J. Harty (Jefferson, NC: McFarland, 2002), 54–63 (56–57); Dorsey Armstrong, "Malory's Morgause," in *On Arthurian Women*, 149–60.

76. Norris J. Lacy, "Mythopoeia in *Excalibur*," in *Cinema Arthuriana*, 33–43 (39).

77. Haydock, *Movie Medievalism*, 71.

78. Haydock, *Movie Medievalism*, 72.

79. MacCurdy, "Bitch or Goddess," 27.

80. Aberth, *A Knight at the Movies*, 22.

81. De Weever, "Morgan and the Problem of Incest," 54–55.

82. Haydock, *Movie Medievalism*, 73.

83. Boorman, Director's Commentary.

84. Kennedy, "The World of King Arthur."

85. MacCurdy, "Bitch or Goddess," 22–23.

86. Boorman, Director's Commentary.

87. Boorman, Director's Commentary.

88. Vincent Canby, "Excalibur (1981). Boorman's 'Excalibur,'" *The New York Times*, 10 April 1981, http://movies.nytimes.com/movie/review?res=9505EFD61138F933A2575 7C0A967948260_(accessed 21 June 2011).

89. Kennedy, "The World of King Arthur"; Boorman, "Director's Commentary." For references to multiple additional (and equally vague) interviews, see Harty, *The Reel Middle Ages*, 86–88.

90. I reproduce here one scholar's incomprehensible analysis, the only such incoherent passage in her entire book, which shows how defeated she was by an attempt to find meaning in the posturing of the film: "it represents a quest for the harmony of the universe, in an attempt to reconcile science and mysticism in the sort of religious syncretism already seen rise to such heights with the success of the 'Celtic' and pagan movements in the 1980s […] the film also deliberately took issue with the perceived individualism and self-preoccupation of the 1980s, by showing the quest for the Grail as an attempt by the individual to find, not himself or herself, but a place in relation to the universe, society and destiny. Attempts have been made to read in *Excalibur* an apocalyptic undercurrent […] combined with the search and desire for a strong ruling hand […]. Perhaps one could rather see a way of turning around the myth of chivalry to reveal the modern ideology of violence, while highlighting the beauty of uncontaminated nature and the importance of the Grail less as an achievement than as a quest" (Ortenberg, *In Search of the Holy Grail*, 210). This analysis also bears little relation to the plot of the film.

91. Boorman, "Director's Commentary," especially on Scene 11, "Arthur and Merlin." For illustrations of scenes from the film, see http://wearemoviegeeks.com/wp-content/merlinexcalibur.jpg and http://nighthawknews.files.wordpress.com/2009/07/morganand-merlin.jpg?w=300&h=190

92. Boorman, Director's Commentary.

93. De Weever, "Morgan and the Problem of Incest," 61.

94. Kenneth M. Hodges, "Guinevere's Politics in Malory's *Morte Darthur*," *Journal of English and Germanic Philology* 104 (2005): 54–79 (57).

95. Hodges, "Guinevere's Politics," 57–60.

96. Hodges, "Guinevere's Politics," 61–62.

97. Hodges, "Guinevere's Politics," 74–75, 79. For additional discussion of Malory's Guinevere as a positive female figure, see Amy S. Kaufman, "Guinevere Burning," *Arthuriana* 20 (2010): 76–94 (76–77, 87–88); Beverly Kennedy, "Malory's Guenevere: A 'Trew Lover,'" in *On Arthurian Women*, 11–34; Edward Donald Kennedy, "Malory's Guenevere: 'A Woman Who Had Grown a Soul,'" in *On Arthurian Women*, 35–43.

98. BBC Woman's Hour Women's History Timeline, www.bbc.co.uk/radio4/woman-shour/timeline/1970.shtml (accessed 21 June 2011).

99. BBC Woman's Hour Women's History Timeline, www.bbc.co.uk/radio4/woman-shour/timeline/1970.shtml (accessed 21 June 2011).

100. BBC Woman's Hour Women's History Timeline, www.bbc.co.uk/radio4/woman-shour/timeline/1970.shtml (accessed 21 June 2011).

101. Mark Mazower, *Dark Continent: Europe's Twentieth Century* (New York: Random House, 1998), 327. For the famous speech see www.margaretthatcher.org/document/106689 (accessed 26 May 2011).

102. Nicholas Wapshott, *Ronald Reagan and Margaret Thatcher: A Political Marriage* (New York: Sentinel, 2007), 76.

103. Mazower, *Dark Continent*, 330–34, 338.

104. Mazower, *Dark Continent*, 341.

105. Mazower, *Dark Continent*, 342, 343–44.

106. Boorman, Director's Commentary.

107. The riots took place on 2 April 1980 in Bristol; on 11–13 April 1981 in Brixton; on 3 July 1981 in Southall; on 4–8 July 1981 in Toxteth; and on 4 July 1981 in Manchester (www.margaretthatcher.org/chronology/browse.asp?t=4&pg=4).

108. Richard C. Thornton, *The Reagan Revolution II: Rebuilding the Western Alliance* (Victoria, BC: Trafford, 2006), 18.

109. "BBC On This Day, 1950–2005: 13 June," http://news.bbc.co.uk/onthisday/hi/dates/stories/june/13/newsid_2512000/2512333.stm (accessed 22 June 2011). There may have been a 1970 assassination attempt in Australia, only revealed in 2009 (Bonnie Malkin and Andrew Pierce, "Queen and Prince Philip Were 'Victims' of Australian Assassination Attempt," *The Telegraph*, 27 January 2009, www.telegraph.co.uk/news/uknews/theroyalfamily/4359649/Queen-and-Prince-Philip-were-victims-of-Australian-assassination-attempt.html (accessed 22 June 2011)).

110. The others were Margaret Beckett (Foreign Secretary), Jacqui Smith (also Home Secretary), and of course Margaret Thatcher. May became Home Secretary in 2010. See "Theresa May Flies the Flag for Women in Government," posted 12 May 2010, www.independent.co.uk/news/uk/politics/theresa-may-flies-the-flag-for-women-in-government-1971727.html (accessed 15 October 2011).

111. For instance, "if Tony Blair and David Cameron are 'sons of Thatcher,' as the journalist Simon Jenkins puts it, the rioters of today are the grandchildren. Prime Minister Margaret Thatcher, who famously proclaimed 'there is no such thing as society,' rapidly privatized state- held assets including railways, steel mills, airlines, coal mines and telecommunications providers. She decimated many public services that tended to the most disadvantaged and vulnerable people in Britain. More importantly, Thatcher abandoned the idea of full employment – a precondition of the welfare state [...]. The enduring effects of this radical socioeconomic engineering are now visible in the U.K., not least in some of the world's highest levels of inequality" (Pankaj Mishra, "London's Rioters Are Thatcher's Grandchildren," 11 August 2011, www.bloomberg.com/news/2011–08–12/london-s-rioters-are-thatcher-s-grandchildren-commentary-by-pankaj-mishra.html (accessed 15 October 2011)).

112. For instance, the cause of the riots was described as "harsh austerity measures finishing off what Thatcher started including privitisation [*sic*] of large chunks of the public

sector, continual erosion of any remaining labour movements, erosion of labour rights, casual-isation of work, underemployment, unemployment, the near constant spectre of crisis, poorly defined class enemies who seem immune to any attack, huge rises in energy prices, increase in VAT etc. …" ("London's Burning: Who's Next?" posted 9 August 2011 on "The Way Home: Go Local, Go Sustainable, Go Now," www.briangordon.ca/2011/08/londons-burning-whos-next/ (accessed 15 October 2011)).

113. See   www.thefirstpost.co.uk/83266,news-comment,news-politics,riots-were-they-mrs-thatchers-fault-or-not (accessed 15 October 2011).

114. The plot descriptions of the series are from the Wikipedia article "Merlin," http://en.wikipedia.org/wiki/Merlin_(TV_series) (accessed 18 October 2011).

115. Sharon L. Jansen, *The Monstrous Regiment of Women: Female Rulers in Early Modern Europe* (New York: Palgrave Macmillan, 2010).

116. Paul Gottfried, "The Trouble with Feminism" (LewRockwell.com, 2001), www.lewrockwell.com/gottfried/gottfried9.html (accessed 31 May 2011).

117. Ortenberg, *In Search of the Holy Grail*, 69–71.

118. Classen, "The Defeat of the Matriarch," 98.

119. Lois L. Huneycutt, "Intercession," in *Women and Gender in Medieval Europe: An Encyclopedia*, ed. Margaret Schaus (New York: Routledge, 2006), 406–7; Dawn Bratsch-Prince, "Ab les mans junctes e genolla en terra": Intercession and the Notion of Queenship in Late Medieval Catalonia," *Catalan Review* 20 (2006): 211–28.

120. Stephen D. White, "Clothild's Revenge: Politics, Kingship, and Ideology in the Merovingian Blood Feud," in *Portraits of Medieval and Renaissance Living: Essays in Honor of David Herlihy*, ed. Samuel K. Cohn, Jr. and Stephen A. Epstein (Ann Arbor: University of Michigan Press, 1996), 107–30; Barbara H. Rosenwein, "Les emotions de la Vengeance," in *La vengeance, 400–1200*, ed. Dominique Barthélemy, François Bougard, and Régine Le Jan (Rome: École française de Rome, 2006), 237–57 (247). A partial exception might be found in the (fabricated) accusation of infanticide as a result of "feminine furor" leveled by the author of one mid-twelfth-century saint's life against Adela of Hamaland; however, most accounts of the feud that she is blamed for precipitating emphasize her political ambition (Régine Le Jan, "La vengeance d'Adèle ou la construction d'une légende noire," in *La vengeance*, 325–40).

121. Nira Pancer, "La vengeance féminine revisitée. Le cas de Grégoire de Tours," in *La vengeance*, 307–24 (310–17).

122. Rosenwein, "Les emotions de la Vengeance," 253–57. There is no sign of the *topos* of the vengeful *domina* in the essays and sources collected in Susanna A. Throop and Paul R. Hyams, eds., *Vengeance in the Middle Ages: Emotion, Religion and Feud* (Burlington, VT: Ashgate, 2010); Kelly Gibson, ed., *Vengeance in Medieval Europe: A Reader* (Toronto: University of Toronto Press, 2009); or Barbara H. Rosenwein, ed., *Anger's Past: The Social Uses of Emotion in the Middle Ages* (Ithaca, NY: Cornell University Press, 1998).

Neomedievalism Unplugged

Pamela Clements and Carol L. Robinson

In recent articles discussing definitions of medievalism(s) and neo-medievalism(s), several themes seem to reoccur; one of those themes is the question of the validity of such scholarship. Karl Fugelso, in his Editorial Note to *Studies in Medievalism XX*, notes that some medievalists consider neomedievalism to be "defending artificial borders that diminish medievalism without establishing valid alternatives"[1] while others question the "validity of neomedievalism."[2] Whether neomedievalism is a subset of medievalism or something distinctive is still a matter of lively discussion; we hope to further that discussion by addressing four themes that have emerged in recent volumes of *Studies in Medievalism* and elsewhere. First is the pedagogical use to which we, as academics, put medievalism, including neomedievalism. Second is the effect upon tenure and promotion for those publishing in neomedievalism. Third is a concern over identifying and defining both medievalism and neomedievalism. Finally, there is a question as to further theoretical possibilities.

It is widely acknowledged that medievalism and neomedievalism have had an effect on medievalists' pedagogy. Almost all of us who teach undergraduate medieval studies slip in an occasional film clip or "modernization," either for comic relief or to advance critical thinking and understanding of the cultural production of images, both in our own time and historically. One could call these overlapping purposes *enlivening, enrollment,* and *enlightening*. There is no need to elaborate on *enlivening*: students respond to references they are familiar with, and we often use those references as scaffold to the less familiar, often difficult work of our courses.

Jane Chance, in her article "Tough Love: Teaching the New Medievalisms," however, identifies one main reason for adding medievalist works to our courses: *enrollment*. In an era when student numbers determine what can be taught, courses in medieval studies have become acutely endangered when enrollments fall. Chance also recognizes:

[…] reduced departmental and university support for the study of the medieval. This is largely related to changes in requirements for the major in English and other languages and literatures and to what our colleagues perceive as requisites for the understanding of our field, which no longer depends (in the case of English Departments) on literary history and genres so much as methodology and theory.[3]

Yet it is not only in English and language departments that support for the study of the medieval has dwindled. The business model of higher education that has taken such a firm grip on our universities and colleges emphasizes practical, vocational goals rather than the traditional study of humanities. Increasingly, university administrators (as well as students and their parents) look askance at study of the past, seeing no obvious connection to the needs of today's graduates. *Obvious* is the operative word here. We who teach courses on the Middle Ages do not have to be convinced, but, sadly, we have to make the effort to convince others that our studies are still relevant. Burgeoning enrollment is an effective tool for convincing department heads and deans that our subjects matter. A little *Monty Python and the Holy Grail* can go a long way toward making such a case for course survival.

However, while practical for purposes of job stability, bolstering enrollment is not the main reason for seducing students into taking our courses. Ideally, most of us want students to learn about and appreciate the *matter* of medieval studies, and many of us ourselves were attracted to medieval languages, literature, history, and the entire multidisciplinary world of medieval studies because of early experiences with Tolkien or T. H. White. We know well that medievalism can lead to curiosity about originary texts and artifacts, and we know that medievalism need not eclipse study of the Middle Ages, even as we recognize that most people will prefer to partake of the popular culture, medievalist, variants. For today's students, the gateway to medieval studies is as fully digital as the rest of their lives. We offer our personal experiences as case studies.

CASE ONE: Clements uses medievalism(s), including neomedievalism, in her hybrid medieval/medievalism courses as well as in her traditional medieval literature courses (such as Chaucer). Her Arthurian literature course, for example, like that of many other professors' special-topics medievalist courses, examines texts both medieval and modern to study the development and cultural embeddedness of Arthurian matter. Indeed, she is submitting this course as an option for her institution's newly-revised core requirements, under the category "Texts and Traditions." Similarly she designed a course centered upon *Lord of the Rings* (*LOTR*) and its sources: student readings include the Anglo-Saxon *Wanderer* and *Seafarer*, parts of the *Kalevala* and *Chanson de Roland*, along with the text of *LOTR* and clips from the Jackson films. Students clamored for it. These two courses deal with medieval and medievalist texts from a culture studies approach, and we have certainly seen students move from an interest in medievalism to medieval studies. Thus, even though the Chaucer class is no longer a requirement for majors, because of these other two medievalist courses, it still makes its enroll-ment. Furthermore, works of neomedievalism can also enlighten students and provide fruitful comparisons with medieval originals. Even within the Chaucer course, Clements plays clips from *A Knight's Tale*[4] to encourage discussion of the differences in ideology between the Chaucer *Tale* and the film's democratizing opposite. Comparing William Thatcher's motto "A man can change his stars" with the heavy emphasis on Fortune in Chaucer's work highlights the Middle Ages' alterity of vision and helps students recognize their own cultural biases. Although she does not teach online, Clements (of course) utilized the many digital materials available, such as Dan Kline's *Geoffrey Chaucer Online: The Electronic Canterbury Tales*,[5] the visual mate-rials at the Canterbury Project,[6] and many more. She also provides online audio versions of the text to help students with their pronunciation and with memorization projects.

CASE TWO: Many of Robinson's courses have begun the movement from the physical classroom to being purely online, but, so far, her medi-eval/medievalistic courses have all been hybrids. Robinson has also taught a hybrid version of Arthurian Literature. As with Clements's medievalistic courses, this course was as much about more contemporary works as it was about medieval sources. Indeed, students were even required to explore a "14-Day Free Trial" of the video game *Dark Age of Camelot*, and students did special research projects tracing and comparing/contrasting contemporary works with medieval sources. Robinson also teaches a course on Geoffrey Chaucer's works, and she regularly takes advantage of the plentiful supple-mental material made available by fellow medievalists (manuscript images, aids in reading Middle English, audio recordings of Middle English, critical texts). Students were required to read Chaucer's works, but they were also required to discuss these works in an online (text-based) forum. For both courses, classes met partially online and partially in the classroom. For the most recently offered courses, enrollment in each was not as high as in the past, and Robinson is proposing to offer the course fully online the next time she teaches it. The Chaucer course is thus becoming increasingly neome-dieval because of its increasingly digitalized nature: students and professor alike are transformed into cyberpunk (virtual online) identities that grapple with online texts, printed books (many of which are increasingly becoming e-books), and supplemental online materials – a multimodal experience. Indeed, Chaucer himself has been digitalized for well over a decade now.

(This is not at all to make the argument that neomedievalist pedagogy is limited to digital classrooms and digital supplements.)

These two cases help affirm, we are sure, the trends in teaching medieval and medievalistic courses both in the United States as well as in other parts of the world. However, such trends are far from established forms of teaching practice. Karl Fugelso observes that:

> Tenure-review boards may be somewhat skeptical of this new field, not to mention the nontraditional media in which they often prefer to work. University administrations may have even more difficulty pigeonholing neomedievalists than medievalists, who are sometimes still treated as if they present a formidable challenge to academic conventions.[7]

Indeed, Robinson (who was lucky enough to have earned her Ph.D. under a committee co-led by a film scholar as well as a medieval scholar) was more recently informed that she is not a medieval scholar, merely a student of medievalism(s). Clearly, prejudice abounds. However, such challenges should not be a reason for avoiding the exciting direction(s) in which medievalism, including neomedievalism, seems to be moving. It is up to those of us who are no longer struggling to establish ourselves to move forward, to further establish medievalism studies. Jane Chance goes even further in arguing for teaching medievalism(s) in the classroom (she uses the term New Medievalism):

> Whether we choose a new historical or a postmodern theoretical approach or we mix media to compare the medieval analogously with the modern, we may find our understanding of the Middle Ages – and our teaching – renewed and refreshed through this treasure-trove of New Medievalisms. Or, to use a more appropriately Tolkienesque metaphor in a more defensive context, for our own Hobbit-like survival as academics in an era when hard-earned skills in language study and understanding of a thousand years of literature, history, and art have all too often been marginalized by our institutions, we may need to open new windows in our disciplinary walls, see what lies beyond, and – like Frodo – take up the journey.[8]

Finding the occasional Frodo (or even Samwise) in our classroom, however, is not the issue; the issue is convincing all of Frodo's cousins and other relatives to also partake in the journey. It does not seem to matter, furthermore, whether the school is a small, private, liberal-arts college (where Clements teaches) or a large, public university (where Robinson teaches completely online): *enlivening* and tailoring for *enrollment* are the only real means for creating opportunities to *enlighten*. Neomedievalism, in this light, might be conceived as a style of medievalism pedagogy, a style inspired by criticism and theory.

Nor is the pedagogy limited to the undergraduate level. Jane Chance notes, "New medievalist Ph.D.s have had to become conversant with contemporary theory, multiculturalism, and interdisciplinarity if they intend to publish and thereby attract teaching positions and receive tenure";[9] and E. L. Risden comments that "as long as a paper still counts for tenure or promotion, why not? If it doesn't follow our courses, our dissertations, or our publishing history in traditional topics, we'll just call it medievalism and hope no one notices, since no one knows what that means."[10] We would like to believe that such approaches to scholarship are in the minority, and we also would like to believe that publications such as *Studies in Medievalism* require higher, stricter standards of scholarly approach. (How often have many of us who have published on medievalism complained of the unappreciated need to be "double-majors" in both medieval studies as well as a more contemporary field?) Yet Risden rightly goes on to say, "We have in medievalism, even in a time of economic recession, a 'growth industry' lots of persons from lots of disciplines want in, and we want to encourage them."[11] Yet – despite this apparent corruption in scholarly practices – there is a growing body of scholarship on medievalism, and yes, even on neomedievalism, and as a small creek flowing to the river of cultural theory, it is being taken seriously. *Studies in Medievalism*, *Postmedieval*, and the online journal *Medievally Speaking* are all peer-reviewed, respected, serious venues. The working group BABEL seems to be covering some of the same scholarly territory. KellyAnn Fitzpatrick points out that neomedievalism might even provide new venues for scholarship, writing, "I suggest we take this as a sign that we should investigate not only what neomedievalism is but what we could do with it."[12] She is referring to the diminishing number of places to publish hard-copy scholarship, at the same time as requirements for tenure and promotion grow ever more stringent and more contingent on publishing. She suggests that digital forms of publication and scholarship may open up new avenues for students of medievalism to exploit.

Resonating throughout the articles in several of the more recent volumes of *Studies in Medievalism* is the ongoing discussion about definitions of medievalism(s), as well as of neomedievalism in particular. Scholarship using theoretical approaches to interrogate medievalist texts is flourishing. Cory Lowell Grewell rightly observes, "The task of defining what exactly constitutes neomedievalism is a very difficult one, as the field is very broad and contains within its purview a substantial number of specific cultural manifestations, ranging in fields from politics to literature to digital media."[13] In a number of the *Studies in Medievalism* articles addressing neomedievalism, words like *fragmented, fractured history, empty signifiers, recursive, unmoored,* and others keep occurring, and these terms all point to neomedievalism as affected by postmodernism. M. J. Toswell also quotes Neil Gaiman using the word "trauma" to describe the dramatic differences between his screenplay for Robert Zemeckis's *Beowulf* and the original text, which he came to at first through a comic-book version. Following Baudrillard, she focuses on neomedieval works as simulacra, calling neomedievalism "a copy of an absent original, a sign that no longer speaks to a semiotic."[14] Lesley Coote associates neomedievalism with the margins of medieval manuscripts, in which playful and disruptive counterarguments to the main text appear.[15] Kevin and Brent Moberly use terms like *recursive*, and *hall-of-mirrors*, and *a world built entirely out of images* to describe the neomedievalist elements of video games.[16] Amy S. Kaufman points out that Kathleen Biddick's definition of *trauma* "relies on remarkably similar descriptors" to our definition of neomedievalism.[17] She points out that neomedievalism "consumes the Middle Ages in fragmented tropes as a way of ensuring against loss."[18] This idea reflects postmodern *pastiche* in which fragmented images are thrust together in often incongruent juxtaposition. David Marshall, in his essay "Neomedievalism, Identification, and the Haze of Medievalism," sees medievalism "as a spectrum of overlapping versions."[19] Citing George Crumb's *Black Angels: Thirteen Images from the Dark Land for Electric String Quartet* (1970), Nils Holger Petersen finds that contemporary avante-garde classical music "provides examples defying […] a distinction" between "historical" and "other kinds of 'uses' of medieval artifacts."[20] Lauryn S. Mayer suggests that "one important element of neomedievalism may have nothing to do with the content of a particular text, but with its forms of production, reproduction, and consumption."[21] Harry Brown sums up what several writers seem to be saying: "Neomedievalism is medievalism transformed by postmodernism."[22] He provides an example:

> By providing a foundation of pseudo-scholarship for numerous works of fiction, *Holy Blood, Holy Grail* marks a significant medievalist moment, as the Templars are uprooted from respected and responsible history and transplanted in the radioactive soil of imaginary history, where they are free to mutate into fantastic new forms.[23]

However, perhaps Mayer is right when she suggests that "the best approach is to worry less about what, precisely, it is and to spend more time thinking about what it does and why it does it."[24] As Nickolas Haydock notes, theoretical discussion of medievalism has been needed and has been a long time in coming. He uses the term *medievalistics* to describe (we think) what has been going on in the last three (or more) volumes of *Studies in Medievalism*:

What I suggest we call *medievalistics* identifies, analyzes, and theorizes particular constellations of these contingencies, especially their influence on the cultural production of alterities and continuities in relation to a distant but not necessarily remote past. This thoroughly contingent, multivalent, and multi-leveled negotiation between the pastness of the past and its presentist applications, the exotic and the immediate, is a proper concern of academic medievalistic studies. Medievalistics has exploded in recent decades, perhaps on the verge of becoming a full-fledged academic discipline in its own right, yet I would argue that it is still poor in theory and (largely as a result of this) continues to occupy a marginal place within medieval studies as a whole.[25]

The energy unleashed by the topics of "defining medievalisms" and "defining neomedievalisms" is a sign that Haydock's *medievalistics* is beginning to bear fruit. Which brings us to where theorizing medievalism/neomedievalism, or *medievalistics*, is going, or might be going. A central part of theory is definition. In "Living with Neomedievalism," we discussed the various possible meanings of both medievalism(s) and neomedievalism, stating that the

> neomedievalism we are discussing is a medievalism that seems to be a direct and unromantic response to the general matrix of medievalisms from which people are partially "unplugged" and thus not at all "so inured, so hopelessly dependent on the system, that they will fight to protect it."[26]

This unplugging aspect of neomedievalism is a crucial function, particularly in light of video games, especially as the virtual realism of these games becomes increasingly *real*, where the lines between fiction and reality in massive multiplayer online role-playing games are ever increasingly and intentionally blurred.

However, perhaps the issue is not so much with the act of unplugging from the fantasy and/or historical realism of the Middle Ages (or even never plugging into them in the first place) as with similarities neomedievalism holds with medievalism(s) in general. "As with 'medievalism,'" writes Richard Utz, "this 'unscholarly' area has met with a tepid response by those intent on defending scholarliness against the onslaught of the tech-savvy hordes who would make forms of contemporary entertainment their academic specialty."[27] One might indeed even argue that a rejection of neomedievalism is practically technophobic. Yet, it may be more of a concern that neomedievalism, like medievalism in general, "has become almost anything we wish, even temporarily, to call it, as long as we may nominally, even dubiously, connect it, by whatever gossamer thread, to the Middle Ages," as E. L.

Risden has suggested, and that "given a possible goal of inclusiveness, that variability and idiosyncrasy, for a time at least, isn't such a bad thing."[28] Is it possible to fear that, because medievalism as a conceived theory has yet to be narrowly defined (even though other theoretical applications such as feminism or even postmodernism have not), neomedievalism poses a theoretical threat? Why cannot neomedievalism, like the New Medievalism of the 1990s, be seen as merely a faction of the greater whole of medievalism(s)? We agree with Harry Brown that, while

> We do not need to disown medievalism in order to legitimate neomedievalism [...]. We do need a new theoretical model, and perhaps a new term, to account for the ways that contemporary culture has appropriated the medieval without quite comprehending (or wanting to comprehend) the Middle Ages, particularly in films and games.[29]

In this emphasis on developing theories of medievalism(s), in examining digital production and performance, and in the many connections with interdisciplinary approaches (film studies, gender studies, and so forth), neomedievalism can have practical advantages in the academy.

For example, neomedievalism is very much about the space-time continuum in a very science-fiction sort of way, which is perhaps why so many have turned to Jean Baudrillard's science-fiction/philosophical concepts. "Baudrillard," according to M. J. Toswell, "uses the simulacrum to posit a discursive Other, to set up a binary. The Other that Baudrillard invokes can never be fully simulated. The simulacrum thus turns in upon itself, having opened a rupture in order to establish a way of critiquing postmodernity."[30] What is delightfully interesting about this notion is that the binary opposition implied by a neomedieval simulacrum lacks any tension. It is not really an opposition, in fact, but simply a passive resistance in two directions. In one direction, the digital-artificial invades the analog-organic (such is the case, as is accurately described by Toswell, of the CGI of Grendel in Zemeckis's *Beowulf*). In the opposite direction, the analog-organic invades the digital-artificial (a video gamer playing an avatar). While Baudrillard's influence upon late twentieth- and early twenty-first-century thought cannot be denied, particularly as his works have inspired cyberpunk science fiction, the binary between that which is Real and that which is Other seems to be an incomplete portrait of what is happening with neomedievalist works. The relationship between medieval historical reality and contemporary fantasy of that reality is complex, just as the interconnectedness between the analog-organic brain and the digital computer is complex. While the neomedieval may be an empty or disconnected sign, it still has meaning, illusionary as it may be. In contrast, Toswell argues that medievalism, which we argue

certainly seems to be presented in more continuous, flowing analog movements, "attempts to ground itself not just in a generalized myth or history,
but in specific representations, in particular constructions, [...] they reach for
a sense of the real."[31] Neomedievalism, Toswell argues, strives more toward
what Baudrillard might call the "hyperreal."[32]

Drawing upon the "hyperreality" of Umberto Eco, the Moberlys argue
that neomedieval works, in the sense that they contain "elements" that "are
amplified and accentuated by the presence of the inauthentic, and function,
in turn, to amplify and accentuate the inauthentic," do not function on a
nostalgic, mimetic level of re-enactment,

> but instead employ contemporary techniques and technologies to
> simulate the medieval – that is, to produce a version of the medi-
> eval that can be seen and touched, bought and sold, and therefore
> owned. Neomedieval works thus abolish what, to [Jean] Baudrillard,
> is the sovereign difference between the real and the representational –
> between the territory and the map.[33]

We would argue, again, that this act of elimination of the line between
fiction and reality is passive-aggressive. Harry Brown also draws from Marxist
theory in his discussion of *Assassin's Creed*:

> Emptied of any contingent historical meaning, the medieval becomes
> more easily traded, more receptive to a projection of the user's own iden-
> tity. In *Assassin's Creed*, Abstergo Industries, the Templars reincarnated
> in the present, embodies popular fears of transnational corporations,
> with their unimaginable wealth, arcane technology, and inscrutable,
> amoral machinations.[34]

Similarly, the Moberlys use Marxist theory to connect the neomedievalist
elements of *World of Warcraft* to the concept of *spectacle*:

> This recursive hall-of-mirrors effect produces a version of the medi-
> eval that is wholly subsumed by its own spectacle. A testament to the
> power of third-stage capitalism to produce and [commodify]. The real,
> the neomedieval spectacle not only demonstrates the power and the
> prowess of the society that produces it, but in doing so, involves its
> audience in an idealized version of the social hierarchy.[35]

It might then also be possible, however, to approach the self-reflexive space/
time and fantasy/reality aspects of neomedievalism (as well as other medievalisms) from other perspectives. For example, alternatively, a less Marxist

approach to historicism might be equally fruitful: Lesley Coote argues that, as with neomedieval works, "Medieval subjects took a similar attitude to their own historical materials and legendary icons, using them to create new meanings in a way akin to that made possible by new technologies and the advent of hypertext."[36] Amy S. Kaufman is right: "Despite its desire to erase time, neomedievalism is situated in time: it just happens to be our time."[37] Such time manipulation obviously affects space manipulation. It is noteworthy that time and space are clearly separate dimensions to a medieval scientist/philosopher; however, to the contemporary intellectual, time-space is one tightly intertwined dimension. This fact emphasizes the large gap of space-time between the Middle Ages and now, which is acknowledged most knowingly by neomedievalist works. *This is one thing that neomedievalist works DO.* As Kaufman puts it: "Neomedievalism consumes the Middle Ages in fragmented, repetitive tropes as a way of ensuring against loss."[38] In neomedievalist works, time becomes both relative and universal – a true dimensional representation. Kaufman observes that the most obvious manifestations of neomedievalist ideology "appear in the post-apocalyptic neomedievalisms of science fiction and fantasy."[39]

However, it is prudent to remember that the entire definition of neomedievalism is not centered around science fiction and fantasy. Another effect of neomedievalism is the potential rewriting of disability and other aspects of acceptance of diversity within cultures. Indeed, Grewell suggests:

> The way that neomedievalism reacts to postmodernism by intermingling postmodern concerns like multi-culturalism and contemporary socio-political issues (such as matters of gender and race) with quasi-medieval fantasy universes characterized by the struggle between good and evil seems to me one of its strikingly definitive facets and one worthy of scholarly exploration. Such exploration, moreover, might go a long way towards detailing some of the particular ways that neomedievalism responds to our contemporary cultural moment.[40]

In fact, it is possible that neomedievalism is a product of too much information. For example, J. R. R. Tolkien's novels are clearly the product of a scholar well-versed in medieval languages and literatures; for the reader to fully appreciate *The Lord of the Rings* trilogy, that reader must be a medieval scholar as well as a scholar of early twentieth-century British literature (the challenge of medievalism scholarship). For anyone else, the books simply create information overload, a symptom of schizophrenia: the inability to take information flowing in (analog) and to categorize and prioritize it into discrete (digital) distinctions. Neomedievalism is a schizophrenic response to information overload, and while that might seem like meaningless dribble to the "healthy" brain, to the schizophrenic brain, it is full of meaning. Thus, as many functioning schizophrenics have learned, a constant reminder of what is real and what is not real may be the only means of truly comprehending the nature of neomedievalism.

To be unplugged from the medieval, then, is not simply a matter of either capitalist exploitation or science-fiction addiction. The concept of being "unplugged" has been complicated by contemporary musicians such as Eric Clapton and Neil Young: unplugged for them means non-electric instruments (acoustic guitars, in particular). However, it is significant to remember that this "unplugged" music is rarely truly non-electric, as everything about the experience is enhanced by microphones and other "plugged" sound equipment, by the electronic video and audio recordings of the performed pieces, and by electronic viewing and listening to these recordings. Crosby, Stills, Nash & Young's song "Guenevere" has become neomedieval in that, while it portends to be of the acoustic tradition, it has been electronically enhanced for recording, and it has even more recently been digitally remastered – illusions of illusions of illusions. Thus, to be unplugged from neomedievalism allows one to better understand all the information (books, television, paintings, radio, libraries, the internet ...) that is jumbled all together when fully plugged-in to the "systems" of information available to us. As Coote observes:

> At one end of the spectrum, the neomedieval encourages the substitution of superficial understanding, the "gist" gathering of cultural bits and pieces, for real knowledge and understanding of the Middle Ages. On the other, it offers the insights of a space in which the medieval can "speak back" from the margins to which it has been confined by the domination of the modern. This is dangerous historiography, which may upset accepted understandings of the Middle Ages in future.[41]

Norman Cantor prophesied that "many of the cultural goals and intellectual assumptions that have molded the twentieth century [will] run down into entropic nothingness, and a new set of ideals will have to be integrated into guidelines for survival and happiness in the twenty-first century."[42] What does this mean for medievalism(s)? What does this mean for neomedievalism(s)? How will this aid in the progressive development of scholarly theory? How will this help those of us struggling to teach medieval history, art, literature, and so forth? How will this help academic institutions develop faculty jobs or help faculty gain tenure and promotion? In the early 1990s, Cantor's answer seems to have been this:

> As this transition occurs, as the familiar ideological signposts of the twentieth century fade away into the enigmatic silence of the super-

seded past, the time-tested spiritual and social ideals speaking directly
to us from the Middle Ages will move ever more centrally on to the
horizons of culture and thought.[43]

But is what has actually happened what he envisioned? While opportunities to teach medieval courses have broadened (as long as such courses
incorporate medievalism entities), they have also narrowed (to become less
often required study material). Furthermore, for medievalists and non-medi-
eval scholars alike, jobs in the tenure/promotion track have been steadily
decreasing. Finally, medieval "time-tested spiritual and social ideals" certainly
moved into the horizon of the first decade of post-apocalyptic 9/11 politics,
where fundamentalists (Islamic, Christian, Jewish) all seem to have pushed
for a movement farther back in time than the Middle Ages. Cantor may
indeed be right, as he declares more optimistically than Umberto Eco that
"everyone has an idea of the Middle Ages" that is "highly personal," "vague
or grossly simple and dogmatically crude, although not thereby to be held
in contempt" as being "corrupt."[44]

As Utz observes, medieval scholars "were not ready to follow" the writings
of Lesley Workman and Cantor in "a move away from the binary distinction between medieval studies and medievalism" that acknowledges "that
all forms of medieval reception participated in the ever-developing images
of medieval culture in post-medieval times,"[45] and that the movement in
the 1990s of the New Medievalists "has proven ephemeral."[46] Utz argues,
"Traditional approaches to the reception of the medieval have yet to develop
the descriptive and diagnostic tools to recognize the revolutionary change
such as a commodifying attitude toward history is bound to engender."[47]
However, Cantor was unable to foresee the cyberpunk apocalyptic cynicism
that has been tainted by Pythonesque self-reflexive humor and a whole-
hearted drive to not only re-live the Middle Ages, but to also knowingly,
laughingly, re-write them. As Utz rightly observes:

> Neomedievalism texts no longer need to strive for the authenticity of
> original manuscripts, castles, or cathedrals, but create pseudo-medi-
> eval worlds that playfully obliterate history and historical accuracy
> and replace history-based narratives with simulacra of the medieval,
> employing images that are neither an original nor the copy of an orig-
> inal, but altogether 'New/Neo'.[48]

The self-reflexive and often humorous antics of neomedievalism remind
the scholar of the lines between the games of gaming (whether in academia,
politics, business, or just in a video game) and the games of reality (beyond
academia, politics, business, and entertainment). It is an emotional safety

mechanism, and perhaps because it functions as such a mechanism, neome-dievalism, as Karl Fugelso has observed:

> [...] has inspired extraordinary passion. Indeed, in my five years of editing *SiM* and many more years of studying (neo)medievalism, I have rarely seen the degree of emotion that was on display during the 2007 conference, in and around the Kalamazoo sessions, and from the readers of Robinson and Clements' essay. Whether for or against the latter, virtually every one of our reviewers expressed themselves in unusually colorful language wrapped around an exceptionally polar position.[49]

A safety mechanism, after all, can be construed as either a silly psychological gimmick (for some) or a vital psychological tool (for others) – either way, it can be unsettling. Quoting *The Matrix* seems to have encouraged many to turn to the writings of Baudrillard, who inspired this film as well as an entire culture of cyberpunk science-fiction enthusiasts. Indeed, Baudrillardian analysis now seems to dominate neomedievalist studies, threatening to consume all other possible approaches in its wake. Yet, this has not happened in all studies. Where do the illusions of Baudrillardian analysis and the realities of other theories collide and/or merge? Clearly, the medieval in motion has become a runaway train, or rather, a runaway computer program. Unplugging, in order to gain perspective and serenity, might be the only solution.

NOTES

1. Karl Fugelso, "Editorial Note," *Studies in Medievalism XX: Defining Medievalism(s) II*, ed. Karl Fugelso (Cambridge: D. S. Brewer, 2011), xi.

2. Fugelso, "Editorial Note," xii.

3. Jane Chance, "Tough Love: Teaching the New Medievalisms," *Studies in Medievalism XVIII: Defining Medievalism(s) II*, ed. Karl Fugelso (Cambridge: D. S. Brewer, 2009), 78.

4. *A Knight's Tale,* dir. Brian Helgeland (Columbia Pictures, 2001).

5. www.kankedort.net/

6. www.lib.rochester.edu/camelot/cphome/stm

7. Fugelso, "Editorial Note," xii.

8 Chance, "Tough Love," 94.

9. Chance, "Tough Love," 78.

10. E. L. Risden, "Medievalists, Medievalism and Medievalismists: The Middle Ages, Protean Thinking, and the Opportunistic Teacher-Scholar," *Studies in Medievalism XVIII: Defining Medievalism(s) II*, ed. Karl Fugelso (Cambridge: D. S. Brewer, 2009), 45.

11. Risden, "Medievalists," 47.

12. KellyAnn Fitzpatrick, "(Re)producing (Neo)medievalism," *Studies in Medievalism XX: Defining Neomedievalism(s) II*, 16.

13. Cory Lowell Grewell, "Neomedievalism: An Eleventh Little Middle Ages?" *Studies in Medievalism XIX: Defining Neomedievalism(s)*, 35.

14. M. J. Toswell, "The Simulacrum of Neomedievalism," *Studies in Medievalism XIX: Defining Neomedievalism(s)*, 52.

15. Lesley Coote, "A Short Essay about Neomedievalism," *Studies in Medievalism XIX: Defining Neomedievalism(s)*, 29.

16. Kevin Moberly and Brent Moberly, "Neomedievalism, Hyperrealism, and Simulation," *Studies in Medievalism XIX: Defining Neomedievalism(s)*, 18ff.

17. Amy S. Kaufman, "Medieval Unmoored," *Studies in Medievalism XIX: Defining Neomedievalism(s)*, 3.

18. Kaufman, "Medieval Unmoored," 3.

19. David W. Marshall, "Neomedievalism, Identification, and the Haze of Medievalism," *Studies in Medievalism XX: Defining Neomedievalism(s) II*, 22.

20. Nils Holger Petersen, "Medieval Resurfacings, Old and New," *Studies in Medievalism XX: Defining Neomedievalism(s)*, 38.

21. Lauryn S. Mayer, "Dark Matters and Slippery Words: Grappling with Neomedievalism(s)," *Studies in Medievalism XIX: Defining Neomedievalism(s)*, 73.

22. Harry Brown, "Baphomet Incorporated, A Case Study," *Studies in Medievalism XIX: Defining Neomedievalism(s)*, 5.

23. Brown, "Baphomet Incorporated," 4.

24. Mayer, "Dark Matters," 75.

25. Nickolas Haydock, "Medievalism and Excluded Middles," *Studies in Medievalism XVIII: Defining Medievalism(s) II*, 19.

26. Carol L. Robinson and Pamela Clements, "Living with Neomedievalism," *Studies in Medievalism XVIII: Defining Medievalism(s) II*, 56.

27. Richard Utz, "*Medievalitas Fugit*: Medievalism and Temporality," *Studies in Medievalism XVIII: Defining Medievalism(s) II*, 35.

28. Risden, "Medievalists," 50.

29. Brown, "Baphomet Incorporated," 2.

30. Toswell, "The Simulacrum," 54.

31. Toswell, "The Simulacrum," 46.

32. Toswell, "The Simulacrum," 50.

33. Moberly and Moberly, "Neomedievalism, Hyperrealism, and Simulation," 15.

34. Brown, "Baphomet Incorporated," 7.

35. Moberly and Moberly, "Neomedievalism, Hyperrealism, and Simulation," 18.

36. Coote, "A Short Essay," 30.

37. Kaufman, "Medieval Unmoored," 5–6.

38. Kaufman, "Medieval Unmoored," 3.

39. Kaufman, "Medieval Unmoored," 6.

40. Grewell, "Neomedievalism: An Eleventh Little Middle Ages?" 40.

41. Coote, "A Short Essay," 32.

42. Norman Cantor, *Inventing the Middle Ages: The Lives, Works, and Ideas of the Great Medievalists of the Twentieth Century* (New York: Quill/William Morrow and Co., 1991), 43.

43. Cantor, "*Inventing*," 43.

44. Cantor, "*Inventing*," 43–44.

45. Utz, "*Medievalitas Fugit*," 34.

46. Utz, "*Medievalitas Fugit*," 35.

47. Utz, "*Medievalitas Fugit*," 36.

48. Utz, "*Medievalitas Fugit*," 36.

49. Fugelso, "Editorial Note," *Studies in Medievalism XIX: Defining Neomedievalism(s)*, xi.

Contributors

EDUARDO HENRIK AUBERT received his Ph.D. from the École des Hautes Études en Sciences Sociales (Paris) in 2011 and is currently the holder of a post-doctoral fellowship at the University of Cambridge. He has published on medieval music, manuscript studies, and medieval historiography and is currently working on a project on the earliest Western notations.

HELEN BROOKMAN is a Stipendiary Lecturer in medieval English literature at the University of Oxford. Her doctoral research, undertaken at the University of Cambridge with the Cambridge Victorian Studies Group, explored translations and editions of Old and Middle English literature produced by nineteenth-century women scholars. She is currently engaged in further research on the lives, careers, and works of three women scholars: Anna Gurney (1795–1857), Lucy Toulmin Smith (1838–1911), and Jessie L. Weston (1850–1928).

HARRY BROWN is Associate Professor of English at DePauw University in Greencastle, Indiana, where he teaches courses in American literature and culture. His first book, *Injun Joe's Ghost*, examines the role of the Indian mixed-blood in American writing of the nineteenth and twentieth centuries. His more recent book, *Videogames and Education*, explores the poetic, rhetorical, and pedagogical relevance of games to the liberal arts. His work in games studies has led him to a more specific examination of neomedievalism in contemporary American culture. In this vein, he has contributed previously to *Studies in Medievalism*. His current work in progress explores historical and literary analogues of ecocatastrophe narratives.

PAMELA CLEMENTS is Professor of English at Siena College (Albany, New York) where she teaches courses on medieval literature, medievalism, science fiction, and poetry. Her scholarship has ranged from Old English sermon studies to medievalism in twentieth-century popular culture. *The Medieval in Motion*, a collection of essays she edited with Carol Robinson, is forthcoming in 2012. She is currently completing a volume of original poetry.

KELLYANN FITZPATRICK is a Ph.D. candidate in English at the University at Albany, where she has pursued her research and teaching interests

in medievalisms, nineteenth-century British literature, and medieval literature and culture. She is currently researching the processes of technological development and production in cloud computing communities while
completing her dissertation on neomedievalism in consumer culture and
academic discourse. Her previous publications address aspects of neomedievalist theory and praxis in digital games, film, and the academy.

JIL HANIFAN is a poet, lecturer in English, and Director of the Writing
Center at the University at Albany. She teaches courses in writing,
poetry and poetics, as well as in contemporary genre studies, such as
horror, science fiction, fantasy or fairy tales. Her poems have appeared
most recently in *Earth's Daughters* and *2River View*. She is currently the
Champion of Kirkwall, and is revered in Ironforge.

MICHAEL R. KIGHTLEY is Assistant Professor of English at the University
of Alabama at Birmingham, where he teaches courses on Old English, Old
Norse, and the history of the English language. His dissertation, completed
at the University of Western Ontario, analyzes how racial theories about the
Anglo-Saxons were transmitted through scholarship to fiction in the late
nineteenth and early twentieth centuries. He has published on *Beowulf*, *The
Battle of Maldon*, and *The Lord of the Rings*, and is currently researching
images of brotherhood in Anglo-Saxon poetry.

FELICE LIFSHITZ is Professor in the Women's Studies Program, with a
joint appointment to the Campus St. Jean, at the University of Alberta. She
has published extensively on medieval religious and cultural history, including
(most recently) the co-edited volumes *Why the Middle Ages Matter: Medieval
Light on Modern Injustice*, *Gender and Christianity in Medieval Europe: New
Approaches*, and *Paradigms and Methods in Early Medieval Studies*. She is
completing a monograph on a series of eighth-century women's manuscripts,
entitled *Gendered Transmissions*, and is embarking on a new study of cinematic medievalism in Europe and North America between 1938 and 1968.

LAURYN S. MAYER is Associate Professor of English at Washington and
Jefferson College, where she teaches courses on medieval and medievalist
literature, literary theory, and popular fiction. Her current research focuses
on collaborative production of meaning in the manuscripts of Trevisa's *Poly-
chronicon*. She has published previous articles on medievalism in online
communities and in computer games.

BRENT MOBERLY holds a doctorate in medieval English literature from
Indiana University. His current academic work focuses on romance, labor, and

spectacle in contemporary computer games and popular medievalism. He has co-authored a number of articles and book chapters on these subjects with his brother, Kevin Moberly. He and Kevin are currently revising a chapter on guilds and spectacular production in contemporary computer games.

KEVIN MOBERLY is Assistant Professor of Rhetoric, New Media, and Game Studies at Old Dominion University. He teaches courses on historical rhetoric, digital mass culture, and computer games. He has published a number of articles and book chapters on New Media, computer games, and digital manifestations of culture. He and his brother Brent Moberly have also co-authored a number of articles about contemporary manifestations of neomedievalism. He is currently working on a book-length study that examines the rhetorical role that computer games play in the late-capitalist culture industry.

E. L. RISDEN is Professor of English at St. Norbert College, where he teaches Chaucer, Shakespeare, Milton, Early British Literature, Classical Myth, and Linguistics. He has published thirteen books, ranging from literary criticism to fiction and poetry, and is currently working on projects on Shakespeare and the problem-play conundrum, narrative theory and the problem of subversion, and Tolkien and the twentieth-century intellectual landscape.

CAROL L. ROBINSON is Associate Professor of English at Kent State University Trumbull, where she teaches courses on medieval literature, medievalism(s), film and literature, Deaf culture, and gender studies. She is co-editor of *The Cultural Influences of William Gibson, the "Father" of Cyberpunk Science Fiction: Critical and Interpretive Essays*, and editor of a forthcoming anthology of essays, *The Medieval in Motion: Neomedievalism in Film, Television, and Electronic Games* (associate editor, Pamela Clements). She has published articles and book chapters on neomedievalism and semiotics in video games, as well as on Deaf culture adaptations of medieval British works, and she is completing a documentary film about the production of Willy Conley's American Sign Language/English play, *For Every Man, Woman, and Child – a modern morality play inspired by EVERYMAN* (co-produced with Daniel-Raymond Nadon and Nancy M. Resh).

M. J. TOSWELL is Associate Professor of English at the University of Western Ontario. She works principally on Old English psalm translations and Anglo-Saxon psalters, but has also published articles on Tacitus, Earle Birney, and W. H. Auden; and for six years edited the journal *Florilegium*.

J. RUBÉN VALDÉS MIYARES is tenured Professor of English at the University of Oviedo, Spain, where he teaches courses on medieval literature, British and Irish cultural studies, and film adaptation. He has published articles on medieval literature, a Spanish edition of Robin Hood ballads, and has co-edited a *Sourcebook of British Civilization* and a collection of cultural studies on the narrativization of history, *Culture and Power: The Plots of History in Performance*. His current research interests are in critical discourse analysis and film studies.

Previously published volumes

Volume I

1. Medievalism in England
Edited by Leslie J. Workman. Spring 1979
2. Medievalism in America
Edited by Leslie J. Workman. Spring 1982

Volume II

1. Twentieth-Century Medievalism
Edited by Jane Chance. Fall 1982
2. Medievalism in France
Edited by Heather Arden. Spring 1983
3. Dante in the Modern World
Edited by Kathleen Verduin. Summer 1983
4. Modern Arthurian Literature
Edited by Veronica M. S. Kennedy and Kathleen Verduin. Fall 1983

Volume III

1. Medievalism in France 1500-1750
Edited by Heather Arden. Fall 1987
2. Architecture and Design
Edited by John R. Zukowsky. Fall 1990
3. Inklings and Others
Edited by Jane Chance. Winter 1991
4. German Medievalism
Edited by Francis G. Gentry. Spring 1991
Note: Volume III, Numbers 3 and 4, are bound together.

IV. Medievalism in England
Edited by Leslie Workman. 1992

V. Medievalism in Europe
Edited by Leslie Workman. 1993

VI. Medievalism in North America
Edited by Kathleen Verduin. 1994

VII. Medievalism in England II
Edited by Leslie J. Workman and Kathleen Verduin. 1995